Strangers at the Gate

THE CENTER FOR CHINESE STUDIES

at the University of California, Berkeley, supported by the Ford Foundation, the Institute of International Studies (University of California, Berkeley), and the State of California, is the unifying organization for social science and interdisciplinary research on contemporary China.

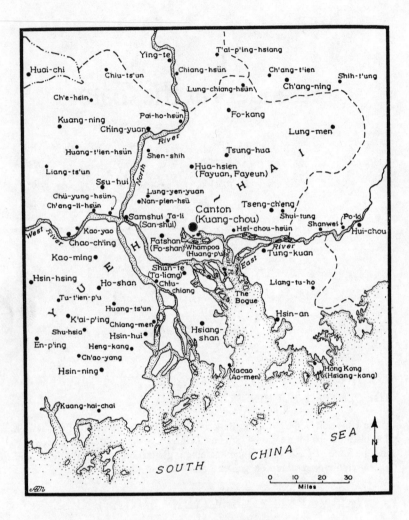

Map of the Kuang-chou delta.

Strangers at the Gate

SOCIAL DISORDER IN SOUTH CHINA, 1839-1861

Frederic Wakeman, Jr.

UNIVERSITY OF CALIFORNIA PRESS

BERKELEY, LOS ANGELES, LONDON

University of California Press
Berkeley and Los Angeles, California

University of California Press, Ltd.
London, England

To Nancy

Acknowledgments

The research for this book was made possible by a two-year grant from the Foreign Area Training Program, under the auspices of the Social Science Research Council and the American Council of Learned Societies. Needless to say, the Program assumes no responsibility for any of my conclusions, but without its support and the help of Miss Dorothy Soderlund and Mr. James Gould the work could not have been completed.

The following people have been more than generous with their advice and aid: Professor Wolfram Eberhard; Professor John K. Fairbank; Professor Kuo T'ing-i; Professor Joseph R. Levenson; Professor Franz Schurmann; Dr. Philip Kuhn; Dr. Irwin Scheiner; my research assistant, Mr. Lin Shang-chien; and the staff of the Center for Chinese Studies at Berkeley. Unless otherwise noted, all translations are mine.

I should also like to acknowledge the services of the many devoted and cooperative librarians and archivists of the East Asiatic Library, University of California, Berkeley; the Hoover Institution, Stanford; the Fu Ssu-nien Library and the Modern History Library, Academia Sinica, Taiwan; the Public Record Office and the British Museum, London.

Transcripts of Crown copyright records in the Public Record Office appear by permission of the Controller of H. M. Stationery Office. In the Introduction, the lines of poetry quoted are from "1887" from "A Shropshire Lad," authorized edition, from *The Collected Poems of A. E. Housman.* Copyright 1939, 1940, © 1959 by Holt, Rinehart and Winston, Inc. Reprinted by their permission and that of The Society of Authors as the literary representatives of the Estate of the late A. E. Housman, and Messrs. Jonathan Cape, Ltd.

Contents

LIST OF MAPS AND FIGURES

LIST OF TABLES

Strangers at the Gate

Introduction

The Taiping Rebellion (1850–1864) was the world's most disastrous civil war. Travelers passing through the once populous Yangtze provinces could go for days without seeing more than rotting corpses, smoking villages, pariah dogs. Ningpo became a "city of the dead," with no trace of its half a million inhabitants, save for the canals, "filled with dead bodies and stagnant filth." Fifteen years of butchery and famine were to cost China somewhere between ten and twenty million souls.

The attrition exceeds the limits of historical imagination. Even worse: the historian, while ashamed to admit he resembles Flaubert's *coeur simple*, finds little of interest in massacre as such. True, the devastation left in the wake of the Taiping Rebellion was a Malthusian corrective that gave those densely populated regions a new lease on life during the years of restoration that followed. But our attention is not drawn again and again to the revolt for that reason. Rather, the historian is attracted because the Taiping Rebellion was a watershed in the flow of Chinese history. In a linear sense, the modern history of that nation emerges from those years of tumult: first, the distintegration of the empire into regional units, then the atrophy and overthrow of the dynasty, and finally the warlord period. Yet, the moment we accept this historical line of descent, confusion arises. Was the revolt a terminal point of one historical process, or the beginning of another? Was the Taiping Rebellion no more than a new form of the perennial Chinese peasant revolt? Or was it an embodiment of new forces that were to shape and change China in the years to come?

It is unfashionable to speak of Changeless China. We continue our efforts to distinguish between types of monarchical change, or to emphasize long-range social, rather than political, developments. Yet, the dynastic cycle *did* exist — if only for the Confucian historians who described it, or for the illiterate peasants who believed that every ruling house was doomed to an eventual time of trouble when the heavenly mandate would pass on to a new dynastic founder. So it had been, and so it would always be: not a progress into a foreseeably different future, but a series of circles, of returns, of repetitions.

This cliché of the Chinese historical imagination was destroyed by the Western assault on Asia. The old circular process was abruptly transformed into a linear one. The Ch'ing empire may well have exhibited the usual symptoms of dynastic decay, but the importance of this traditional decline paled beside the corrosion, not of a ruling house, but of the very concept of a Confucian dynasty. China was drawn inevitably into a global history that she had never made.

Before the European Renaissance there had been no world, no global, history. For many there had been no globe at all. Europe, the Middle East, Africa, Asia, the Americas — each had been what Toynbee has called "intelligible historical units." There had been mutual intercourse, even impingement — the Mediterranean World being the most famous example; but each was a historical sphere unto itself. The Roman "embassies" to the Han dynasty, even the Nestorians and Arabs of the T'ang period, had been travelers to another time, another place, another world. Only once, during the reign of the Mongols (1280–1367), was there any real bridge between China and the Mediterranean World. The Ming dynasty (1368–1644) effectively severed that link. By the eighteenth century, the greatest land power in East Asia had been politically and ritually sealed into its own hermetic sphere of activity. All that came from outside that civilization was merely barbarian, not worthy of consideration, hardly worthy of fear.

But during this period of oblivion, a new global history was being made. It became conceivable for a European sea captain to sail sixteen thousand miles for a cargo of spices or silks. It even became conceivable, as time went on, for English or Dutch supercargos to rule regions half a world away. Clive's victory at Plassey saw the birth of a new stage in man's development: the Europeanization of the "Third World."

> It dawns in Asia, tombstones show
> And Shropshire names are read;
> And the Nile spills his overflow
> Beside the Severn's dead.

And with that, Europe itself began to change. By 1768, Hargreaves' jenny and Arkwright's water frame were being used to spin cotton in England. Less than fifteen years later, Cort's puddling process was refining pig iron. By 1835, even France's backward metal industry was producing a third of a million tons of pig iron, and Alfred Krupp had introduced the steam engine to his crucible steelworks. The globe, for better or worse, was becoming an economically different, an industrially new, world.

Yet China remained temporally and spatially apart from this process of human revolution. The longer her isolation continued, the more jarring the shock when the cultural enclosures of this last, great, independent historical unit were shattered. The drama of that sudden blow is well known — the seizure of foreign opium by Lin Tse-hsu, the first naval battles, British razzias and blockades — in short, the Opium War (1839–1842) and the opening of China.

Now the two processes — internal and global — merged, even became confused. Familiar events were endowed with new, unrecognizable meanings as the historical context changed. A symptom of traditional decline could presage total change. Hence the confusion, even among contemporaries, over the implications of the Taiping revolution: rebellion or revolution, traditional or new?

Modern historians have used four major arguments to show that the Taiping rebels were not just traditional bandits in slightly different garb. The first hypothesis is a form of Marxist reductionism, which insists that Western economic imperialism created a new class of treaty-port coolies and tea-carrying boatmen who were driven into unemployment by the Opium War. It was the participation of this *lumpenproletariat* which gave the rebellion a genuinely protorevolutionary character.

The second argument is based on the role played by the gentry who eventually suppressed the revolt. In the past, local gentry had always been offered a choice during any time of revolt. They could support the reigning dynasty, or they could come to terms with a promising rebel leader in hopes of grooming their own candidate for the dragon throne. This time, Taiping attacks on the normally accepted status of the Confucian literati deprived the gentry of any choice at all. Sheer self-survival forced them to support a weak dynasty rather than a socially threatening revolutionary movement.

The third, and most subtle, certification of change suggests that the Emperor of the Taiping Heavenly Kingdom was a new sort of ruler. Hung Hsiu-ch'üan and his followers did not simply believe that the Manchus had lost the immanent Mandate of Heaven. Rather, they accepted a new and foreign source of transcendent legitimacy — God in Heaven — which supplanted the Confucian notion of kingship.

Finally, many have claimed that the communal property systems and chiliasm of the rebels represented a new kind of utopianism which was quite foreign to China, and could only be found in the Christian texts available to Hung Hsiu-ch'üan.

For each of these arguments, of course, there exists a refutation. The Marxist is told that his *lumpenproletariat* was no more than the simple "unemployed vagabonds" (*wu-yeh yu-min*) of traditional Chinese texts. The gentry thesis is countered by citing supporters of the Taiping Heavenly Kingdom among degree-holders, or by insisting that not enough is yet known about specific local opposition to the rebels to warrant such blanket statements. Opponents of the third argument maintain that comparisons of immanent and transcendent kingship apply only to the last, dynastic phase of the rebellion and are based on a narrow philological analysis which ignores other, traditional aspects of Taiping rule. And finally, it is held that Hung's utopianism was drawn not from the Bible but from the native tradition of mystical Kung-yang Confucianism.

In short, while all can agree that an understanding of the rebellion is a necessary prerequisite to an understanding of all of modern Chinese history, few can share common definitions. This is so partly because, to use Marc Bloch's distinction, there has been a confusion between causes and conditions. Clearly, South China's social disorder after the Opium War "caused" this unrest to develop. Just as clearly, the Western impact "conditioned" the form that development took. In either case, the search for origins pulls the historian back in time and east in space to the crucible of that disorder and conflict: Canton during the first twenty years after the Opium War.

We know Canton well. Its role as a meeting ground between Chinese and Europeans has been exhaustively studied. Its foreign factories, its Cohong, its "viceroys," have all been presented to us in travelers' accounts, in official archives, in diplomatic histories. But all around this elaborate mercantile and administrative structure lay the larger society of South China, in ferment during these years of turmoil. Scholars fretted over China's military impotence, landlords organized militia, tenants joined secret societies, clans struggled one against the other for local wealth and power. In short, underneath that overlying surface of official history, there burgeoned mass fears, mass hopes, mass movements.

These were not two different worlds, of course. Never can a neat and simple line be drawn between this sort of local history and national or imperial or world history. But, after all, is it not this convergence which makes this time, this place, of interest? Chinese villagers stone an Englishman, and Palmerston rages in London. Whitehall pressures Peking, and a peasant is beheaded in Kwangtung. World history weaves in and out of local happenings, and China is changed.

And so, in the end, the search for Taiping origins turns into a different kind of study, the dissection of a new historical unit: Canton, Kuang-chou, Kwangtung, South China — it has a coherence all its own.

Let us engage in local history.

PART ONE

San-yuan-li

THE POLITICS OF PATRIOTISM 1839–1841

I

The San-yuan-li Incident

The long walls of the Bogue forts,
　　So strong, so thick;
The great general's confident air,
　　So full of pride.
But the black barbarians came from afar,
　　Invaded this land of peace,
Nightly belched their cannon-fire
　　Before our towered gates.

Admiral Kuan falls and dies in bitter battle,
Sitting, looking, none to save,
　　Who can pity him?

The women of Kwangtung weep to the gods
　　above.
White bones lie across fields,
　　Flocks of sheep asleep.

　　　　　　Sun I-yen, quoted in A Ying,
　　　　Ya-p'ien chan-cheng wen-hsüeh chi (1957)

In the spring of 1841 the Chinese and the English faced each other across the great port of Canton. It was the second year of the Opium War, a time of false starts, of aborted negotiations. January had brought another British attack on the Bogue fortifications, this one costing the Chinese two forts, most of their fleet, and five hundred men. Ch'i-shan, the Manchu, had seen no alternative but to negotiate a cease-fire: the Convention of Chuenpi (January 20, 1841), which gave England Hong Kong, six million dollars, and the right to communicate directly with high Chinese officials in Canton. Neither Peking nor London were to want such a settlement. Still, Captain Charles Elliot, the British plenipotentiary, took pains to keep his side of the agreement, until new Chinese defensive measures incited another British attack on February 26, just as

Ch'i-shan was being replaced by the Emperor's cousin, the more militant I-shan. Again, there was a series of inconclusive meetings, while I-shan's deputy, Yang Fang, tried to square the Tao-kuang Emperor's orders to annihilate the barbarians with yet another enemy occupation of the Bogue forts and the tragic death of old Admiral Kuan. Increasingly impatient, British forces moved closer to the city. On March 18, 1841, they occupied the foreign factories. Severely threatened once again, the Chinese officials at Canton allowed the British to resume trade.[1]

The March armistice was followed by two months of careful watching and waiting. The Chinese leaders tried to restore their shattered defenses. Ch'i-shan had tried to economize by disbanding two-thirds of the navy. Now the authorities ordered a special levy of "water braves." Southeast and southwest of the city, where the people of the suburbs were "packed like the teeth of a comb," special barricades were erected. Fireboats were built, and a five-ton cannon was cast at Fatshan. Reinforcements came in from Szechuan, Kweichow, Hunan, and Kiangsi, increasing the local garrisons by forty-five thousand men. Thirty-six thousand local "braves" were trained.[2] And throughout, Captain Elliot and the newly arrived army commander, Major General Sir Hugh Gough, watched with fearful misgivings.[3] By early May, both sides recognized the inevitability of another clash, but the Chinese were to precipitate it. Yang Fang had wanted to wait for more reinforcements; but on the night of May 21, I-shan, hoping for a glorious victory, secretly ordered his fireboats to attack the British fleet anchored just off the city.[4] The naval action that followed was almost predictable: in the next few days, the English sank seventy-one junks, dismantled the shore batteries and razed the waterfront. Yet, the heart of the city remained inviolate. In spite of the British capture in 1840 of Chusan, the Cantonese still felt that if the barbarians tried to land, they would be no match for Chinese and Tartar infantry. The British themselves realized that a mere naval victory would not be enough; junks, fireboats, gun emplacements — all could be rebuilt. The city would have to be humbled. On May 23, the new shallow-draft steamer, the *Nemesis*, had discovered that it could move upstream beyond Canton and anchor close to shore behind the city's defenses. On the morning of May 25, while I-shan awaited an assault from the South, General Gough landed a force of Indian and British soldiers north of Canton, marched east across the paddies, and captured the five Chinese forts on the heights just outside the north gate of the city — heights that put the city below them at their mercy.[5]

On the morning of May 27, Gough was leaving his bivouac to order

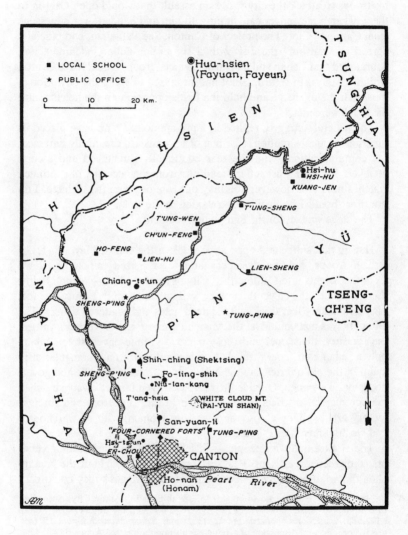

Map of the San-yuan-li area.

his troops to attack the city walls, an assault that would open Canton to them, when a messenger caught up with him and handed over a message from Captain Elliot. The prefect of Canton, She Pao-shun, had officially agreed to "ransom" the city with a six-million-dollar indemnity, and guaranteed that I-shan and all extraprovincial troops would leave Canton within six days. In return, Elliot had promised to spare the city. Gough must halt the offensive and hold the British position on the heights until the terms were met.[6]

The general, enraged, replied in a private note: "You have placed us in a most critical situation. My men of all arms are dreadfully harassed, my communications with the rear continually threatened and escorts attacked. My men must suffer dreadfully from the necessity of continued watchfulness. For however you may put confidence in the Chinese, I do not, nor should I be justified in relaxing in the least."[7]

The stage was set for the San-yuan-li incident.

During that sultry and oppressive week at the end of May, 1841, the British troops, fighting dysentery and fever, gazed impotently down from the heights into Canton, the "City of Rams" (*Yang-ch'eng*). Below them stretched the eleventh-century wall, six miles of it, twenty-five feet high and twenty feet thick, with sixteen gates and scattered towers. The Old City was just behind it: the Manchu quarter, the Governor's yamen, the treasury, magazine, and those narrow, granite-paved streets where only a sedan chair could travel. And beyond that, in a rectangular strip south of the old quarter, lay the New City with its own walls and governor-general's yamen. Outside the ramparts, even farther away, stretched the commercial districts, running down to the waterfront and foreign-factory area, spilling across the river into Honam, with its warehouses and wealthy merchants' houses.

The city teemed with people — at least half a million* jostling vendors, shopkeepers, artisans. Peasants came from throughout the Kuang-chou delta, attracted by the two shillings daily wages† they could earn

---

*In 1908, there were said to be 590,847 inhabitants in Canton City. According to a municipal census taken about twenty-five years later, the number had risen to 1,122,583. See: *Shina shōbetsu zenshi*, 1:22; and *Kuang-chou chih-nan*, 15 (see n. 8). For a general discussion of Kuang-chou's population, see Appendix I.

†A carpenter earned seven shillings. Young children, sorting tea, were paid three pence a day. At the same time, incidentally, English railroad navvies were only earning five shillings a day half a world away. It is impossible to estimate the size of the city's unskilled labor force at this time. One hundred years later, there were only about forty thousand laborers in Canton: 5 percent of the male population. See: Lee, *Modern Canton*, 93; *Chinese Repository*, 4:193 (May,

unloading and hauling the goods that poured into Canton: salt, fish, rice, and sugar from the coastal towns of Kwangtung, carried by Ch'ao-chou junks; from Kwangsi, rice and cassia; from Yunnan, copper, lead, precious stones, and gold. Fukien sent earthenware, tobacco, grass cloth, sugar, camphor, black tea and umbrellas. From Chekiang came silk piece goods, fans, and fine embroidery. Anhwei sent green teas; Hunan, Hupei, and Honan, their rhubarb and drugs.

Canton returned bird's nests, sandalwood, foreign luxury articles. Sixty-seven thousand men, women, and children wove cottons, silks, and brocades.* Others manufactured coarse chinaware and cheap glass, shipping it by the boatload to the rest of the empire. Large jewelry firms polished and set cornelians, agates, topazes, pearls — netting millions of dollars a year. Cabinetmakers and joiners made the finest toys and furniture in China. Ivory, imported from the South, was carved into intricate and exotic shapes. Like a magnet, the city attracted raw materials and men, spewing them forth again, altered and enhanced.

Beyond Honam, the urban landscape melted into the rich delta lands and alluvial soils of Shun-te *hsien* (district or county). At its northern extremity, the county was almost a series of islands, crisscrossed by countless offshoots of the Pearl River. And far to the south, nearly out of sight, were the domains of old landed families whose scions staffed the empire's bureaucracy. Around the sprawling homes of these gentry lived smaller freeholders and tenants who were the great silk cultivators † of Kwangtung.[8]

Looking away from the city, the British troops gazed northwards into the famous White Cloud Mountains (*Pai-yün-shan*), which divided Nan-hai and P'an-yü counties. There Su Tung-p'o loved to wander during his days of exile in the South, and there the poets of Kuang-chou held their wine-drinking contests. West of these mountains, along the main

---

1835–April, 1836); C. R. Fay, *Life and Labour in the Nineteenth Century* (Cambridge, 1947), 171; Morse, *International Relations*, 363–366; Lai Hsin-hsia, "Ti-i-tz'u ya-p'ien chan-cheng tui chung-kuo she-hui te ying-hsiang," 114.

*The local manufacturers copied European weaves more effectively and cheaply than any other Chinese could. Most of the actual weaving was done by individuals who sold their articles to wholesalers. Even though some cottage weavers sold their woof as soon as it was ready to large-scale entrepreneurs, the larger sort of weaving establishment was relatively rare. See: FO 17/30, Gutzlaff's report, Incl. 1, Desp. 4, Jan. 10, 1839.

†In 1819, the mulberry orchards of Shun-te and Nan-hai counties together covered over 15,000 acres, and provided employment for "several hundred thousand" households. See: Li Wen-chih, *Chung-kuo chin-tai nung-yeh shih tzu-liao*, 1:82, 431–432.

road running out of the Great North Gate, lay the "ninety-six villages," separated from each other by hills and rice paddies, copses and irrigation ditches. It was a moderately wealthy region. The year-round residents had small but productive holdings, and during the hot months, some of the wealthier folk of the city migrated there to elaborate country villas.[9] In the center of these villages, separated from the British soldiers on the heights during these last hot days of May by a set of hills and ridges, sat the little village of San-yuan-li.

By British military standards, the troops behaved exceptionally well during their eight days on shore. There was almost no rowdiness, no drunkenness, no disobedience.[10] And yet, with five thousand English and Indian troops roaming through the countryside, there was bound to be friction. There was no question that the British looted.[11] In fact, the very word, "loot" (of Indian derivation) was first used by the English during the Opium War. Foraging was even systematized: if a household donated food or animals to the English, it was given a placard to post as protection above its door.[12] San-yuan-li was particularly subject to these raids.[13] A contemporary account told of night patrols breaking down gates and fences, seizing livestock, stealing clothes.[14] A few peasants were upset by the British gun emplacements which disturbed the *feng-shui* (geomancy); others by the soldiers marching through their rice fields.[15] But those were minor annoyances, the fortunes of war, not the sort of thing that would normally drive a peasant to violence. It took two other sorts of incidents to enrage the local population.

The first occurred when an officer of the Thirty-seventh Madras Native Infantry, visiting a joss house called "Twin Mountain Temple" (*shuang-shan ssu*), opened some of the tombs to see how the Chinese embalmed their corpses.[16] The ancestor-worshipping Cantonese could hardly appreciate the curiosity of a barbarian military officer. The prefectural gazetteer later listed five instances of British troops "lewdly plundering" the temples, "opening graves and scattering the bones about."[17] Nothing could have enraged the properly filial Chinese any more than this sort of desecration; and they were undoubtedly right when they believed that at least some of the graves were opened in search of treasure.*

The second type of offense — rape — occurs during any military occupation. At the time, the British refused to acknowledge this, but seven years later Sir John Davis — then Plenipotentiary — admitted that

---

*At the time, though, S. Wells Williams' *Chinese Repository* (10:530) insisted that such indecencies had been carried out by Chinese camp followers.

sepoy troops had indeed violated native women around San-yuan-li.[18] If *hsiao* (filial piety) was offended by tomb robbing, *i* (righteousness) was most certainly aroused by having one's own, or one's neighbor's, wife molested. Add to that the racial antagonism toward "black" Indian troops, and we can begin to understand some of the fervor that swept the countryside.

On May 29, 1841, a British patrol stopped in the hamlet of Tung-hua, near San-yuan-li. Some of the soldiers forced their way into the home of a man named Chang Chao-kuang and attacked the women of the household. A fight broke out, and the villagers armed themselves with cudgels and hoes to drive out the troops. Then, beating gongs, they assembled the peasants of the neighboring villages. Every male between sixteen and sixty was armed with some sort of weapon, usually a sword or a spear, and the women were ordered to set aside food and water as rations. As more and more braves joined the original force, barricades were thrown up on all the surrounding roads and ambushes were prepared. At ten o'clock the next morning, under a searing sun, five thousand of these armed men gathered on a hill in front of the British camp. Assembly sounded almost immediately. General Gough, leaving his second-in-command, Major Burrell, in charge of the main British position, ordered an advance by the Twenty-sixth Cameronian Regiment, the Thirty-seventh Madras Native Infantry, and the Bengal Volunteers. The Chinese braves promptly retreated three miles, seemingly driven off. Gough, seeing some of his men dropping out of the ranks with sunstroke, then ordered the Bengal Volunteers back to the main camp. The Chinese forces remained where they were. Slowly, more and more peasants joined them: 2,000 irregulars from the northwest, partially armed with guns; then, 500 trained "river braves" from Shih-ching. By now there were 7,500 men on the hill. Exhilarated by the reinforcements, the Chinese suddenly hoisted banners and began a slow advance in the face of enemy rocket fire. The British fell back, regrouped, and decided that the Chinese would have to be dispersed before nightfall lest they attack the main camp. And so, at 1 P.M., a general attack was ordered by Major General Gough. The Third Company of the Thirty-seventh Madras, under Lieutenant Hadfield, was sent off to the left, to open communications with the Twenty-sixth Cameronians (15 officers and 294 men) who were advancing on a large village. The rest of the Thirty-seventh moved off to the right, driving the Chinese line back three miles. Satisfied that they had averted any danger to their encampment, the Thirty-seventh began to withdraw, when a violent summer rainstorm that had been brewing in the mountains swept down upon them. Dazed by the fury of the storm, general and staff cut off from the troops, flintlocks useless, the unit began to stumble about blindly, trying to find its way out of the paddies.

"The rain had completely obliterated every trace of a foot-path. All before us was one sea of water. At times the leading files would suddenly disappear in some deep pit or ditch, which it was impossible to guard against. The thunder and lightning were perfectly terrific." [19] Passing through T'ang-hsia village, the uneven line of troops was set upon by Chinese militia, but they fought a successful rearguard action all the way back to the hills, where they rejoined the general at 4 P.M. Shortly after that, the Twenty-sixth Cameronians, who had encountered precisely the same conditions and had lost the last man in their column, also straggled in. It was only then that they realized that Lieutenant Hadfield's company had not reached the Cameronians, but was still out there, wandering in the rain among seventy-five hundred Chinese braves.

When the storm had swept over his company, Hadfield lost sight of the Twenty-sixth, and ordered his men back toward the city. The Chinese militia, knowing which direction he would have to take, sent a unit, under a militiaman named Yen Hao-ch'ang, around the enemy to intercept them at a small river village near Niu-lan-kang. When Hadfield's company had strung itself out along the narrow path that ran through the hamlet, Yen attacked. In the turmoil, a sepoy was snatched from the ranks by a pike, and a young ensign named Berkeley left the protection of the line to try to save him. Yen himself led the men that surrounded Berkeley, hacking at him with knives and swords. Another brave picked up the ensign's fallen musket, and in spite of the dense rain, managed to apply his own match and to lodge a ball in Berkeley's arm before the ensign was rescued and the troops reformed beyond the river on a small ridge. By now none of their muskets would fire, but although their bayonets were a poor defense against long Chinese spears, the militia did not close in. Suddenly the rain stopped, and the British ran to a small copse nearby where they formed a defensive square to give the sepoys time to remove the linings from their caps and clean out the wet gun barrels. New cartridges were inserted, and as the Chinese began to move in, the Indians managed to get off three or four ragged volleys. Then, as suddenly as it had stopped, the rain began to fall again, as fiercely as before. By now it was growing dark, and the British reformed their defensive square, relying solely on fixed bayonets, while the militia staked out the area with torches to keep any of the English from slipping out of the trap, and sent off for more men from the neighboring villages.

During all of this the main British force had sent out two companies of marines armed with new Brunswick muskets, percussion locks relatively immune to moisture. Attracted by the blazing torches, they fought their way through the encirclement, dispersed the militia units, rescued Hadfield and his troops, and returned to camp by 9 P.M. Total losses for the day: one private killed, one officer and fourteen men wounded.

Only then, only after this initial success, did the larger numbers of militia congregate around San-yuan-li. On the morning of May 31, when the news of the victory had spread, 12,000 more volunteers joined the original 7,500, and massed on the hillside again. Meanwhile, General Gough, furious over the engagement, had sent a message to the prefect, She Pao-shun, warning him that he would attack the city if hostilities continued.

"At length the prefect arrived, and assured the general that the movements of these peasants was quite without the knowledge or sanction of the authorities, and that he would immediately send off an officer of rank to order them to disperse to their houses." [20] Then She, along with the magistrates of Nan-hai *hsien* (Liang Hsing-yuan) and P'an-yü *hsien* (Chang Hsi-yü), and a British captain named Moore, walked across the ridge toward the militia. When they reached the braves, the Chinese soldiers refused to let Captain Moore through their ranks, and the three Chinese officials went on alone. Then, according to Liang T'ing-nan's famous account, the officials told the gentry leading the braves that "Peace has already been signed, and since the foreigners can no longer invade us, you must let them go." They warned the gentry there that they would be fully responsible for any incidents.[21] While the peasants grumbled and threatened, the gentry quietly slipped out of the crowd and returned to their homes. Leaderless, the irregular braves slowly and begrudgingly dispersed.

By the afternoon of June 1, 1841, the British had re-embarked, and Canton was again left to itself.[22]

That was the San-yuan-li incident: to the British only a skirmish, not to be reported in either Elliot's or Gough's official correspondence, but to the Chinese a great popular victory. Tales of heroism, complete with a peach-garden oath, began to circulate almost immediately after the affair. As local lore had it, the gongs of San-yuan-li had summoned more

than 25,000 men from 103 villages *before* the battle. A poet-leader of
the braves later described the stirring scene:

> Cherishing the Ch'ing, we embody loyalty and
>   righteousness.
> All the militia stand bravely erect,
> The gentry who lead and the peasants who fight.
> The first, leading the infantry and heading the
>   river men,
> Are the claws of the dragon, planning and scheming,
> While the tiger-troops are marshalled in lines.[23]

The official account given in the local gazetteer may have exaggerated a
bit when it stated that ten British were killed; but less meticulous sources
went far beyond even that distortion by claiming one hundred British
dead. Ch'i Kung himself heard that the British had offered ten thousand
silver dollars to ransom their many dead from the San-yuan-li troops.[24]
But records, facts, were really unimportant. What mattered was that a
generation of Cantonese believed that peasant troops had smashed the
British attacking force.

> They roared like thunder before San-yuan-li:
> A thousand, ten thousand, assembled at once,
> Righteousness behind rage, and rage behind the braves,
> While the villagers' force broke the enemy's ranks.
> Fields and villages — all must be manned.
> None waited for the drum's snare to awaken his zeal.
> Wives were of one mind with their heroic men,
> Mattocks and hoes turned to weapons at hand.
> Around the hamlets, far and near, flashed the
>   Banners of every color and hue.
> One brigade, then a hundred, over the hills beyond,
> While barbarians looked on and suddenly paled.[25]

Through all of this the official and semi-official records became distorted.
Contemporaries such as Hsia Hsieh, Liang T'ing-nan, and even Wei
Yuan, completely exaggerated the importance of the incident:

> The foreign soldiers also earned the ill-will of the people by giving way
> to plundering and lust; and as 1500 of their number did this the day
> after the peace, on their way down from the Square Fort to the Mud
> Rampart, the exasperated villagers of San-yuan-li surrounded and killed
> 200 of them, including the General, Po-mai-hsia-pi (Bremer?), whose
> head was as large as a bucket, and whose baton, orders and double-
> barrelled pistol were taken. . . . Elliot hastened to the rescue, and, as

the crowds of villagers became more numerous, had to seek the assistance of the prefect. . . . If orders had been given to surround and slay the foreign soldiers, and take the foreigners prisoners, we might have held them as hostages, ordered the ships beyond the Bogue, and then discussed terms at leisure, entirely as it should have suited us.[26]

Little wonder then that Chinese Communist historians have enshrined this incident. Out of the humiliating military defeats of the Opium War they have been able to extract a great popular victory, blemished only by the cowardice of Ch'ing officials. Today on the mainland, every child's history book contains an account of this battle. Every tablet, every shrine to the San-yuan-li dead, has been carefully tabulated by the local history bureau of the province: a Bunker Hill and an Alamo, rolled into one. Add to that the Marxist search for origins, and you have the first popular movement against foreign imperialism:

Because popular, nationalist;

Because popular, peasant-led;

Because popular, spontaneous.

Each of these assertions has to be examined, not because we need a convenient strawman ("protonationalism" or "anti-imperialism") to knock down, but because the San-yuan-li incident was a vital prelude to so many of the problems that inflamed South China during the following twenty years: the militia movement, the Taiping revolt, secret societies, clan wars, and the antiforeign movement. Unless San-yuan-li is clearly understood, what came after will seem meaningless.

II

The Militia of Kwangtung

> We make Proclamation to all the Gentry and
> Elders, the shopkeepers and inhabitants of the
> outer villages and hamlets along the coast, for
> their full information. Pay you all immediate
> obedience hereto, assemble yourselves together
> for consultation; purchase arms and weapons;
> join together the stoutest of your villagers, and
> thus be prepared to defend yourselves. — Lin
> Tse-hsü, militia proclamation*

The peasant braves of San-yuan-li were not a new phenomenon for the
Chinese. Officially organized militia had been used since the *fu-ping* of
the sixth century A.D. And at least since the early sixteenth century, local
gentry had unofficially trained their own militia whenever regular defense
methods failed. In fact, gentry militia could almost be considered a normal form of local defense in times of social crisis, part of the political
breakdown we associate with the dynastic cycle in Chinese history.
Because of this, there was usually a clear theoretical distinction between
official levies of mercenaries, called *yung* (braves), and local self-
defense units, called *t'uan-lien* (militia). In any given situation, *yung*
usually appeared long before *t'uan-lien*, for the simple reason that they
were the first recourse of local government if regular troops were either
inefficient or insufficient. Genuine local militia, on the other hand,
would appear only if the crisis continued and if a particular area's local
notables had both enough power and enough interest to lead them.[1]

Kwangtung province had its own version of the mercenary braves in
the *yung* of Ch'ao-chou prefecture (around what was later Swatow) and
of Tung-kuan county (lying just in back of the Bocca Tigris channel
on the east side of the Pearl River). These were semiprofessional fighters

---

*Translated by the British from a placard. See: FO 17/32, Incl. 2, Desp. 37,
Aug. 1839. For an order issued by Lin Tse-hsü to local officials shortly after this
militia proclamation, see: Lin Tse-hsü, *Lin wen-kung ch'üan-chi* (1963), 6:9-a to
9-b.

nurtured by clan and boundary wars. Indeed, the province developed what later came to be a military tradition among its poorer families.* But besides providing "bare sticks," local rowdies who enrolled as *yung* in *ad hoc* armies for pay, Kwangtung also had a long history of genuine local *t'uan-lien*. This was because of the singular presence of endemic coastal pirates, whose periodic raids had long forced rural areas to organize militia.

In the summer of 1807, for example, armed bands began to harass the coastal villages of Hsiang-shan *hsien*† with more than usual ferocity. The following year, the pirates spread upstream to San-shui, at the confluence of the West and North rivers. Late that winter, Hsin-hui was struck, just down the coast from Macao. This raid set a pattern for most of the later ones. Villages were burned and looted, and several hundred men, women, and children were kidnapped.[2]

Involved in a commercial crisis with the British,‡ the governor and the governor-general at Canton did little to combat the pirates until July, 1809, when imperial troops under Brigade General Hsü T'ing-kuei fought a pitched battle on the Hsiang-shan coast. The Ch'ing soldiers were routed, and fled back to the *hsien* capital, looting and plundering on the way. At that point two crucial decisions were made. A local *chin-shih*§ named Cheng Ying-yuan provided rations for the looting, starving troops, while also "summoning village braves" to guard the coast and keep soldiers away from the villages. At the same time, the governor-general of the Liang-kuang, Pai Ling, ordered the coastal prefectures to arm and train local militia under official control. The weapons that were then distributed to these village units were to be recovered by the district magistrates after the pirates were repulsed.[3] Cheng's initiative and Pai Ling's proclamation began a period of intense militia activity. At least three other local defense movements were started:

---

*In the modern Nineteenth Route Army, for instance, four out of every five men were from Kwangtung. Of these, 10 percent came from the North River area, 30 percent from the East River, and 60 percent from the southwest corner of the province. See: Han-seng Chen, *Agrarian Problems in Southernmost China* (Shanghai, 1936), 110, and appendix, table 31.

†Present-day Chung-shan, the arid county on the west side of the Pearl River, stretching down to Macao.

‡In 1809, the Ch'ing government forbade the importation of opium into Canton. Although this crisis was resolved, and although the British later helped repress piracy, most of the local gazetteers associate the rise in piracy with the foreign crisis.

§A successful candidate at the Peking metropolitan exams, usually translated in English texts as "doctor."

In Hsiang-shan county, Li Tso-yuan and the local magistrate revived the *pao-chia** registries and formed *t'uan-lien*.[4]

In Nan-hai *hsien*, a *chü-jen*,[†] Chou Tuan-p'ei, joined several walled villages into a militia league, headquartered at Ta-lan.[5]

Again in Nan-hai, Ch'en Kuan-kuang, a *chü-jen* and local tutor from K'uei-kang, "summoned braves" and "organized them into militia units."[6]

By then, the scattered groups of pirates had flocked to the banner of a single leader, the infamous Chang Pao. This larger band was now capable of besieging the cities of the delta, although Chang tended to avoid strongly defended Hsiang-shan and Nan-hai, and concentrated on less militant counties. The summer months of 1809 saw a series of raids in the rich river lands of rural Shun-te and P'an-yü, but there, too, the local peasants armed themselves and eventually drove Chang Pao back downstream to the sea. A month passed. Then the pirates reappeared in the less populous county of Hsin-ning, far down the southern coast. From September 10 to October 8, they ravaged the district — burning, kidnapping, killing. Then, moving up the river system west of the Bogue, Chang led three hundred junks on another foray into P'an-yü and Shun-te before the militia drove him back.

That was the last great raid of 1809. Piracy was never stamped out, but its virtual exclusion from the "inner waters" (*nei-ho*) was largely a tribute to *t'uan-lien* in existence thirty years before the Opium War. Militia and mercenaries were used sporadically in Kwangtung during the years that followed, always on call if local conditions got out of hand; but nothing as concerted and as thorough as the 1809 militarization occurred again until the Opium War broke out.

In 1838, the Grand Council issued a set of injunctions against the opium trade. Canton complied by arresting many of the local buyers. However, that only drove the distribution system into other channels. Instead of transporting opium openly, the buyers either hired and armed

---

*The *pao-chia* system, of great antiquity, registered every rural household under an elaborate control system, ten households forming one *p'ai*, ten *p'ai* forming one *chia*, ten *chia* forming one *pao*. *Pao-chia* — as they functioned on paper — were designed to ensure that no individual or household disturbed the social order. Each family guaranteed the public behavior of every other family around it through this complex of interlocking units which finally merged at the top under one family selected as *pao-chang*, which was responsible to the local magistrate. During the eighteenth century, however, the *pao-chia* registries were generally not kept up to date, and the system gradually broke down.

†A successful candidate at the provincial exams, usually translated as "master."

local *liu-mang* (troublemakers) for their boats, or bribed official patrol craft.[7] Once the provincial officials realized that their navy had been corrupted, they dismissed the petty officers in charge of river patrols and put the boats directly under the command of local civil officials. When this failed to stop the trade, Lin Tse-hsu and Admiral Kuan T'ien-p'ei went so far as to hire detectives, who were secretly planted among the crews.[8] But the bribes were too high. Everyone proved corruptible, and the navy remained hopelessly compromised. So accustomed were the sailors to selling their services that they even refused to fight when war broke out. During the Battle of Chuenpi, for example, the naval commander had to pawn his own clothes so that he could promise each man a two-dollar bonus if he would go into battle.[9]

If it were necessary to spend extra money on official troops, why not hire mercenaries? After all, the waters around Canton swarmed with the junks of the Tanka, the boat people. True, they were a proscribed class, forbidden to take official examinations, but they were superb seamen. A local saying described them as "vermin on land, veritable dragons afloat." [10] And so, some time after March 12, 1840, Lin Tse-hsu memorialized the Emperor:

> Since you can only control traitors with traitors* and attack poison with poison, Kuan T'ien-p'ei and I have secretly considered using the large and small fireboats which were constructed during peacetime. Then we could hire each household of boat people, telling them: "Why not attack here? Why not defend there?" Each boat would be under the command of one or two privates or petty officers, who could hire and use these people as water braves.[11]

Paying each recruit six dollars a month, plus an extra six dollars to the soldier's family, Lin shortly assembled more than five thousand such "water braves." The funds for this force were subscribed by the Cohong,† local salt dealers, and the Fu-ch'ao junk merchants. And, if we can believe one-tenth of what the Tanka were officially credited with doing, their later record was meritorious.[12]

There were obvious risks to such a policy. After all, it meant arming thousands of potential troublemakers and rebels. But it was effective and, as far as Peking was concerned, cheap. The only alternative to imminent

---

*Lin was aware, of course, that the seamen who served aboard the opium-runners, or sold supplies to the British, were Tanka. *Ergo*, it takes a thief to catch a thief.

†The association of Chinese merchants in charge of trade with the West. See chap. 4.

war deficits was to shift the cost of defense to the provinces. There were ample precedents for this in the suppression of the White Lotus Rebellion at the end of the eighteenth century, and they happened to agree with the Tao-kuang Emperor's own personal avarice. Therefore, after the British took Chusan in July, 1840, the Emperor ordered that locally financed militia be used to defend the maritime provinces.[13] This in turn made central military financing more and more difficult. As autarchy spread, local resources became available only for local use; and so it grew difficult to send official troops from one province to another. When Lin Tse-hsu wanted to get troops from Kiangsu, for example, grain stations which were supposed to feed the soldiers on their way south were either empty or jealously guarded by local residents. Under these circumstances, it was only natural for Lin and his successors to turn to Cantonese levies to replace and reinforce their garrison troops.[14]

But there was even more to the militia policy than all that. Lin Tse-hsu himself was infatuated with the very concept of militia. As governor-general of the Hu-kuang in 1837, he had found village braves most effective against Lan Cheng-tsun's rebels. And as a Confucian moralist, he was also emotionally attracted by the ideological justification for such militia: *pai-hsing chih i*, "the people's righteousness." Again and again, he threatened to turn this ultimate weapon on the British. In March of 1839, for example, he warned the foreign merchants that if they ignored his ban and continued trading, "groups of patriots will be assembled within moments, to exterminate you with ease."[15] And three months later, when the British anchored off Kowloon point, he warned Elliot that unless the merchant vessels registered immediately at Canton or returned to Britain, the coastal population would arise and, in a rage, wipe out the barbarians.[16] These threats were not mere device or rhetoric. They were part of a genuine mystique. To Lin and some of the other late Ch'ing officials, the People were the great imponderable of Confucian history. The People could save or destroy, restore or overthrow. If ever morally mobilized, they could not be beaten. Even as defeat piled upon defeat, that faith did not lessen.

Much of this mystique was derived from the Confucian concept of *min-pen*: "the people as the trunk [of society]." But that was not all. The shattering sense of military impotence which the Chinese felt during the Opium War — the overpowering and ubiquitous *Nemesis*, the inexplicable ease with which the British troops overran their positions — turned them to *any* techniques their own civilization could muster in its defense, even if this mean using the heterodox or the profane.

Anyone who has dipped into Chinese heoric literature, the *wu-hsia hsiao-shuo* (tales of chivalry), is familiar with the legendary boxing masters, the swordsmen, or the *ch'i-kung* adepts who could levitate at will or shatter a wall with a flick of their finger. Irrational, popular, superstitious, even infantile — these tales integrated the fantasies of generations of literate Chinese. A scholar, no matter how rigid his tutors, was aware of this tradition. In fact, images and themes present in both orthodox and heterodox styles of thought suggest that the gap between the two was not so wide as the Emperor's *Sacred Edicts* would indicate. For one thing, both stressed the importance of the inner man, of complete self-control. The boxing master by definition had to be a supremely moral creature, uniting thought and action. The immoral but skillful swordsman *had* to lose to the fighter who achieved inner serenity. Furthermore, both the heterodox and the Confucian traditions (particularly Kung-yang Confucianism) defined learning as the total mastery of a series of truths.* Those truths had levels of meaning, so that at any one time the student might believe himself adept, only to discover yet another mystery based on a deeper meaning. Just as the *t'ai-chi-ch'üan* shadowboxer practiced for years before intuitively understanding the significance of his exercises, so did the scholar memorize all of the Classics before mastering their meaning. This magical view of skill and attainment may have characterized traditional thought in general. At the very least, it certainly permitted a scholar to share some of the sentiments of the secret-society boxing master. Philosophical Taoism abetted this. Sung Lung-yuan's gloss of the *Tao te ching*, a favorite edition of the Kung-yang school, was filled with allusions to the inner man, the mysteries of learning, and control over the powers of the universe.[17]

The fact remained, though, that heterodoxy might have been tolerable as fantasy, but remained socially unacceptable to the Confucian bureaucrat who rationally abhorred popular Buddhism, popular Taoism, and the mumbo jumbo of secret societies. To believe fully in this subcurrent of thought was to reject civilized learning. But after the resounding defeat at Chuenpi on January 7, 1841, Chinese officials began to turn in desperation to the hidden techniques and mysterious skills associated with that tradition. Hence, the reiterated schemes to employ ocean divers who could spend hours under water, *ninjitsu*-type bandits, trained monkeys, secret-society assassins — in short, anything to defeat the barbarians.[18] In a way, this recourse to the secret, the hidden, the irra-

---

*Lin Tse-hsü was, of course, a follower of *chin-wen* Confucianism, which accepted the Kung-yang commentary to the *Spring and Autumn Annals*.

tional foreshadowed the later Boxer convulsions, when the dynasty itself turned to that other, darker strain of Chinese culture. Little wonder, after all of this, that the more hopeless China's military position, the more currency such ideas procured. Not that a man like Lin Tse-hsu ignored other techniques, for he was one of the forerunners of the self-strengthening movement. The point is, both Western weapons and secret-society arts were merely techniques, allowing the scholar momentarily to retain his own ideological purity.

If the militia flourished under Lin, they at first waned under his successor, Ch'i-shan. This was partly due to Ch'i-shan's own distrust of armed and roving vagabonds, but the decision was really made by Peking.[19] Once the Emperor received the news that the British had been pacified by Ch'i-shan and were returning South, he immediately ordered a reduction in military expenses, asking each province to dismiss unnecessary troops. On September 26, 1840, eight hundred Fukienese braves were returned from Chekiang "in order to save on excessive costs." By October 27, the capital had been informed that all of Kiangsu's village militia had been disbanded, and less than a month later that two thousand militia had been demobilized by I-liang in Kwangtung.[20]

The peaceful interlude quickly passed. Immediately after the Battle of Chuenpi, Ch'i-shan could think of only one way to reinforce the battered, unmanned Bogue forts. Overcoming his fear of armed irregulars, he ordered that 5,800 braves be recruited in Tung-kuan, Nan-hai and P'an-yü *hsien*.[21] The Emperor agreed that this was necessary, even while Ch'i-shan was being dismissed.[22] Then, the pattern repeated itself with I-shan. Like any good Tartar, he was initially suspicious of using the traditionally rebellious Cantonese as militiamen. How easily they could turn into rebels! Far better, he thought, to import *yung* from Fukien than to hand out arms to local village groups, as Lin had done.[23] But by March, 1841, the simple problem of defending Canton overrode any objections he might still have had. Virtually on the eve of the San-yuan-li incident, he found himself officially ordering "the two *hsien* of P'an-yü and Nan-hai to secretly defend themselves immediately."[24]

Prefect She Pao-shun had lied to General Gough that morning on the heights. The officials were indeed sponsoring the militia of the ninety-six villages.

III

The Gentry and San-yuan-li

> Thirteen local men, filled with concern,
>   Pledged an angry oath at the edge of Niu-
>   lan-kang:
> Never to retreat, never to waver,
>   Of one mind to follow their chosen path,
> Without a thought of death.
>
> Liang Hsin-fang*

Local government in nineteenth-century China rested on a delicate balance between the powers of the district magistrate and the gentry.† The latter were indispensable agents of central control in a vast agrarian empire ruled by a thin layer of appointed officials. Without the cooperation of this local elite, a magistrate could not hope to collect taxes and police the district. Social welfare, public works, defense, education — all were at one time or the other left to the gentry.[1] In spite of Confucian universalism (*t'ien-hsia*), the state did not pretend to total administrative control. That great society below the governing edifice was largely left to its own devices until disasters — famine, flood, corruption — threatened the ruling house's mandate. Dynastic self-protection was usually the criterion for interference. Hence, the state perpetually sought only one form of totalism: the eradication of heterodox (*hsieh* or *yin*) teachings which competed with or threatened official Confucianism. In practice, of course, the alternate set of values (popular Buddhism or Taoism) were acculturated and not wiped out; but the "gentry and elders" of the empire were recurrently exhorted to counter these doctrines with moral

---

*Kuang-tung-sheng, "Kuang-tung jen-min," 279 (see chap. 1, n. 22).

†The word "gentry" is used as loosely as possible here. Though often defined only as degree-holders, the gentry actually formed a local class of prestigious notables who may or may not have held official rank. Their position was both economic (drawing rents, furnishing credit) and political (representing their local communities, functioning as a recruiting ground for the bureaucracy). See: Maurice Freedman, *Lineage Organization in Southeastern China*, 53.

suasion and indoctrination: monthly readings of the *Sacred Edicts*, the honoring of filial behavior, maintenance of Confucian temples, and so forth. In truth, these ceremonials only served to enhance the gentry's local status, but that was what was most important. The gentry's presence in a locale guaranteed the conservation of official values there, for they embodied and diffused the social beliefs that had held the civilization together so long and so successfully.* In times of order their support was vital: in times of crisis, crucial.

However, there was another side to the coin. The magistrate had to lean heavily on the local elite, but if the gentry were allowed to appropriate too many of his functions, he could find himself emasculated of real power. The gentry mediated local disputes. What if they actually began dispensing justice and assuming police powers? The gentry gathered funds for local defense. What if they actually began collecting taxes?

Let us temporarily equate local power (accompanied by gentry or elite status) with large landholdings. Given the Malthusian pressure on land, given the usury and rack rents that characterized so much of Chinese agrarian history, and given simple economic rationalism, we would expect a landlord to increase both his holdings and his rents whenever and wherever possible. There were limitations, of course, and the most obvious one was the simple problem of rent collection. If pushed too far, tenants might refuse to pay, or turn into bandits, or even resort to *jacquerie*. Therefore, the wealthy landlord needed the magistrate and his police to ensure local order and his legal rights to rent. Beyond a certain point, however, the need shifted. If local conditions worsened, then it was the magistrate himself who had to have the gentry's financial and military support to restore the status quo. And even if the mandarin succeeded in doing that, he faced a further problem. The instruments of victory — militia units or unusual financing devices — now rested in landlord hands. Sometimes the magistrate could recover his full powers. Then a complete restoration was possible. But at other times, depending on the severity of the original crisis, he would find that the local notables were using those very instruments to strengthen their own local hegemonies. Ultimately, the magistrate might even see his tax surpluses begin to decline as more and more land was acquired by the rural elite, who

---

*Gentry culture as such was a symbol of order and stability. In 1841, one of the devices used to convince those who had fled Canton that things were restored to normal was to announce that there would be an *ad hoc* examination of the students in Canton's private academies. Over half the refugees were said to have returned. See: Liang T'ing-nan, *I-fen chi-wen*, 3.

were either taxed at a legally lower rate or not entered on the fiscal registers at all.[2] At this point, of course, most officials simply threw up their hands and doggedly insisted on maintaining their own revenue by increasing the tax burden on any remaining small freeholders, in turn worsening the social crisis.

If the crisis actually reached the stage of a peasant rebellion, then a final danger arose — the riskiest of all as far as the dynasty was concerned. No peasant rebel could hope to "change the mandate" without the coaching and concurrence of important gentry in areas he threatened or militarily controlled. Until then, he simply remained a prepolitical social bandit. Therefore, it was a cardinal, though unspoken, point of Ch'ing policy not to allow literacy to come into too close a contact with mass force. The gentry could not be allowed to master and eventually use the people they helped control. For this reason, the architects of the early Ch'ing control system of *pao-chia* had emphatically refused to let members of the gentry become *pao-chang*, or heads of the control units.[3]

In sum, the two forces balanced on a perpetual seesaw: gentry power versus bureaucratic power. If one went up, the other went down, in a perfect inverse ratio. The gentry constantly tended to appropriate local power. The bureaucracy just as constantly moved toward centralization, "de-feudalizing" that centrifugal force.

This model of the gentry-bureaucratic seesaw is extreme and exaggerated. In truth, matters were never quite so neat and stereotyped. The magistrate shared interests with the local notables, and the local notables, often through the clan, shared strong interests with the peasantry they were supposed to exploit. After all, the gentry, according to the only definition Sinologists can seem to agree on, were official degree-holders; their status was legitimized by the polity, their charisma was "derived." Since rank held the prestige it did, wealth inevitably led to office; and that meant accepting certain Confucian ideals that tempered the harsh strains of naked self-interest, and held the civilization together. Still, there was a balance of power, and it had to be maintained. Tipping it too far on the distaff side would break the power of the central state. In earlier times, this might merely have brought a new dynasty, a new reconstitution of central control. In the nineteenth century, with the Western erosion of Confucianism and the mandarinate, it meant fragmenting the polity itself into local and regional units. As far as Kwangtung was concerned, this fragmentation began not with the Taiping Rebellion but with the Opium War.

That local balance of power first shifted when opium smoking was suppressed. Opium had been used medicinally in China since the T'ang period. In the early seventeenth century, it became an addictive drug. It was not, however, until Hastings' Bengal Council created the Opium Monopoly in 1773, and the lucrative triangular trade was established between India, China, and England, that the drug traffic really began to flourish. By 1816, 3,210 chests of opium were being imported annually into Canton; by 1831, 16,500 chests; and by 1838, 40,000 chests. The imperial government had banned opium smoking in 1729, but the prohibition had been so ignored that further edicts were issued in 1796 and 1800, finally forbidding any importation of the drug at all. There were periodic arrests, periodic threats; but little was done to limit the trade until the Tao-kuang Emperor acceded in 1821, full of reforming zeal and appalled by the heights to which the trade had soared.[4]

Angered by the lack of enforcement of existing laws, the Emperor first tried to use the principle of magisterial responsibility. Any official whose area contained opium would be fined on a sliding scale. This bureaucratic technique failed for obvious reasons.[5]

By 1829, opium had changed the balance of trade. China began to *export* silver sycee. On January 10, 1830, another imperial edict was issued, expressing alarm over the rising cost of silver south of the Yangtze. Opium was still flooding the country because the river patrols were collaborating with the smugglers.[6] Provincial officials began to send in precise intelligence of the trade, exposing the distribution system: Lintin, the "fast crabs," internal trade routes. Canton was the key to the trade. If it could be stopped there, the supply would be cut off and the drain on silver ended. And so, on July 4, 1831, the Emperor ordered the governor-general of the Liang-kuang to "exhaust his body and soul" to break up the trade in Kwangtung.[7]

At about the same time, measures were taken to arrest native opium-growers. The Emperor ordered local officials to revive the defunct mutual-responsibility units of the old *pao-chia* system. Once enrolled, each member would guarantee that each of the other four members was not growing opium, by signing a "mutual-responsibility bond" (*hu-pao kan-chüeh*), antecedents of the bonds that Lin Tse-hsu forced the British merchants to sign eight years later.[8]

Those three policies — official enforcement of existing laws, arrests of smugglers, and arrests of native growers — should have ended the matter, but there was the usual problem. When the governor of Kwangtung, Lu K'un, reported that he had registered the population in *pao-chia*, collected bonds, and completely wiped out opium addiction in the province, the Emperor tersely noted on the side of the memorial, "This cannot be true."[9]

By the summer of 1836, it was clear that more opium than ever was coming in and more silver being shipped out. It was then that a new voice was heard. Hsü Nai-chi, vice-president of the Sacrificial Court, and an old hand at things Cantonese,* memorialized the Emperor on May 17, 1836, humbly suggesting that prohibition was not the answer. After all, was not the loss of silver bullion the heart of the problem? Morality aside, why not legalize the opium trade, but only for barter?[10]

The Emperor agreed to consider the proposal for legalization, asking that the high officials of Kwangtung memorialize in answer. In July, the hong merchants warmly supported Hsu's suggestion; and in September, the governor-general of Kwangtung and Kwangsi, Teng T'ing-chen, cautiously agreed that prohibition was impractical. "The more severe our laws are, the more ingenious are the private smugglers." Instead, a state opium monopoly should be established. After the drug was obtained by barter, it would be taxed like any other trade item, and those wishing to distribute the drug would have to bear a certificate from the Hoppo.†[11]

As far as the Canton interests were concerned the solution was perfect; state revenue would increase, the Hoppo's share of squeeze would be higher, and the Cohong would be able to tax-farm a very profitable trade. Above all, it would curtail corruption in Kwangtung. That, after all, was their strongest point; either the Court insisted on the severest of measures, which would probably be impossible to enforce, or else illegal interests would grow and grow and grow.

The following month, October, 1836, the moralists replied. Three high officials memorialized.

Chu Tsun, vice-president of the Board of Ceremonies, flatly stated that infraction was no reason for annulment. Opium was evil, "a flowing poison" that ruined "the minds and morals of the people."[12]

Yuan Yü-lin, censor for the Kiangnan circuit, warned that if opium were legalized, everyone would use it. Existing laws should be enforced with severity.

And, most important, Hsü Ch'iu, supervising censor of the Board of War, stated that the only logical alternative to legalization was not trade

*Earlier in his career, Hsü had been director of the Yueh-hua Academy in Canton, and provincial judge of Kwangtung.
†The Chinese superintendent of foreign trade. See chap. four.

regulation, not registering native growers, but the strict and draconian punishment of opium merchants, be they native or foreign.[13]

On the one side, then, were those who either were part of the "system" at Canton, or felt reluctant to prosecute millions of native smokers and dealers; and on the other, those who felt the vice was a menace to the moral, physical, and economic health of the empire. It was that old debate of Chinese administrative history: the tender versus the tough-minded, Ssu-ma Kuang versus Wang An-shih. For the "moralists" shared almost a legalist point of view: the laws must be prosecuted, regardless of human cost or social inertia. The *gestalt* was there: social reformism and the distrust of mercantile interests, huge solutions and massive techniques, accompanied by the mobilization of large numbers of people. In short, interference by the polity in society.

Needless to say, the Emperor sided with the moralists. In late 1836, he commanded Governor-General Teng to "apprehend all those traitors who sell the drug, the Hong merchants who arrange the transactions in it, the brokers who purchase it wholesale, the boatmen who are engaged in transporting it, and the naval militia who receive bribes."[14] On June 2, 1838, the final and most drastic solution was suggested by the director of the Court of State Ceremonial, Huang Chüeh-tzu: let the Emperor promulgate laws ordering the *smokers* to stop within a certain period or be executed.[15] It was that which led the Emperor to ask for the opinions of the provincial governors and governor-generals. It was that in turn which brought Lin Tse-hsu's proposals (and his own record of successful opium suppression in Hupei and Hunan) to the Emperor's attention. And it was that which ultimately led to his appointment as imperial commissioner at Canton, with instructions to prevent the sale and smoking of opium.

Long before Lin's arrival in March, 1839, the governor-general of the Liang-kuang, Teng T'ing-chen, had begun a vigorous campaign against the opium traffic, even though he had remarked to an associate that opium smoking was so commonly practiced that to ban it would be like prohibiting tea. His attitude was so well known, in fact, that later when Lin did begin his opium suppression campaign, many people approached Teng and asked him to moderate the Imperial Commissioner's zeal.[17] But at the time he carried out the Emperor's orders faithfully. By January, 1839, 345 offenders had been arrested. As yet, however, there had been no real attempt to punish the addicts themselves.[18] Hsin-pao Chang has correctly pointed out that the suddenness of the shift to strict enforcement under Lin Tse-hsu has been exaggerated.[19] What he failed to emphasize, however, was the shift from an attack on the traders to an attack on the smokers. This change, which had been at the heart of Huang Chüeh-tzu's famous memorial, was given legal form in the thirty-nine-article statute against opium, which provided that eighteen months after the law had been promulgated (June 15, 1839) any smoker would be sentenced to death by strangling.[20] Armed with these powers, Commissioner Lin initiated a sweeping campaign against addiction in Kwangtung.

In addition to punishing all trafficants and merchants severely, and setting up a sanitarium just outside the city gates where addicts could turn themselves in for a cure, he instituted an elaborate and complex control system. (1) For the transients who moved in and out of the city, he ordered a set of registers to be kept by innkeepers and landlords, and presented for official inspection every five days. (2) For officials, soldiers, and yamen clerks, he established five-men mutual-security groups. (3) For smokers, dealers, and peddlers within the city, he ordered severe penalties, and high rewards to be given to informers. (4) And for smokers in the rural areas, he ordered the institution of *pao-chia*.[21]

This last step was the most important of all. Lin had publicly proclaimed in March, 1839, that the old *pao-chia* had failed to work because its guarantors were not dependable. Now, looking for dependability but ignoring one of the cardinal precepts of rural control, the Imperial Commissioner decided to include the gentry (*shen-shih*) in his new network.[22] As he explained to the Emperor:

> I venture to believe that even though the addicts are good at concealing [their addiction], and the suppliers clever about receiving their goods, it is still very difficult to keep one's neighbors' eyes and ears closed to such depraved behaviour. And so I have once more issued instructions to each of my subordinates to select public-spirited and upright gentry in each village to arrange and establish clan organizations (*tsu-tang*) whose heads and deputies shall enroll and investigate *pao-chia*, so that the better elements will be protected and the bandits attacked. If there are malefactors, then they will be apprehended.[23]

In theory, a rural census was compiled in each district, and the local gentry chose men of high moral quality, or the heads of clans, to act as their deputies. These deputies were supposed to see that door tablets were posted for each of the five-family mutual-security groups thus founded.

This policy had two serious effects. The first was a simple matter of dislocation and terror. Many smokers were decapitated, others thrown into jail or Lin's sanitarium. Some people refused to admit the parties of soldiers that were sent to search their houses. Others barricaded the streets.[24] As Gutzlaff described it retrospectively: "The prisons were crowded with victims, the innocent being the major part; many died in them, informers prospered, capitalists were purposely involved in crimes to get hold of their property, all legal trade was at an end; and strange to say, the introduction of the drug was, when the panic had passed, resumed with greater vigor."[25]

Secondly, it made the Commissioner himself depend heavily on gentry enforcement. Just as Lin opened an opium-collection and information office at the Temple of Longevity (*Ch'ang-shou ssu*) in Canton, so did the gentry establish their own surveillance bureau in the Great Buddha Temple (*Ta-fo ssu*) within the city walls.[26] Outside the city, Lin followed Governor-General Teng's suggestion and authorized a Hsiang-shan notable, Huang Tsung, to form militia units to arrest and execute "traitors" and opium dealers at his own discretion.[27] In other instances, rural *pao-chia* were changed by prominent local notables into militia units.[28]

Thus, one of the unforeseen results of the Commissioner's vigorous attack on opium addiction was the official sanction of gentry control of *pao-chia* and nascent *t'uan-lien*. When that was accompanied by gentry participation in militia activities during the Opium War, the vital balance of power between local official and local notable began to shift in favor of the latter.

During the Opium War, the militia of Kwangtung operated at three levels. The highest, which was the most closely controlled, was the level of braves (*yung*), who were commanded by regular military officers. Next came gentry-sponsored militia, which were either under strict official control or in close contact with Canton. Finally, there were the genuine *t'uan-lien*, which were usually sanctioned by provincial officials but operated independently of bureaucratic control. The descending order, therefore, was official to personal, central to local, formal to informal.

Yung were simply hired soldiers. In July, 1840, Canton's prefectural government opened a canopied recruiting office just in front of the foreign factories. Would-be braves lined up by the hundreds and tried to lift a one-hundred-catty weight. If successful, they were signed on at six dollars a month by the colonel of the Kuang-chou regiment, and attached to a regular army unit.[29] Occasionally, a local man with a military background, which often included banditry or piracy, would be awarded brevet rank and given funds to commission boats and men.[30]

Next came the intermediate level, where the gentry acted as agents of the provincial government. Some, like Yang Yung-yen, were no more than traditional *mi-yu* (private secretaries).[31] Others, higher in rank, served as liaison between Canton and the gentry of the rural *hsien*. K'ung Chi-tung, for example, was a noted scholar from Lo-ko-wei in Nan-hai. After getting his *chü-jen* degree in 1818, he had become Department Director of Schools, passed his *chin-shih* in 1833, and was eventually appointed an assistant proofreader in the State Historiographical Office at the capital. When the Opium War broke out, he was in retirement; but he agreed to become an informal military aide to the governors and governor-generals at Canton. Because of his local standing and close relationship with many important members of the gentry throughout the prefecture, he was able to help Lin Tse-hsu, I-liang, and Ch'i Kung manage local defense.[32]

The gentry whom these intermediaries reached often contributed defense funds to the provincial government. Whether these were actually joint subscriptions by clan and local organizations is impossible to say, but the sums were often considerable. Ch'a Wen-kang, of En-chou in Nan-hai, gave enough money to staff several local forts.[33] And a local notable from Tung-kuan named Ch'en Pei-yuan contributed over 70,000 taels for local harbor defense.[34] Presumably, though the sources fail to mention it, these acts of patriotism were rewarded with official rank.

Finally, there were other rural leaders who had trained their own militia and found themselves absorbed into the official hierarchy when they were given command of a local fort or gun emplacement.[35]

Below the intermediate level, still more personalistic, were the genuine *t'uan-lien*. Although they may have existed as skeletal organizations long before the war,* they were not given official recognition until the opium-suppression campaign. Then, some of the gentry were commissioned to register the population and protect their areas against "traitors."[36] And in March, 1841, when hordes of people fled the threatened city for the rural areas, even more gentry were asked by local officials

*Local histories often stated that their direct antecedents were gentry mediation organizations, used to "resolve difficulties and settle misunderstandings." See, for example, *P'an-yü hsien-chih*, 20:31-a.

to keep the people in line and "watch over things."[37] However, many local notables formed *t'uan-lien* even without the imprimatur of Canton. To the gentry and officials out of office, such activities met a need for action, action that they felt was necessary in the face of the authorities' impotence. Lin Tse-hsu, for example, remained near Canton long after his disgrace, training eight hundred volunteers at his own expense.[38] And if patriotism was not a motive, there was always the danger of looting bands. P'an K'ai in Shun-te county, Hsieh Tse-sen in P'an-yü, Wu Ssu-shu in Hsiang-shan — each man formed such *t'uan-lien*.[39]

The militia movement, if it can be called that, crystallized around the defense of Canton in May, 1841. According to Hsia Hsieh, all of the militia used in the defense of the city came from either Nan-hai, P'an-yü, Hsiang-shan, or Hsin-an* counties. In theory at least, they were based on the *hu-ch'ou-ting* (household levies) system, whereby each household (*hu*) provided one conscript for every three adult males (*ting*). One hundred conscripts formed the traditional *chia*; eight *chia*, a *tsung;* eight *tsung*, a *she*; and eight *she*, a *ta-tsung*. In practice, though, one area's *ta-tsung* might be one-quarter the size of another's. This was because the *hu-ch'ou-ting* network was simply superimposed on preexisting local militia, for in only ten days, all of the volunteers were supposedly collected and transported to Canton.[40]

Only the Hsin-an braves proved to be any help in defending the city. On May 24, they cooperated with Tartar troops attacking some of the British vessels. The other militia units, particularly those from P'an-yü and Nan-hai, had put themselves under the command of officials by May 22, but on that very evening they straggled into a mob and got out of control. Their presence was militarily negligible.[41] The importance of the "movement" was that the Ch'ing officials, in an effort to mobilize the countryside against the British invaders, had gathered together tens of thousands of local males and gotten their blood up. As soon as the truce was signed, these irregulars, infuriated and inflamed, having never really had a chance to fight, were looking for any sort of provocation.[42]

On May 25, 1841, thirteen scholars from the San-yuan-li area met at the village of Niu-lan-kang, where British troops were later ambushed, to plan the organization of a militia in their area. The men swore a blood oath, chose three leaders, and split up to arouse the countryside.

*Hsin-an is the *hsien* from which the New Territories were excised in 1898 to form part of the Colony of Hong Kong, the island of Hong Kong itself having originally been a minor offshore island of the same *hsien*.

The best known of the three, and the man who had asked local authorities to sanction this meeting, was Ho Yü-ch'eng, a famous local writer and *chü-jen*. He proceeded to the northeastern part of Nan-hai, and took charge of militia activities there and across the border in P'an-yü county.[43]

The second, Wang Chao-kuang, an expectant assistant district magistrate, who had earned a sixth-rank button for military merit, presumably in the Opium War, organized six Hakka villages in P'an-yü.[44]

Finally, an influential local notable, Liang T'ing-tung, from En-chou, west of San-yuan-li, combined the "twelve local schools" of his region into a defense command.[45]

Beneath these three major leaders were several other organizers who commanded individual units during the San-yuan-li incident itself: Ch'en T'ang, P'an Shih-ying, Liang Ts'ai-ying, and Ch'ien Chiang—a name which we will encounter later.[46]

Their *t'uan-lien* did not resemble the official paper structure of the *hu-ch'ou-ting*. Instead of *tsung* or *she*, they were organized under "banners" (*ch'i*), usually inscribed with the characters "righteous people" (*i-min*) and the name of the particular village. The last was most important, for each of the *t'uan-lien* represented someone's own village. The irregulars tended to retreat or advance behind the banner of their particular town, and not that of any other unit. There was a unit banner for the entire assembly, a black flag, which was designed to ward off evil spirits and was taken from the Buddhist temple at San-yuan-li. But the essential character of the irregulars remained unchanged.[47] They were a lumped-together assemblage of specific, localistic village units.

If each of the militia represented such particular loyalties, how did they function together at all? How were the nuclear villages transcended in the first place? How, in fact, was this "spontaneous" popular movement held together?

As we have seen, the gentry provided the cement. Only at that level of action could the countryside transcend the *hsiang* (village) and form extensive organs throughout an entire area. Usually a gentry organizer would form a cohesive *t'uan-lien* around one town, as Lin Fu-hsiang,*

---

*Lin Fu-hsiang (1814–1862), a Hsiang-shan man, had studied both military science and the Classics, the latter under the famous Cantonese scholar, Huang P'ei-fang. Huang introduced Lin to She Pao-shun and Ch'i-shan, both of whom were impressed by the young man's defense plans for Canton. After the battle of Chuenpi, when riverine defenses were in such a deplorable state, Ch'i-shan commissioned Lin to recruit "water braves." By May, 1841, Lin Fu-hsiang had trained over five hundred men and assembled a fleet of sixteen junks, which pa-

who led the "river braves," did at Shih-ching. When he had assembled his men, he persuaded the elders of the neighboring villages to enroll their banners under his. Large gongs were then distributed, so that an emergency at one village would bring the others to its aid.[48] From such integral nuclei, other, less tightly organized "banners" could be extended; but gentry leadership, not peasant spontaneity, was the essential factor.

The Kwangtung Historical Research Society has been able to show that most of the secret societies in the area joined in the incident, which, of course, would be quite compatible with gentry leadership and would in no way alter the nature of the movement. However, it has further claimed that "proletarian" elements from the city also participated.

When the news of the initial victory reached Canton, some of the silk-brocade weavers put down their looms and marched to San-yuan-li en masse. Those workmen, called *chi-fang-tsai*, were artisans whose factory had traditionally been associated with a Buddhist temple in their quarter of Canton. They had been especially prominent during the Ch'ien-lung period as a lusty group that boxed, drilled with swords and halberds, and formed a kind of drum-and-bugle corps that participated in popular festivals.[49] In short, they were exactly the same sort of organization that one finds in modern day Taipei: boxing and sword-fighting societies which give exhibitions at local *pai-pai*. There they are usually called *fu-le-she*, and although their organization resembles that of a secret society, they are known to local authorities as "correct sects" (*cheng-p'ai*), and not as "heterodox sects" (*hsieh-p'ai*).* The most important thing about the *chi-fang-tsai* was not their "proletarian" origin but the fact that most of the men who worked in the factory came from En-chou, where Liang T'ing-tung had organized the "twelve local schools."

The conclusion is inescapable. The uprising was neither purely spontaneous nor peasant-led. It was another in a long series of militia organi-

---

trolled the waters west of the city. He was actually defending the shoreline north of Canton when Gough landed there, and he resolved — since his was the only trained Chinese unit operating in that area — to establish a defensive nucleus near Shih-ching. After the Opium War was over, Lin Fu-hsiang slipped out of public view, re-emerging during the Taiping period as a major rebel adviser. Eventually, he was killed by Tso Tsung-t'ang's forces at Ch'ü-chou (Chekiang). See: Hsien Yü-ch'ing, *Kuang-tung wen-hsien ts'ung-t'an* (Hong Kong, 1965), pp. 41–43.

*The only European parallels that come to mind are the *compagnonnages* of late eighteenth- and early nineteenth-century France.

zations that depended upon the careful, sanctioned leadership of the gentry.

And yet, in the end, one hundred and three villages did flock to San-yuan-li's banner. Could sporadic rapes possibly have driven twenty-five thousand peasants to arms? Or was the San-yuan-li incident, as many historians believe it to be, the first manifestation of modern Chinese nationalism?

IV

Traitor in Our Midst

> The more wealthy classes absorb their very existence in trade; commerce is the invariable topic of conversation, the most important pursuit, the highest object of pleasure, and the very goal of all their wishes. — Charles Gutzlaff, "A Dissertation upon the Commerce of China," Jan. 10, 1839*

The Pearl River delta was once a jungle land of tropical animals and fierce Thai tribesmen. Then it was part of Nan-yueh: an amorphous barbarian region comprising Kwangsi, Kwangtung, and Annam. Ch'in Shih Huang-ti "pacified" the area in the third century B.C.; but Canton, then the Nan-hai *chün* (commandery), was only an outpost of Chinese civilization in the midst of marauding southern tribes (*Man*). Later, a Ch'in general named Chao T'o founded the independent kingdom of Nan-yueh, and built Canton's first walls and palaces. Conquering Han armies restored central control, and made the city their command post for all of the Southeast. But as soon as China entered that dark hiatus between the end of the Han and the beginning of the Sui (A.D. 220–589), Canton ceased to belong to a central empire.

In the early seventh century Nan-yueh was reconquered. Then, under the powerful T'ang dynasty (618–906), Kuang-chou began to change. Slowly, the hostile *Man* adopted Chinese names, Chinese dress, Chinese habits. Northern immigrants started to farm its river valleys. Degraded Confucian officials spent their terms of exile in its back-country yamens. Modern Kwangtung† slowly took shape.

Canton progressed with it. As its administrative importance grew, so did its role as a major trading center. For, even though Kuang-chou was cut off from Central China by a ring of high mountains, it did stand at the doorway to Southeast Asia. Under the T'ang, roads were built, the

---

*FO 17/30, Incl. 1, Desp. 4.
†The name "Kuang-chou" was not used until A.D. 210, nor "Kuang-tung" until 1150.

famous Mei-ling pass cut, and Canton's trade soared. Then disaster struck. In 758, Arab and Persian raiders attacked and devastated the city. A little over one hundred years later, just as Canton was recovering from this shock, the notorious rebel, Huang Ch'ao, demanded that the T'ang court give him the command of Nan-yueh. When Ch'ang-an refused to deliver this tempting plum into his greedy hands, the rebel chief loosed his men to plunder and burn the city. One hundred and twenty thousand foreigners were killed and Canton was almost destroyed.[1]

Had the city been merely a military post or an administrative center, it might not have been rebuilt after each of these disasters. But by the eighth century it could boast a thriving population of two hundred thousand Chinese, Arabs, Jews, Singhalese, Indonesians, and Persians — all busy feeding the exotic tastes of the T'ang with gems, rare woods, drugs, and incenses, in exchange for Chinese silks, slaves, and porcelains.[2] This flourishing trade and the revenues drawn from it were more than enough to encourage local officials to revive Canton. One of the constants in the long history of Kuang-chou was the way in which the bureaucracy mulcted commerce. Canton, like some of China's other international ports, was a prize to be fought over fiercely by provincial and central officials. Eventually, the revenue ended up in provincial hands. Not until the Ch'ing period (1644–1912) was the trading system centralized. Then the ritualization of what we now know as the "tributary system" was used not only to appropriate revenue but to control elements disturbing to the Confucian state.[3]

The earliest challengers were merchants, a class which had come into its own after the Sung Period (960–1126). The very word "challengers" may be of European inspiration and hence misleading, because there quickly developed a relationship between merchant and official that worked to the benefit of both.[4] Nevertheless, wherever and whenever large-scale trade existed, the Confucian state made certain that it was controlled. In Canton, the Cohong was created. To its dozen or so members it guaranteed a monopoly of foreign commerce. To the Emperor's trade superintendent, the Hoppo, it represented a physically available source of revenue, grouped into manageable and docile hostages. And to the state at large, it served as an instrument of control over the second set of challengers, the Westerners.

There is no ambiguity here. "Challengers" is indeed the right word. The history of Kuang-chou up to the thirteenth century had been one of slow Chinese expansion southward. In the seventeenth century the mobile shifted. The outside world began to impinge upon China. At

Canton the mercantilist forces of the West met the monopoly forces of the Chinese world.

At first glance, there is a close resemblance between the European mercantile companies and the Chinese Cohong. Both held monopolies originally designed to fill the coffers of the state. But there were three essential differences.

First, European mercantilism consisted of a complete fiscal triangle: Crown, Company, and State Bank. The Chinese system had only two components, State and Cohong. Banking credit was missing, hence the commercial instability of the Cantonese.

Second, the Cohong, in a manner quite without parallel in Europe, guaranteed the foreigners to the Chinese official world. Their unwilling role after 1736 as security merchants was part of the same local regulatory system that had been imposed on Chinese commerce. Thus, whatever efforts the East India Company and the Cohong might have made in common toward furthering trade was opposed by the constant restrictions of the Hoppo. In the eighth century, T'ang overlords so "squeezed" the Canton trade as to force it to shift to Hanoi. The same pressures existed in the eighteenth century. Several times the British tried to trade elsewhere; but the local markets at Amoy or Chusan were too quickly saturated, and their own mandarins just as avaricious. The Company always returned to Canton; and always it faced the same set of hidden exactions, measuring fees, arbitrary customs duties, and "cumshaw." [5]

The third difference was not so obvious, but it existed nonetheless. The European mercantile companies were dedicated to the extension of commerce. The Cohong merchants fought for its restriction under their own control by trying to corner a portion of an existing market. Trade increased almost in spite of their efforts; but it *did* increase, and at an amazing rate throughout the late eighteenth and early nineteenth centuries. Huge fortunes were made on both sides. The wealthiest member of the Cohong, Howqua, estimated his personal fortune in 1834 to be twenty-six million silver dollars (U.S. $52,000,000). His palatial home in Honam with its five hundred domestics, its pleasure gardens of the "ten thousand pines" (*wan-sung-yuan*), was famous throughout China. [6] And there were other successful traders: a colony of merchants from Ningpo; hundreds of Shansi bankers who had settled in the city to handle the extensive cotton trade with northwest China and lend out their bullion; or the four thousand Fu-ch'ao* junk merchants, who sent their ships

---

*Fukien, Ch'ao-chou. These junk merchants originally came from what is now Amoy (Fukien) and Swatow (Ch'ao-chou).

across the waters of Southeast Asia, controlled most of Canton's floating capital, and acted as brokers for trade with the interior.[7]

Yet, for all of their enormous wealth, the merchants of Kuang-chou earned neither ultimate honor nor power. Foreigners from treaty-port days on have made much of the Confucian contempt for commerce. Things were never quite so simple, but there did exist a genuine official animus toward the Canton mercantile interests. The revenue they brought to the coffers of the state may have been important, their houses large, and their local influence great; but they were always mere merchants.

The city reflected this; Canton was no Hanseatic burg. Administratively split in two parts by the P'an-yü and Nan-hai county lines,* it was not even politically integral. It was the *sheng-ch'eng* (provincial city), not the *shang-ch'eng* (commercial city); for the mercantile quarter lay outside the city walls, almost an illegal encroachment. In a European context such merchants might have evolved into genuine capitalists; like their Flemish counterparts, they were originally *negociatores*, living on the fringes of society.[8] But Chinese society was bureaucratic, state-centered. Tax-farming or monopoly capitalism was the only sure road to wealth. Instead of being an independent, vigorous class that challenged a ruling aristocracy, the Cantonese merchants lived in symbiosis with the state and its mandarinate. Status honor being what it was, wealth invariably led to the purchase of office, or conspicuous consumption in the scholar-gentry manner, both of which dissipated capital. Thus, the merchants of China were perpetually servile to the honored symbols of that society, the gentry.[9]

Paradoxically, this emulation of the gentry way of life elicited contempt and disdain, for a county landholder envied the great establishments of Honam. He may even have felt threatened by the degree-purchasing wealth of that mercantile way of life. Most traditional

---

*The eastern half of Canton fell under the administration of P'an-yü *hsien* which ran twenty-five miles east and west, north and south. There the delta lands ended, and the villages were scattered, linked by a passable system of roads instead of rivers or canals. As one moved north from the docks of Whampoa, the plains of P'an-yü gradually became arid, leading into small foothills where every possible bit of ground was cultivated. The western half of the city belonged to Nan-hai *hsien*, running eighteen miles to the west and thirty-five miles north and south. Its topography combined P'an-yü and Shun-te's, though delta lands predominated. Almost as wealthy as Shun-te, it was just as densely populated with silk cultivators and farmers. Its less fertile hillsides were green with sugarcane, ranking it just below Ch'ing-yuan county in that respect. See: Li Wen-chih, *Chung-kuo chin-tai nung-yeh shih tzu-liao*, 1:453–4.

societies consider trade immoral,[10] and such feelings in China were blessed by Confucian doctrine. However, they were not directly expressed in diatribe. Instead, there seemed to be a lingering resentment of the city and its trade among Kuang-chou's local notables. A kind of Joachinism developed that identified Canton itself with immorality, decadence, and even social treason.

This rural-urban distinction must be kept in mind, because it accounted for so much that then seemed puzzling. The British, for example, were astonished at the *volte-face* of 1841 when San-yuan-li erupted. Elliot had been convinced that the interests they shared with the Cantonese would permit a *modus vivendi* to be arranged so that trade could continue while war went on in the North. After the March truce, She Pao-shun had told him that the imperial commissioners would let him know when and if the Emperor ordered hostilities renewed, so that they could mutually arrange a token battle at a safe distance from the city.[11] To Elliot this proved that the local authorities were only going through the motions of war, and that real motives shared by the Canton interests and the British made a settlement possible.

> Indeed, there is evidence of all kinds, that the people of this great city, so dependent upon Foreign Trade, have been pushed by the Court to the verge of endurance, and when we had happily placed ourselves in a situation of mastery over Canton, it at once became manifest that the local government had no choice between immediate exclusion with the hearty dissent of the masses of the people (if not their open insurrection); or an immediate, direct, and formal disregard of the Emperor's will. The late adjustment in fact is little short of a separate arrangement by the Province of Canton, and it cannot be disturbed without immediate consequences, of such moment to the whole Empire as is hard to think the High Officers here, or the Court itself, will dare to induce. The City and Trade of Canton and the whole Province are flourishing . . . under the protection of the British Flag, and the people perfectly understand they would be subject to a recurrence of renewed oppression by their own Government . . . the very hour that our protection is withdrawn.[12]

What Elliot failed to realize was that *form* could be more important than "real" interests, for Chinese political resentment originally stemmed from the British refusal to act within the formal pattern of tributary *li* (rites). Such niceties seemed unimportant to the British plenipotentiary, who had initially been quite willing to use the established forms of intercourse between inferior and superior just so that he could get across the new content of his diplomatic message to the Chinese.* What seemed important to Elliot were the sentiments of the city populace, who so clearly favored peace and commerce. Even his attack on Canton would not drain that reservoir of good will.

> The purposes I had in view were to break up the large contingent force from the other provinces assembled at Canton; to destroy the formidable aggressive preparations of the last few months before we went north-wards again; and to tame the spirit and cripple the resources of the government by dismissing the Imperial Commissioners and laying a heavy contribution upon the Imperial Treasury in part-satisfaction of the just demands of H.M. Government.[13]

But he did not propose to harm "the vast and rich city before us, and its immense unoffending population."[14] Hence, his willingness to accept the ransom, in spite of Major General Gough's anger at a leader as "whimsical as a shuttlecock," who thought more of "present trade" than "national honour."[15] To Elliot, forbearance was a noble gesture: "I believe the safety of this great and rich city from destruction, or from mischief of any kind, is one of the most memorable examples of high discipline and forbearance recorded in military history."[16]

Captain Elliot's sincere belief in these shared interests also convinced him that England should appeal directly to the "people." Proclamations were translated into Chinese and posted publicly. Once, he even cleared one of his placards with the Chinese prefect.[17] Such proclamations usually insisted that the British fought only China's officials and not its people. The Cantonese were reminded that the English were "the real protectors of the city," and were asked to "consider whether the troops of the other provinces now among them were not the real scourge of the inhabitants."[18] Unfortunately, such "spurious" (*wei*) placards did not have the desired effect. It was to be expected that officials would be angered by such an obvious usurpation of Chinese imperial authority.[19] But the local gentry were also enraged.[20] The barbarians had intruded on *their* home ground. Proclamations were traditionally the gentry's way of influencing the peasantry, and the gentry controlled rural Kuang-chou. That was the fundamental British miscalculation. They failed to see that

*Trying to succeed where Napier had failed, Elliot was willing to petition (*ping*) through the Cohong, instead of insisting on direct communication (*chao-hui*) with the governor-general. He believed that all that mattered was imparting the news that he was a political representative and not a commercial agent, even if it meant using a subservient form of communication. Palmerston vetoed the petitionary *ping* and insisted that Elliot communicate directly with the governor-general. See: W. C. Costin, *Great Britain and China, 1833–1860*, 31–37.

the split was not between rulers and ruled, but between city and country. Repeated appeals to the urban populace would bring the countryside to arms, because — as time went on — the rural inhabitants grew more and more suspicious of the city's collusion with the enemy.[21]

There was no question that the citizens of Canton and the English did indeed share certain interests. Elliot was even told that the Cohong formally petitioned Lin Tse-hsu, begging him not to disturb the province's trade by declaring war.[22] Whether or not that was true, Lin himself was genuinely convinced that the hong merchants had betrayed their country for the sake of commerce.[23] This put the Cohong at a more than normal financial disadvantage. Even in peaceful times the security merchants were "squeezed" on every possible occasion.[24] From 1773 to 1832, their *recorded* contributions to the government totaled four million taels, while it was estimated that the Wu family alone had actually given ten million.[25] During the Opium War, their efforts increased, for they had to guarantee their good faith. After the Emperor told I-liang to squeeze the costs of a new navy out of the Cohong, one of their members contributed a fully equipped, modern gunboat, built by Fawcett of Liverpool.[26] But contributions, however magnanimous, only guaranteed further victimization. The mercantile class, and that vast group of go-betweens that we know as "compradors," remained under suspicion. The Manchu officials in Canton were thoroughly convinced that thousands of Chinese were potential, if not actual, collaborators. "Putting out of view those who are actual traitors . . . the rest dwell indiscriminately with foreigners. The utmost intimacy has grown up between them."[27] Hundreds of laborers worked for the British at Macao and Hong Kong. Thousands more supplied food and provisions. It was simply not considered "unpatriotic" to deal with the enemy. Commissioner Lin did all he could to enforce trade and labor boycotts. *Pao-chia* were established around the foreign enclaves. Fishing boats were theoretically allowed to carry only one day's provisions. Special militia were formed just to enroll potential deserters to the British.[28] The officials and the "righteous" gentry were disgusted and worried by fraternization. The mayor of Peking even suggested restricting all native boats to inland waters.[29] But the populace remained apathetic until the panic of March, 1841.

As the Bogue forts fell once more with ridiculous ease and the *Nemesis* terrorized the countryside, as mobs fled the city and panic spread, there began a search for a scapegoat. It was then that all of the antiurban and antiforeign sentiments expressed by the gentry and latent among the peasantry began to merge. Suddenly, "traitors" were everywhere and anywhere, opening the gates of China to the barbarians.

The word "traitor" (*han-chien*) had been used indiscriminately in this context long before the Opium War. The Chia-ch'ing Emperor, for example, so called those Chinese traders who pretended to be Siamese tributary envoys.[30] By at least 1823, opium smugglers were also being called *han-chien*.[31] Even Chinese who merely dealt with the barbarians in a commercial or diplomatic way felt the sting of that accusation. Especially treacherous were those who had "betrayed" their culture by teaching the barbarians the Chinese language, or by writing documents for them.* The man who translated Flint's petition in 1759 was thus decapitated as a *han-chien*. And similar denunciations were heard much later during the Napier affair† when the British ignored all precedents by posting a Chinese placard outside the factories. At that time, Leang A-fah‡ was handing out religious tracts to the scholars when sitting for the provincial examinations. The authorities simply assumed that he was the "traitor" who had written the proclamation for the English. For that act of treachery he was hounded by the Chinese police from Canton to Macao, and he later fled to Singapore.[32] Even under normal circumstances, however, a foreigner who knew how to read Chinese would be careful not to stop and scan a native poster for fear that his comprador would be punished for letting him learn the language.[33]

Finally, when the Opium War began, the word "traitor" was used so indiscriminately that it came to include the entire commercial establishment of Canton. After Lin Tse-hsu declared a boycott against the British in December, 1839, he fulminated constantly against the city's merchants, calling them *chien-shang* (treacherous merchants) for continuing to trade.[34] In fact, his memorials in the spring of 1840 gave the impression that his worst enemy was not the British but the countless

*To the Confucian, civilization was a set of techniques. Mastery of them, including literacy, meant dominance over the uncivilized, the unlearned, the weaker. For a Chinese official's discussion of this, see Li Shih-yao's memorial on the Flint episode in 1759: *Shih-liao hsün-k'an* (Historical Materials Published Thrice Monthly) (Palace Museum, Peiping, 1931), *t'ien*:307-a.

†Lord Napier was sent to China in 1834 by Palmerston to regularize Sino-British trade relations after the abolition of the East India Company monopoly the previous year. Unfortunately, his attempts to communicate directly with the governor-general at Canton had led to a trade embargo, a British show of force which failed to impress the Chinese, and an embarrassing loss of face for the English.

‡Leang A-fah was one of Morrison's rare Christian converts. His pamphlets greatly influenced the Taiping leader, Hung Hsiu-ch'üan.

merchants, boatmen, and coolies who dealt with the enemy. Personally, of course, Commissioner Lin held nothing but disdain for the Cantonese traders. When he first arrived in Canton, one of his initial acts was to threaten the Cohong with the execution of one or two of its members.[35] Howqua* then begged for an audience with the Commissioner, and a meeting was arranged at the Yueh-hsiu Academy. As soon as Howqua was ushered in, he obsequiously offered Lin Tse-hsu full use of his family's financial resources in the conflict to come. Lin contemptuously replied, "This Great Minister does not want your money. He wants your head, and that is all." Then he ordered Howqua imprisoned. Reportedly, the merchant desperately sent vast sums of money to Peking and bought his way out of this indictment. Certainly, he never forgot the Commissioner's enmity. Later, during the Taiping troubles when Lin was named governor of Kwangsi and seemed about to return to favor, Howqua took precautions by sending money to suppress the rebels, along with packets of foreign medicine for the ailing official.[36]

Trading with the British, selling them food, even working for them — that was understandable. But the public began to join in the outcry when collaboration approached treason, as Chinese pilots helped guide British ships up the treacherous backways of the Pearl River.[37] Officially, the Imperial Commissioner tried to lessen his own disgrace by throwing all blame on the ubiquitous "traitors" who had undermined his river defenses. Unofficially, the people of Kuang-chou began a witch hunt. Suddenly the militia were as busy killing *han-chien* as killing Englishmen. Over twelve hundred hapless victims were murdered in the San-yuan-li area alone. Marauding banner troops indiscriminately accused simple peasants of treason, using that as an excuse to loot at will.[38]

The need for a scapegoat was understandable. The opponent had to be generalized into a silhouette, the omnipresent "traitor." The British were out of reach, unavailable. Accumulated frustration, despair, and fear could find an outlet only on nearer targets. For the gentry, perhaps, it was a more intellectual reaction. To the Confucian, failure must stem from a moral cause. In this case it was the spiritual degeneracy of certain segments of the population that had lived too long "in intimacy" with the barbarians. As the *Chung-yung* put it: "If you correct yourself and do not demand perfection of others, then you will be without resent-

---

*This was actually Wu Ch'ung-yueh, the fifth of the famous Howquas. He took over the family firm in September, 1833. See: Liang Chia-pin, *Kuang-tung shih-san hang k'ao*, 226–234; Arthur Hummel, *Eminent Chinese of the Ch'ing Period*, 867–868; Wolfram Eberhard, *Social Mobility in Traditional China*, 82–84.

ment. . . . The Master said, 'It is like the gentleman at archery: when he misses the target, he turns to his own self.' " [39] In another sense, it was only too human. Inexplicable stress often makes its victims search for treason in the ranks. Witness the nativism of the American Red Scare of 1919–1920: a defense against inner turmoil by enforcing order on external life, purging a society of its alien elements. [40]

And so, for the Cantonese, the figure of the "traitor," the *han-chien*, coagulated all of the antiurban, antimercantile and antiforeign sentiments described above. The purism, the "righteousness," of the rural gentry came to be shared by the peasantry.

V

We and They

Shall we expect the myriads of people to endure this, just to sit and watch? At first the will of the people was not united, but now they have joined together to pledge an oath, rescinding the peace arranged by you officials. . . . If you should obstinately continue to follow your mistaken ways, we shall repair our arms, form our righteous troops into ranks, urge our robust braves to exert their strength and our sturdy scholars to perfect their plans, so that when the call to arms is answered, we can once again have peace on our rivers and seas. — Gentry proclamation, May 28, 1841*

When the British attacked Canton in May, 1841, the Ch'ing defenses simply collapsed. While the garrison troops "lolled about the city," alarm spread.[1] What were the authorities going to do? Who would protect the city? Tension mounted until one unfortunate incident precipitated mass panic. I-shan, dismayed and worried, was disembarking from his gig at the waterfront. A gang of coolies, who had been eating at a stall in front of the Great Buddha Temple, put down their bowls of congee and ran in front of the Commissioner's retinue. There they blocked his way, demanding to know what was being done to save them. The Manchu was infuriated by the impertinence of the mob. Without hesitation, he ordered his lictors to seize several of the coolies' spokesmen and decapitate them on the spot. When the marketplace crowd saw their heads roll into the river, they gave way in terror and confusion. The city descended to chaos. Many fled with the deserting soldiers through the gates. Others began to plunder the foreign factories. Fights broke out between the militia and the banner troops.[2] One Chinese official reported: "Innumerable bodies strewed the streets. All discipline was lost; a confused clamour filled the ways, and everywhere I observed plunder and murder. Several thousands of our soldiers ran

*Kuang-tung-sheng, "Kuang-tung jen-min," 280 (see chap. 1, n. 22).

away, after loading themselves with robbed goods, and then pretended they had lost their road in pursuit of the enemy."[3]

Within the city, many citizens begged their officials to sue for peace. Liang T'ing-nan wrote: "Since the army crouched in one corner, conducting only halfway measures and not marshaling to meet the enemy, the people clamored like rushing water, saying that the soldiers were not to be depended on. The city would certainly be destroyed, and the barbarians would enter to burn and loot. And so, supporting the aged and leading their children by the hand, they went crying to I-liang, begging him to take measures of expediency."[4]

Conscientious gentry outside the walls were disgusted by the spectacle within the city. Some offered to send militia, but the authorities, afraid of more rioting and looting, turned them down. Now there was no recourse. Who knew what would happen when the British troops stormed the city from the heights? In desperation, the ransom agreement was signed.

In spite of local authorization for the ransom moneys, which were provided largely by members of the Cohong, this was an informal, unapproved accommodation.[5] The Court was not told of the "bribe." Instead, the defeat was glossed over with tales of local bravery. Peking was assured that continued hostilities would only have given local thugs the chance to loot and burn the city, just as they had plundered the foreign factories.[6] Therefore, as far as the Emperor was concerned, there had been no barbarian victory. If the English wished to humble Peking, they would have to carry the campaign to the North.

Locally, another sort of rationalization occurred. On the one hand, the British had pulled out. As time passed, this permitted the peasantry to fabricate tales and legends of village self-defense and popular heroism. On the other hand, everyone remembered that it was the higher officials, many of whom were Manchus, who had cowardly agreed to the ransom. A new myth was thus created. The Cantonese had really defeated the British, but before they could wipe them out they had been betrayed by their own "treacherous" rulers, who were in collusion with the merchants of the city. This belief was probably the most important single motive of the later antiforeign movement. It literally determined the fate of the empire, for any official who thereafter adopted a moderate policy toward the barbarians could be accused of collaboration and treason.

When She Pao-shun later had to pay an installment of the ransom, he was forced to assume a disguise and meet Elliot in secret. He rightly feared that if he were recognized handing over the funds, there would be an uncontrollable popular revolt. In the eyes of the people, She Pao-shun and other officials had "sold out their country" (*mai-kuo*).[7] With scorn and contempt for their rulers, the peasants sang:

> What a roar the cannons made,
> Elliot lay in wait by the walls.
> San-yuan-li hemmed in on all sides
> While the "Four-cornered forts"
> Were crushed like an egg.
>
> Howqua was best of all,
> Begging for peace with six million dollars!
> *Ch'i-ch'i li-pai.**
>
> Eight thousand catties never even fired:†
> Just enough to melt in the flames.
> Ain't that so, ain't that so?[8]

Traditional "tribute ideology" literally kept the barbarians in their place before the Opium War. While the sun and the moon revolved around a Confucian world, the strangers who came from afar to be "cherished" by a benevolent Emperor were assigned their restricted spheres of insulated activity. Sinocentrism was a corollary of smugness and security. True, the barbarians were not always regarded with complacency, for, like animals, they could be unpredictable and dangerous.‡ But that awful erraticism could be stabilized. Official uneasiness aroused by the barbarians' commercial presence was alleviated when the foreigners were physically confined to the factory area. Similarly, the mass fears of the Chinese about barbarian unpredictability were assuaged by mentally restricting the behavioral patterns of these big-nosed Europeans to categorized stereotypes.

One of the most astonishing things about the Chinese documentary record of foreign affairs during the early nineteenth century is the almost complete omission of any personal characterization of foreign envoys. By nature, of course, "officialese" generalizes the particular. But to the Chinese statesmen of the 1840's, Englishmen such as Elliot, Bonham,

*A rhythmic line.

†This refers to the five-ton (or 8,000-catty) cannon cast at Fatshan, which was never fired and which was eventually smelted by the conquering British.

‡In the 1800's Cantonese mothers often quelled their children's weeping by threatening to throw them to the *fan-kuei*, the bogeyman foreigner. See: *Chinese Repository*, 11:326 (Jan.–Dec., 1842).

or Davis were seldom names and usually were just "barbarian headmen" (*i-shou*). All foreigners were uniform — cutout figures without faces or individuality, possessing nothing but group characteristics.

For one, all barbarians were profit-seeking.[9] This axiom so blinded Chinese policy-makers that Hsü Kuang-chin and Yeh Ming-ch'en were actually incapable of understanding Palmerston's notion of national honor. As long as trade continued and the economic appetites of the commercial barbarians were sated, why argue about getting into Canton City?

Foreigners were also immoral and debauched: *yin*, or "lewd." Every year, the Hoppo regularly warned the barbarian merchants not to satisfy their libidinous dispositions by hiring young boys or courtesans.[10] Nor were foreign women allowed in the factory area.* The unprecedented arrival of several English and American ladies in April, 1830, almost led to a complete stoppage of trade.[11]

After 1841, when complacency was succeeded by fear, these cultural stereotypes assumed a threatening aspect. "Concept formation," or what Lefebvre has called a *nivellement d'idées,* created categorized viewpoints that underlay racial prejudice.[12] Categorization — which enables man to group impressions in manageable units — "saturates all that it contains with the same ideational and emotional flavor."[13] Thus, during periods of extreme social or emotional stress, such categories can bring order into a disordered world by creating generalized whipping-boys. In short, prejudice, and eventually racism, can emerge from stereotypes such as we have examined above. Suddenly all Jews are avaricious, all Japanese treacherous, all Negroes criminally inclined.

The barbarians were profit-seeking. It was a short step from that to a fear of economic exploitation. Surprisingly enough, long before the days of Leninism, the Cantonese began to feel that every foreigner was plotting to seize China's wealth.[14]

All foreigners were lewd. It was an equally short step from that stereotype to genuine sexual fear. Sexual xenophobia often saturates virulent racism. Witness the heavy penalty paid by the Southern Negro for alleged rape, and the fearful rumors of his sexual prowess. Witness the Nürnberg laws and the frightening sterilization experiments of the Nazi death camps. And witness the fact that some of the more glamorous

---

*One might also argue that this was because the Chinese could not tolerate an integral community of barbarians. As long as the strangers perched on the edge of the empire in a state of impermanence (without women) or exclusion (like Macao), they remained cultural clients.

courtesans of Taiwan's "gay" quarters become unacceptable to Chinese customers once they have consorted with American soldiers. We have seen how reports of rape inflamed the peasants of San-yuan-li. The greatest single incitement, according to every source consulted, was the rumor that British troops, usually Indians (whose dark skins had shocked the already prejudiced Chinese), were molesting native women.[15] Eight years later, during the height of the entry crisis, a British observer guessed that similar sexual charges were the most common of popular accusations.[16] And the anti-Christian propaganda that swept Central China twelve years after that almost always identified foreign religion with debauchery, accusing the barbarian priests of magically enticing Chinese women so that their own men could not sexually satisfy them afterwards.[17] In short, early xenophobia and sexual hysteria coincided in China. The sexual drive being the most powerful of all, sexual fears are the most explosive. They are also indissolubly linked to racism because they concern one of the most fundamental of national emotions, the sense of origins — what makes me different from him, and us from them.

The xenophobia of the Cantonese antiforeign movement was not the cultural we-and-they distinction of Confucian tribute ideology. After 1841, the mild cultural stereotypes changed into racial categories. However, those categories were not nationally inclusive. The "we" of the Cantonese was bounded by Kwangtung. The focus was the province, even the ecumene of Canton, the "community of speech."[18] This was xenophobia in its most literal sense: fear of strangers, any strangers. When Hunanese troops were brought into Canton in the spring of 1841, the local gentry persuaded the authorities not to let the soldiers leave the city, because of the high rate of venereal disease that was supposed to prevail among the men from Hunan. When the soldiers stole out at night anyway, rumors spread that they were sleeping with Cantonese women; and some of the braves of Nan-hai and P'an-yü decided to ambush a party of pleasure-seekers. When they caught them, they butchered the Hunanese until "the corpses and bodies were piled high." Those that escaped were chased back through the city gates by militiamen, who screamed that they were *han-chien*.[19]

This was not nationalism. In fact, a strong sense of national identity is not usually found among peasants in such societies. There are too many other particular loyalties: village, sib, land, or even dialect. China suffered from what Deutsch has called "an uneven distribution of overall social communication."[20] The polity, the bureaucracy, held the empire together; but whenever it foundered, the country tended to break up into smaller areas of relative discontinuity, areas which can be viewed as either economic or linguistic regions. The province of Kwangtung was just such an area, and provincial loyalties were high. An antiforeign placard of the period read: "Our Kwangtung is a country of learning, and we are scholars who belong to the militia units, knowing what resources you Kweichow donkeys possess.* Therefore, we raise our righteous banners and pledge to wipe out you devils' spawn. Let the rebellious bandits hide their heads and flee secretly back to their own country if they want to go on living." [21]

Chinese from other provinces often stressed the uniqueness of the Cantonese. They were considered uncommonly bellicose,[22] and they were often looked down upon as serpentine *Yeh-man* (savage southern barbarians) whose habits were bizarre and uncouth. Somehow, Northerners always think of the Cantonese as eating something ungodly, such as newborn rats ("honey peepers"), raw monkey's brains, fried snake, or sauerkraut of buffalo curd.[23] The corresponding Cantonese reaction is an intense, though defensive, pride in their origins. It is not uncommon to find articles in twentieth-century magazines written by people from Kwangtung who claim that their province is the most Chinese of all areas. While the rest of China was sullied by barbarian Mongol and Manchu invasions, Kwangtung remained "pure." Cantonese is also the dialect closest to archaic Chinese. The family, which is the basis of Chinese culture, is stronger there than anywhere else.[24]

Such an obsession with origins and "purity" is typical of regions that are marginal or peripheral to a great national or cultural complex. Quite often the most outspoken of nationalists come from such areas, as if they were quicker to feel the need to possess an organic past: Napoleon from Corsica, Hitler from Austria, Stalin from Georgia. To take a more recent example, the *pieds noirs* of Algeria were self-consciously even more French than the Parisians. This obsession with origins which existed in Kwangtung may even have partially accounted for the bitter Hakka-Punti wars. Certainly, the large number of differing linguistic

---

*Kweichow has no donkeys. One was imported once. A tiger saw it high in the mountains and was terrified by its braying. Approaching it cautiously, the tiger circled round and round the creature until the donkey kicked at it. The tiger immediately took courage and ate the animal. The moral was: "A donkey looks so big, one thinks that it must be very strong; and brays so loud that it must be very powerful. As long as it did not display its powers, the savage tiger did not dare to attack it and eat it up; but when it displayed them, its doom was sealed." See: Wolfram Eberhard, *Chinese Fairy Tales and Folk Tales*, 261–262.

communities around Canton forced people to distinguish ethnically between "we" and "they." In addition, their long period of foreign contact gave them another sense of uniqueness. The inner group is aware of itself only when it faces an outer group.[25] Therefore, xenophobia was almost a natural reaction for the Cantonese once the security of their political universe had been shattered by the British. The provincial focus of that xenophobia was probably a good conditioner for later nationalism. Once you had "Cantonese" and "barbarians," you were bound to have "Chinese" and "Manchus." It was no mere coincidence that Sun Yat-sen's revolutionary *Hsing-chung hui* found its origins in the Canton area. But during the San-yuan-li period, this provincial xenophobia was only protonationalistic. It lacked that sense of universal application which is so necessary for a politically viable ideology. Above all, it lacked revolutionary potential. Like most preindustrial movements of its sort, it was a "legitimism of the barricades," in which the traditional rulers still represented the cultural norm.[26] The fact that the San-yuan-li mob broke up when the officials frightened off the local gentry showed how necessary the gentry were for ideological cohesion, for anything transcending village stone-throwing. Without a potential of its own, without some larger unit of loyalty like the "nation" or the "Chinese people," the peasantry could not agitate individually, except against racial stereotypes like "pigs" or "rapists." It was not nationalism but urbocentrism — the defense of the specific, particular city of Canton — that held the antiforeign movement together.

San-yuan-li was an ideological watershed because it marked the beginning of antiofficial agitation and fervent antiforeignism. A long period of conceptualization, accompanied by individual strain, had suddenly found a formal organization, the popular militia. The isolated individual suddenly realized that his irritation and wrath were "socially sanctioned."[27] Thanks to gentry intervention and the storm of the Opium War, the rural peasantry around Canton had become politicized. They had realized the exhilaration of mass power.[28] Once mobilized, they would settle down only with great difficulty. That was the pattern for the future, and it would literally determine China's foreign policy during the risky decades ahead. As one of the San-yuan-li leaders demanded triumphantly after the battle: "How can we look on the barbarian soldiers with fear? How can we think them ferocious now?"[29]

PART TWO

Strangers at the Gate

THE POLITICS OF RESISTANCE 1842–1849

VI

Righteous or Rebellious?

> We do not need official troops, nor the help of the state. . . . If we do not kill every one of you pigs and dogs, then we are not true sons of the Han, nor a land founded by the Gods themselves. At a single summons, we shall go forth, to lose ten thousand men without retreating. We shall hack, we shall kill, we shall destroy all of you. If you ask others to calm us, we shall not heed them. We shall do our best to flay off your skins and eat your flesh. Let it be now known that we shall massacre you with cruel ferocity. — Gentry placard posted June 5, 1841*

The gentry of Nan-hai and P'an-yü had discovered a new formula for military success in June, 1841: the people's will (*min chih i-chih*). How could the barbarians oppose them now? The people, the gentry, and even the officials were of one mind. The distressing fratricide of the South — *han-chien* versus the righteous — would cease. The nation's soul would be healed, and spirit would triumph over matter.[1]

There was no doubting the sincerity of the people's "zeal" (*fen*). Long after the San-yuan-li affair, bands of patriotic militia continued to hunt down "traitors" and to attack British boats or landing parties near Whampoa.[2] All that the gentry had to do was to convince the local authorities that this zeal was neither misplaced nor potentially rebellious. Petitions poured into the governor-general's office, pleading for official support. "You must know that we are all educated, versed in the Classics. We have a deep grasp of [the principles of] righteousness."[3] Ho Yü-ch'eng, the *chü-jen* who had led the San-yuan-li irregulars, asked that the local scholars be allowed to form a militia bureau for the entire county of P'an-yü. The peasants, he assured the governor-general, genuinely understood "righteousness," and the gentry could vouch for their political reliability.[4]

*Cited in Kuang-tung-sheng, "Kuang-tung jen-min," 290 (see chap. 1, n. 22).

The local gentry had several reasons for keeping the *t'uan-lien* alive. First, there was the immediate problem of protecting rural areas from vagabonds, marauding deserters, or bandits. A wave of social disorder had been generated by the Opium War. During the British assaults on the city, tens of thousands of people were dislocated. One Chinese official estimated that eight or nine of every ten families living in the suburbs had been forced to flee to the countryside or to seek refuge inside the walls of the old city.[5] Bandits, many of them ex-militiamen, "rose like locusts." Secret societies came into the open, to rob and plunder. As conditions worsened after demobilization, many local notables became convinced that only by preserving the *t'uan-lien* could they defend their families, their farms, their villages.[6] Others sincerely believed that the defense of the city, if not of the empire, against foreign incursion depended upon such local initiative. Certainly, the banner troops could offer no help after their miserable failure in May of 1841. "If today's soldiers are like this, then we can see what those of later days will be like; if one province's troops are like this, then we can see what those of the Empire will be like."[7] Above all, however, men like Ho Yü-ch'eng could not bear the thought of letting the militia movement lose the emotional momentum it had gathered after San-yuan-li.

Several militia bureaus were opened just after the famous incident.[8] But the real institutional successor to that *levée en masse* was the *Sheng-p'ing she-hsüeh* (local school of approaching peace). One of the minor leaders at San-yuan-li, a man named Li Fang, took it upon himself to rebuild the local school at Shih-ching.* When the school was founded in 1764, it had serviced eight villages in P'an-yü and five in Nan-hai *hsien*. Since then it had fallen into disrepair, but during the excitement in May, 1841, the decrepit ruins had been used as Lin Fu-hsiang's militia headquarters. Now it was to become the largest militia bureau of the time.[9] By the end of the year, from fifteen to eighteen similar bureaus, all under the nominal leadership of the Shih-ching office, had been set up in the local schools of the region. The collective name for this federation of militia was taken from the central office: the *Sheng-p'ing she-hsüeh*.[10] Li Fang remained the actual organizer, helped by a staff of four other local leaders. By 1842, however, the nominal director and figurehead of the organization was Ho Yü-ch'eng's prestigious friend, Liang T'ing-tung. Thanks to his participation, local gentry contributed

---

*Shih-ching, site of the later "Shektsing League," lay on the border of Nan-hai and P'an-yü counties, north of San-yuan-li. The *she-hsüeh* there still stands and is now used as a primary school for the district.

more than twenty thousand taels, and each of the fifteen or eighteen local *t'uan-lien* boasted an approximate membership of ten thousand.[11]

Just how centralized was this federation of militia? Li Fang's administrative bureau took seven of the twenty thousand taels to recruit a hard core of mercenaries, since the "outer" *t'uan-lien* were only composed of temporary levies. In fact, Li eventually moved his headquarters from Shih-ching to Chiang-ts'un,* where he could recruit *yung* more easily. But even seven thousand taels could not last forever. By 1843, little was heard of the league. Yet the *Sheng-p'ing she-hsüeh* was to appear and reappear during the next twenty years, following the fluctuations of war and rebellion. For long periods of time it would exist only as a paper organization. If the government discouraged militia, it became inactive. If a crisis should arise, its bureaus were reopened. In 1849, for example, the gentry of the two counties contributed the enormous sum of 440,000 taels to the *Sheng-p'ing* league to help in the defense of the city.[12] And thanks to its continued existence, the villages of northeastern Nan-hai and northwestern P'an-yü developed a vigorous local tradition of rural self-defense that would stand them in good stead during the Taiping troubles. More than anything else, though, the *Sheng-p'ing she-hsüeh* set a pattern for all later militia.

It was relatively easy to summon twenty-five thousand peasants for a three-day battle. But how does one routinize popular fervor? What institutional device could be used to regularize the levies? There was always *pao-chia*, but that was a passive control organ, not a positive form of social organization. The answer lay at hand in the "local school."† Whenever clan elders or the gentry of an area wished to form a transvillage organization, the *she-hsüeh* provided a "nodal point for local co-operative endeavour."[13] In 1836, for example, village leaders near Whampoa had become alarmed by secret-society activity. Twenty-four of the villages built a common hall under the guise of a "local school" at a market town on the south side of Honam island. There the elders met under an elected president to try miscreants and bind them over to the district magistrate.[14] Thus, while a common hall (*kung-so*) might be called a "local school," it also functioned as a meeting place for multivillage organizations. Even though denouncing a clansman for secret-society membership was politically correct and welcomed by the local authorities, this kind of independent municipal or clan activity

---

*Chiang-ts'un is in the northwest corner of P'an-yü on the borders of Hua-hsien and Nan-hai.

†See Appendix II.

operated outside of sanctioned channels. The Ch'ing emperors had long been suspicious of any local activity that was not officially recognized. Since the *she-hsüeh* were semiofficial and eminently Confucian in tone and function, they provided a "cover" for communal or gentry activity. One of the important functions of Kwangtung's "local schools," for example, was to mediate clan wars.[15] "At the time when robbers and bandits were quite numerous in Kuang-chou, and had already fomented serious disturbances, every hamlet and walled village established publicly organized local schools, and collected funds to run them, asking the local gentry to arbitrate in order to mediate legal disputes."[16] Above all, the *she-hsüeh* played a vital role in the development of *t'uan-lien*.[17]

In fact, the existence of the militia movement in Kuang-chou during the Tao-kuang period was one other reason for the renascence of so many local schools that had fallen into disrepair or ruin during the intervening years. As institutional expressions of the militia, the *she-hsüeh* served as recruiting depots, treasuries, meeting halls, posting

TABLE 1

LOCAL SCHOOLS AROUND SAN-YUAN-LI

Name	Founded as a School	Militia participation
Shih-ching	1764	Headed Sheng-p'ing league.
Ho-feng	1766	Joined San-yuan-li irregulars.
T'ung-sheng	1801	Contributed 1,000 men to the Sheng-p'ing league.
Kuang-jen	1824	One of the "twelve schools" which participated at San-yuan-li. Later, it was occupied by Triads during the Red Turban rebellion.
Fo-ling	1827	Originally founded by 24 of the villages around Hsiao-kang. Ho Yü-ch'eng headquartered here. After 1841, it led the antiforeign movement in its region. Also used by rebels during the Red Turban revolt.
Lien-sheng	1837	Prominent at San-yuan-li.
Hsi-hu	1841	Prominent at San-yuan-li.
Ch'un-feng	1841	A center of antiforeignism in the 1840's.
T'ung-wen	1841	Prominent at San-yuan-li. Involved in later antiforeign movement.
Lien-hu	1841	Provided many irregulars at San-yuan-li.

SOURCE: Kuang-tung-sheng, "Kuang-tung jen-min," 293–295.

places, and drill grounds. More than anything else, they helped legitimize the movement in the eyes of suspicious local authorities.

After the ransom of Canton in May, 1841, provincial officials gave their first thoughts to the restoration of the city's shattered defenses.[18] To save on costs, Ch'i Kung and I-shan thought that militia could be used for the reconstruction. They even suggested that military colonists be settled around the Bogue to combine farming and fighting.[19] Peking's obsession was finance.[20] The burden of a large standing army was almost intolerable. In Kwangtung, for example, each soldier cost four taels per month just for upkeep. Military colonists and locally financed militia would reduce those expenses.[21] Besides, had not the Cantonese *t'uan-lien* fought more bravely than the garrison troops? Shortly after San-yuan-li, the governor-general of Fukien and Chekiang, Yen Po-tao, implored the Emperor to utilize the ardor of the people, as expressed at San-yuan-li, by sponsoring a coastal militia movement throughout the country.[22] The Court was unquestionably pleased with the victory at San-yuan-li but felt some doubt about the unqualified use of *t'uan-lien*. The Emperor had warned Ch'i Kung on June 28, 1841, that "There are unforeseen consequences [to militia]," and asked him and I-shan to report as fully as possible on the use of irregular troops in Kwangtung.[23] Their answering memorial described the feats of the *t'uan-lien* in glowing terms. They were skeptical of some of the exaggerated accounts, but there was no question that both Ch'i Kung and I-shan felt that the normally apathetic, treacherous, and anti-Manchu population of Kwangtung had suddenly proved to be a tremendous boon to the dynasty. This was the one thing that could be salvaged from the ruins of policy in the South. And so they asked that "reliable gentry" be encouraged to organize militia which could be used to build river barricades and patrol roads around Canton. However, the Emperor's ancestors had had too much trouble with Kwangtung in the past to give him much confidence in their loyalty now. For the time being he laconically endorsed the reconstruction plans and reserved his judgment on the militia.[24]

I-shan, Ch'i Kung, and I-liang remained undaunted. In early September, 1841, they memorialized the Emperor again, presenting a master plan for the development of Kuang-chou's militia. Since the imperial reinforcements garrisoned at Canton were plagued with diarrhea and fever and were rapidly running through their grain supplies, why not send them back to their home provinces and draft irregulars in their place? Boldly the officials told the Emperor that some steps had already been taken: "We have already selected certain members of the gentry, namely Hsü T'ing-kuei and Huang P'ei-fang,* to go out into the villages in all four directions to summon the gentry and people, and train militia." Since then the gentry of Nan-hai and P'an-yü had enrolled thirty-six thousand braves, all young, healthy fellows, full of vim and vigor, well armed and well trained.† Their leaders were loyal and upright local gentry, who had assured the governor-general in their own words: "We are all profoundly aware of the Dynasty's deep compassion and how it has enriched [the country] for the past two hundred years." Moreover, these leaders were in full control of each of the village bureaus, which had conscientiously subscribed to the federation's bylaws. "In addition, bandits run boldly along the roads near the sea-coast. The counties of Hsiang-shan, Hsin-an, Hsin-hui and Tung-kuan have seen since last year [several examples] of bitter and shameless conflict between the local officials and the people. . . . What a calamity [it would be] not to muster this public zeal in the defense of the city." Finally assuaged, the Emperor agreed to the request and gave his full approval to the gentry militia.[25]

This initiated a year of government-approved *t'uan-lien* activity, from October, 1841, to October, 1842. I-shan himself even held a public dinner in January to collect funds for the militia. The *Sheng-p'ing she-hsüeh* flourished and grew.[26]

Then came the end of the Opium War in August, 1842. On October 1, 1842, after the news had reached them, the magistrates of Nan-hai and P'an-yü ordered the *t'uan-lien* to disband.

> Whereas the affairs of the English having compelled us to station soldiers, and to collect volunteer companies of militia for the defense of every place, this is to declare that peace having been re-established, on a certain day, every body of troops wherever placed for the defense of the county, and all the companies of militia, must immediately disband and return home, thus affording quiet alike to the soldiers and the people, and not retarding their usual occupations.[27]

But had the war really ended? Did the concept of warfare between national equals even exist for the Chinese at this time? Mencius once wrote, "Imperial correction (*cheng*) is when a superior punishes an inferior. Enemy states (*ti-kuo*) cannot correct each other."[28] Thus, unresolved conflict between equally powerful enemies remained outside

---

*Huang was an eminent classicist, and one of the eight directors of Canton's famous literary academy, the *Hsüeh-hai-t'ang*.
†This, of course, was the *Sheng-p'ing she-hsüeh*.

the hierarchical scale of civilized Confucian behavior. To accept the notion of "national enmity" was to concede that the barbarians confronted China as an equal *ti-kuo*, "enemy state." Therefore, after 1842, the English were still kept within the traditional, soul-satisfying scheme of things by being classified as rebels, "revolting" (*ni*) against the universal figure of the Emperor. Only a formal gesture of acquiescence, like the symbolic kowtow, could restore the balance.

Thus, many Chinese recognized no change at all in their relationship to the British after the Treaty of Nanking was signed. In January, 1843, one of the Cantonese militia bureaus told the governor-general, "The British rebels are secretly stirring up trouble north of the city."[29] The rebels would still have to be "pacified." And this meant that local militia would have to continue to exist.

In July, 1841, two other San-yuan-li leaders, Wang Shao-kuang and Kao Liang-ts'ai, had decided to create a copy of the *Sheng-p'ing she-hsüeh* on the other side of the White Cloud Mountains in northeastern P'an-yü. They called their organization the *Tung-p'ing kung-she* (public office of the eastern peace). Because both were expectant assistant district magistrates, they received enthusiastic official and gentry support. The *Tung-p'ing* league was never as large as its paragon, mustering only about nine thousand irregulars, but it did unite Hakka and Punti in that area, and even built a small munitions plant with gentry subscriptions.[30]

When *t'uan-lien* were disbanded in October, 1842, Wang and Kao dissolved their *kung-she*. Three months later, for unknown reasons, they decided to try to get official permission to reopen their bureaus. The device used was a common one, employed before and after this incident. The gentry leaders asked the governor-general to give them permission to erect a stone tablet honoring one of their heroic braves. Had this request been granted, it would have sanctioned further militia activity.[31]

One year earlier such a petition would have been readily accepted. But the *t'uan-lien* had changed since 1841. The ideal militia leader trained and armed farmers, who returned to their villages as a corps of minutemen, ready to march out whenever the gongs of battle sounded. This was fine as long as the peasantry around Canton was committed enough to give up their spare time to drill and train. By early 1842, though, much of the popular fervor aroused by the San-yuan-li incident had died down, and the gentry found itself forced to hire permanent militiamen, who were distributed throughout a given district and billeted in local schools.[32] By uprooting the locally unemployed, the militia bureaus thus helped create a group of landless, well-trained and armed *condottieri*, who had to be kept under gentry control. Therefore, when the war ended, the militia may have been "officially" disbanded, but probably even more soldiers of fortune were put on *t'uan-lien* payrolls — if only to prevent them from becoming outlaws. In short, once professionals were involved, the militia system became self-perpetuating, since disbandment meant the instant creation of paramilitary gangs of rowdies.

Worse yet, once the war was over, some members of the gentry withdrew their patriotic support. By default, the organizations fell into the hands of the less "righteous." Then, and earlier, a local squire could not simply approach a village tough and ask him to join his militia. There had to be social intermediaries, men who could function at both levels of society.* Often these were lower gentry, *sheng-yuan*, who could not personally found "local schools" because they had neither prestige nor official contacts.[33] Every militia group relied heavily on such men. For the *Tung-p'ing kung-she*, for example, it was an organizer named Lo Pao-kuang.[34] Some of these men were even drawn from other provinces: minor degree-holders attracted to Canton in search of fame and fortune against the British. There they simply waited for an opportunity to prove themselves, "drifting about, sojourning in the provincial capital" (*liu yü sheng-ch'eng*).

In November, 1840, a band of such men fell under the control of a persuasive military adventurer named Ch'ien Chiang. Ch'ien typified the more successful soldiers of fortune of his time. Born in Chekiang, he had spent his boyhood studying books on sorcery and military tactics. A scholar's life, he told his friends, was a waste of time. Besides, it blunted one's military keenness. Nevertheless, Ch'ien did try to pass the exams, failing several times, and finally bought a *chien-sheng* degree.[35] Restless and ambitious, he left for Kwangtung when the Opium War began. There he heard that the rural gentry of Kuang-chou wished to fight the British by "summoning together town and country vagabonds" and falsely entering them on the militia registers as local *ting*. He promised his cohorts that the organizers of such "vagabonds" could earn both money and military rank if they succeeded. The idea sounded wonderful; the only problem was that none of his lieutenants were Cantonese. Ch'ien Chiang solved this by having them pretend to belong to clans whose names were inscribed in Canton's Confucian temple (*Ming-lun-t'ang*).

---

*There was an avoidance of face-to-face relationships even in normal activities in South China. Land transactions, minor quarrels, betrothals, the determination of produce prices — all required the use of middlemen. See: Daniel Kulp, *Country Life in South China: The Sociology of Familism*, 1:99.

Then Ch'ien approached a local notable named Su Lang-jao, who provided him with funds collected by his village's militia bureau. Placards were promptly posted all over the waterfront, offering each new recruit a bonus of two dollars for joining.* To give the whole affair an air of legitimacy, regulations were even carved on wood and hung up in the *Ming-lun-t'ang*. Exactly what happened after this is difficult to say. Ch'ien, by all accounts, led a militia unit at San-yuan-li. Some even insist that he headed the mob which burned the foreign factories in December, 1842. Yet he was later accused of having squandered Su's funds on wine, women, and song. By April, 1843, however, he had enough standing as a militia leader to bluff his way into the governor-general's yamen and demand to be appointed director of local defense.[36]

At this very moment, a heated national debate was taking place over the militia.[37] Should organizations like the *Tung-p'ing kung-she* be allowed to exist? On the one side stood those who felt that *t'uan-lion* expressed the righteous will of the people.[38] Ch'i Kung memorialized: "We always consider the people our country's foundation (*pen*). If the people's feelings are resolute, then the power of the country will be strengthened. This is what the foreign barbarians really fear, and this is what we within the country must pay the most attention to."[39] The opposition, led by Ch'i-ying, warned that *t'uan-lien* could easily get out of hand.[40] The people were "righteous." But if China should pursue a moderate foreign policy, angering the local militia, it might find these "patriotic" braves turning into dangerous rebels. The question was really one of control. How much power did the higher and more reliable local gentry exercise over the *t'uan-lien*?

This question was inadvertently answered by Ch'i Kung when he rashly jeopardized the very gentry he wished to support by losing his temper at the bold effrontery of Ch'ien Chiang. When he had the adventurer arrested, † the case quickly reached Peking and helped convince

---

*For some reason, vendors of salted vegetables around the docks often joined such militia. See: FO 228/126, Meadows' report, Incl. 1, Desp. 9, Jan. 7, 1851.

†Ch'ien Chiang was eventually exiled to Sinkiang. There he found that his reputation as an activist had preceded him. For he had almost become a symbol of the hard-line policy that Ch'i-ying and others seemed to be betraying. His fame spread among the garrison troops on the frontier, and he was soon pardoned. From Sinkiang he traveled to Peking, to hang about the ministries, offering schemes and suggestions which were generally ignored. Some of the important officials of the capital, however, took a liking to him and tried to arrange for an extraordinary appointment. This was refused. Embittered, he was supposed to have responded with alacrity when news of the Taiping victories reached Peking. "My genius cannot be hid," he proclaimed, and then sneaked out of the capital

the Emperor that the militia units were falling into the hands of those who, "in the name of public interest, pursue private ends, hypocritically using Confucian temples to post proclamations," which "aroused and deluded" (*shan huoh*) the people.[41]

Thus, by the summer of 1843, the highest levels of the government had decided that the potentially rebellious militia would be permanently disbanded. In truth, the *t'uan-lien* continued to exist clandestinely in Kwangtung during the mid-'forties, both in defense of local order and as instruments of the antiforeign movement.[42] But as far as national policy was concerned, the militia would not regain their legitimate and "righteous" character until Hsü Kuang-chin used them so triumphantly in 1849.

in an old cart to join Hung Hsiu-ch'üan at Wu-ch'ang. There he was said to have presented the Taiping Emperor with a grand scheme for the conquest of China. Lo Erh-kang has shown that this meeting never occurred but that Ch'ien ended up, along with other local militia experts, in Lei I-hsien's *mu-fu* (tent government) at Yangchow. There seems little doubt that Ch'ien did indeed "invent" the new form of taxation known as "likin." Its success went to his head, and he became so arrogant that eventually even Lei became angered by his protégé and had him decapitated. See: Lo Erh-kang, *T'ai-p'ing t'ien-kuo shih pien-wei chi* (A Collection of Discussions on Forged Facts, Objects, and Books about the Taiping Heavenly Kingdom) (Shanghai, 1950), 117–149.

VII

The Entry Dilemma

> The authorities stand in awe of the people, instead of the people standing in awe of the authorities. — Foreign Office Dispatch from Lay to Pottinger, May 1, 1844*

From 1842 to 1849 the politics of Kwangtung were dominated by a single problem: the Chinese refusal to allow the British to enter the city of Canton. The diplomatic entanglement was simple enough. The second article of the English version of the Treaty of Nanking gave the British the right to reside in the "cities and towns" of the five treaty ports. The Chinese text only allowed them to "reside temporarily at the ports of the cities." This misunderstanding simply formed the legal nexus for a set of forces that impelled the two governments into one dangerous confrontation after the other.[1]

British policy was characterized by the "clash between the merchants' folklore, which pictured the infinite potentialities of the China Trade, and the official conviction that this vision had been grossly exaggerated."[2] During the years after the Nanking settlement, the newly formed British Chamber of Commerce in Canton carried on a voluminous correspondence with the powerful Manchester Chamber of Commerce. This mercantile bloc became convinced that the disappointing trade returns at Canton after 1844 were the result of British official reluctance to force their way into the city, and the Chinese imposition of inland transit duties. This conviction was expressed again and again to Palmerston by the Manchester Chamber of Commerce.[3] And even after Davis took action in 1847,† these British commercial interests remained dissatisfied, demanding a "more firm" policy to "overcome the unruly rabble of Canton."[4]

English officials could not ignore these voices. After all, commerce was England's prime diplomatic motive in the Orient. Only after 1852,

*FO 228/40, Desp. 8.
†See chap. 8.

when the Mitchell Report* introduced the principle of Chinese economic autarchy, did the government begin to realize that trade did not necessarily follow the flag.[5] But during the 1840's, British officials in China were constantly forced to bow to Manchester's demands that Canton — and China — be opened to English commerce. Certainly, there were fluctuations. In August, 1841, the Whigs resigned to Peel's Conservatives, and Lord Aberdeen began a period of retrenchment at the Foreign Office, a reaction to flamboyant Palmerstonian diplomacy. Guizot was soothed, the Queen visited Louis Philippe, and Asia quieted down. Eventually, of course, the Potato Famine and the Free Trade Crisis defeated Peel's ministry. By December of '46, the Whigs were back: Lord John Russell at 10 Downing Street, Palmerston at Whitehall. Immediately, Peel's foreign policies were reversed. England broke with France over the Spanish marriage question, and Palmerston vigorously began to promote British interests in Asia.[6] In China this attack settled on the Canton entry question. Three hundred foreigners in Canton were stuffed into twenty-one acres of the old factory area. Stifled, frustrated, envious of colleagues in Shanghai — their Chamber of Commerce's demands for entry grew increasingly strident.[7] Consuls and plenipotentiaries had come to feel more and more that Britain could no longer afford to let herself be humbled by the mobs of Canton. As long as the Chinese kept the barbarians out of the city, Kwangtung's officials would continue to scorn British power and secretly to impede trade.[8]

Their Chinese counterparts — particularly the Liang-kuang Governor-General and Commissioner for Foreign Affairs, Ch'i-ying — faced an even tighter set of pressures because of the empire's military weakness. Masataka Banno has brilliantly described Ch'i-ying's dilemma:

> He was closely connected with Grand Councillor Mu-chang-a, who held the real power in Peking and had led the peace party at the time of the Opium War. The foreign policy of Mu-chang-a and Ch'i-ying, however, was essentially a variation of the "barbarian management" strategy, and its aim was to preserve as far as possible the established regime. In the background there was an antiforeign mood in Peking officialdom and among the literati and officials generally throughout the empire, and in Canton there was a violent antiforeign movement. Consequently, the policy of conciliation within the framework of "managing the barbarians" rested on an extremely precarious

*The Mitchell Report, an analysis of Far Eastern trade prepared for the British Foreign Office in 1852, suggested that China was economically self-sufficient. This was the first hint that the Manchester merchants' dream of an unlimited market of 400 million customers within the borders of the Ch'ing empire was no more than a myth.

equilibrium maintained by the influence of Mu-chang-a's clique, by the skill-ful maneuvering of Ch'i-ying, and by the persisting memory and fear of British military strength.[9]

The most unstable element in this equilibrium was the virulent xeno-phobia of Canton.

On September 16, 1841, when the official "betrayal" at San-yuan-li was still a recent memory, the prefect of Canton, She Pao-shun, went to the examination hall in Canton to administer one of the prefectural exams. Results of an earlier test had shown that the scholars of Nan-hai county had scored first over all. When She arrived, the students from Nan-hai and P'an-yü began to boo, shouting: "All of us have read the writing of the sages and know rites and proper decorum. We will not take an examination given by a traitor." They threw their inkstones, driving him from the examination hall. When the Nan-hai and P'an-yü magistrates tried to soothe the students, the mob accused the officials of "wearing dirty white hats instead of pure, precious golden hats," and added that they should wear their honorary peacock feathers on the front of their hats instead of on the back. The meaning was painfully obvious to the two officials, both of whom had helped She Pao-shun break up the mob of irregulars at San-yuan-li. But finally the magistrates managed to calm the candidates, who still refused to take the examina-tion unless the prefect resigned. The public storm was so great that She Pao-shun submitted his resignation and was temporarily succeeded as prefect by I Ch'ang-hua.[10]

This was perfectly legitimate agitation. The rebukes were Confucian, and the students had not rioted until they had already proved their worth by all accepted standards.* Traditionally, there was a distinction between riots directed against the abuses of local officials, and rebellions directed against the established system or dynasty. Hostility had to be expressed loyally and locally.[11] In fact, a local official could often serve his Emperor better as a whipping-boy. As far as the official was concerned, though, the ignominy of such an incident meant resignation or worse. As far as Peking was concerned, such agitation might eventually lead to actual rebellion. A moderate foreign policy, then, could be fatal to either party. It did not take Ch'i-ying long to realize this, but by then it was too late.

---

*Later anti-foreign riots often took place during examination periods, when rural scholars, fervently xenophobic, gathered together in the prefectural capital, laboring under immense emotional strain. See: Paul Cohen, *China and Christianity: the Missionary Movement and the Growth of Chinese Antiforeignism, 1860–1870*, 86, 90–95, 105–106.

He was already caught between two millstones: British demands and the antiforeign movement.

As soon as the Cantonese gentry received news of the Treaty of Nanking, protest began. Placard succeeded placard, rumors fed on other rumors.[12] The public became alarmed. On December 2, 1842, a public meeting was called to set matters straight. As one group of gentry tried to read a manifesto urging calmness and moderation, another broke into vociferous argument and the meeting dissolved in confusion. To compound matters, the badly timed visit of several foreign wives to the factory area seemed to confirm new rumors that the British were planning to enter the city immediately. As a last resort, the governor-general and governor jointly forbade placards, meetings, and the public denunciation of official policy.

The following day, December 7, 1842, the entire affair erupted into violence. A lascar, strolling near the factories, got into an argument with a fruit vendor and stabbed him to death. The irate mob that quickly gathered turned on the foreign factories, burning some to the ground. The next day, more gathered to loot the smoking ruins. Only then did the authorities clear the area with two hundred Chinese troops. However, Ch'i-ying quickly and apologetically paid a large indemnity, and decapitated ten of the mob's ringleaders.[13] His policy of firmness seemed a total success. Public agitation suddenly died down, and matters apparently returned to normal.

Seven months later, in July, 1843, Ch'i-ying felt confident enough to announce that Canton would soon be opened to the barbarians. To his surprise, this was met with the same round of petitions, placards, and meetings. This time Ch'i-ying told the British plenipotentiary, Pottinger, that it was no use, the people were too excited. The British would have to wait until public sentiments changed. Pottinger, still slightly embarrassed over the lascar's senseless act of violence, acquiesced.[14]

This was followed by a three-year hiatus. Pottinger was getting along too well with Ch'i-ying to raise a seemingly unimportant issue, Lord Aberdeen wanted no adventurism, and the British Chamber of Commerce was too busy counting its profits to think of disturbing the booming Canton trade. There were minor irritations, of course, but mutual good will made accommodations possible.[15]

In 1844, however, Pottinger retired as plenipotentiary. His successor was an old China hand, Sir John Francis Davis,* who was convinced

*Davis had been an interpreter for the East India Company, and accompanied Lord Amherst's embassy to Peking in 1816.

that Britain's failure to subdue the "rabble" of San-yuan-li had been one of the great mistakes of the Opium War.[16] A year as plenipotentiary convinced him all the more that the city question was the key to Chinese responsiveness. On March 22, 1845, Davis told Ch'i-ying that the Chinese authorities had prevaricated long enough. The stipulations of the Treaty of Nanking must be fulfilled. Ch'i-ying answered, just as he had before, that popular emotions were too agitated. He could not guarantee the safety of the British if they did enter the city. Davis, fettered by Aberdeen's caution, had to admit that antiforeign incidents had increased during the past few years. But if the British could not formally enter the city, at least they could ask for Chinese protection for Englishmen wandering through the countryside. Time and time again, parties of casual hikers had been reviled, robbed, or stoned in the rural hamlets where antiforeign feeling was the strongest.

Six months of desultory discussions at the consular level followed. Consul James MacGregor first met with the prefect of Canton, and the magistrates of Nan-hai and P'an-yü in June, 1845. The Chinese insisted that the only safe promenade area was just around the foreign factories. They justified their firmness quite simply. An insertion in the sixth article of the Chinese version of the Supplementary Treaty stated that British residents could not go into the countryside around the treaty ports beyond distances jointly fixed by the local district magistrate and British consul, "due regard being had to the dispositions of the people" (*ke chiu ti-fang min-ch'ing*).[17] This new impasse lasted for three months. Finally, thanks to a combination of threats and cajolery, MacGregor persuaded the magistrates to post official proclamations outside the city. These placards informed the people that the foreign merchants had been trading in Canton for two hundred years and had brought great benefit to the area. The Emperor himself had decided on peace because the Chinese and the barbarians formed one great family. Furthermore, the merchants, just like the Chinese, loved to exercise. The people must not interfere with their harmless excursions.[18] These Confucian platitudes did little to change the people's hostility. Besides, the magistrates posted only ten such placards in inconspicuous places.[19] MacGregor, disgusted by their lack of cooperation, continued to plead for compliance until the Nan-hai magistrate frankly admitted that the officials dared not "incur the odium of the people" by appearing too proforeign. Only an imperial edict, he assured MacGregor, could alter such unvarying popular hostility. Such an edict would take three months to obtain.*

---

*By express courier, it would really have taken only about one month.

Finally, MacGregor played the last card in his hand. He warned his counterpart that if entry was once again postponed, the British would not return Chusan* to the Chinese.[20]

Ch'i-ying, realizing that the recovery of Chusan would be a great diplomatic triumph for his and Mu-chang-a's policy of "managing the barbarians," had been looking forward to paying the last installment of the indemnity on January 22. Now MacGregor was warning, with Davis's approval, that payment might not be enough. China would have to show some good faith over the entry matter.[21] Accordingly, Ch'i-ying decided to try once again. On January 13, 1846, an official proclamation announced that the foreigners would have to enter the city. Gentry opposition to this state policy was approaching sedition. Denunciations must stop.

This was the showdown. The rural gentry had already warned Ch'i-ying that "our villages" would disobey official orders if he allowed the British to enter.[22] In turn, the Governor-General was trying to do what She Pao-shun had done at San-yuan-li: threaten the gentry themselves so that they would exercise their control over the peasantry and calm the agitation. In 1841 the gentry had panicked. This time they picked up the gauntlet. On January 14, placards posted on every street corner announced that the barbarians would be massacred the moment they set foot in the city. If the security merchants tried to protect any of them, they would meet the same fate. Canton's high officials were not only weak but naïve.

> They do not reflect that the English barbarians are born and grow up in wicked and noxious villages beyond the pale of civilization, have wolfish hearts and brutish faces, the looks of the tiger and the suspicion of the fox, and that the cause of their not presuming to covet our Kwangtung consists only in their not getting into the city to make inquiries respecting the true state of the country and hear the reports on affairs.[23]

In the meantime, Ch'i-ying had secretly sent the prefect of Canton, Liu Hsin, to discuss the entry matter with the British. Somehow news of this meeting was leaked to the public. As rumor had it, the prefect was actually setting the date for barbarian soldiers to march through the city gates. On January 15, Liu Hsin returned from his meeting. On the way into the city, he found his official progress deliberately blocked by

---

*According to article 12 of the Treaty of Nanking, Chusan was to be returned to China when the Opium War indemnity had been completely paid.

an insolent coolie sitting in the middle of the road. Immediately, the prefect ordered his lictors to seize the coolie by the hair and flog him. The watching mob of several thousand city dwellers began to mutter. "The officials dispense with the *tao* of the Ch'ing to welcome foreign devils. They consider us, the people, as their fish and meat." Alarmed, Liu ordered his carriers to take him back to his yamen. The procession moved away but the mob followed, and the retreat turned into a rout. When Liu reached the yamen, the mob pushed his guards aside and followed him inside. Some even broke into his living quarters and set fire to his official robes, shouting, "If he is going to serve the barbarians, he cannot again be an official of the Great Ch'ing." Others chased the prefect on into the back garden, where he escaped through a gate into the governor's residence.[24]

This was a genuine urban mob, the *menu peuple* whose riots filled the pages of the British *Blue Books* during the 1840's. Disturbance excited them, and they excited disturbance. They were always ready to change from a peaceful marketplace crowd to a yowling, screaming mob, terrifying foreign merchants and native officials alike. The preindustrial cities of central and southern Europe once had their urban mobs, too. There the populace lived off a resident court, the Church, or an aristocracy, because the city itself had little or no industry. This distinguished Rome, Naples, Palermo, or Istanbul from London or the Flemish cities, where the guild was the basic form of mass social organization. Canton, of course, had some industry, but its guilds were merely protective associations, hardly expressing a distinct class interest. Therefore, its urban mob was not politicized. Political action was urbocentric, imbued with municipal patriotism, for there were no specific class loyalties. When its behavior did transcend urban *jacquerie*, it became "legitimist" — first, because it spoke in the name of the Emperor, and second, because it used a traditional cliché to indict the prefect: he was feeding on the people like a parasite, treating them as "fish and meat." Yet there was a new and disturbing tone to the accusations. The prefect was parasitic because he was too proforeign. The city mob had begun to equate its own leaders with the foreigners. This kind of identification occurred elsewhere under similar circumstances: the Flemish revolts, Wat Tyler's rebellion, the Taborites — all identified their ruling classes with foreign allies or interests, hitching the powerful emotions of xenophobia to inarticulated social disrest. In each case, the revolt preceded a period of strong national awareness. As with the cases cited above, Chinese class discontent and "nationalism" were being joined into one, potentially revolutionary, set of attitudes. The Emperor still represented ultimate legitimacy, but here were the beginnings of later revolutionary anti-Manchuism.

This time the rural gentry and the urban mob were not satisfied with the mere resignation of the prefect. When the provincial treasurer and the provincial judge tried to quiet the city, agitation only increased. By the morning of January 16, 1846, the officials had lost their nerve. The judge and treasurer denied that they had ever intended opposing the "righteous" people. The barbarians would have to be kept out of the city.[25] This proclamation was quickly followed by an abject apology from the governor-general, Ch'i-ying, and the governor, Huang En-t'ung: They were deeply ashamed of the way they had been forced to bow to barbarians' demands in the past, but now they had no intention of favoring the barbarians over the Cantonese. Ch'i-ying even pretended that he had only wanted to test public opinion. He had never really intended to let the barbarians enter in the first place: "If the people are really all averse to the English entering the city, how should We be willing to act quite contrary to their feelings, and in a devious spirit, comply with the prayers of the English? Do not cherish feelings of doubt and suspicion."[26]

The Kwangtung extremists had scored a clear victory, unmarred by the belated arrival of the imperial rescript that had been promised in December. The Emperor's message to the barbarians was sprinkled with the usual homilies — "mutual friendship," "cherishing the men from afar" — but the British were granted only a vague permission to trade at Canton. Ch'i-ying used the rescript to order the local gentry not to placard or act in a disorderly manner under the pretense of "public righteousness."[27] But no one was fooled. The Governor-General had lost enormous face. His only possible consolation was that the British, fearful of seeing a moderate driven out of office by fanatics, had shelved the entry matter. On March 11, the British, French, and Americans announced: "His Imperial Majesty having stated that after a lapse of time when tranquility is insured, it will be safe and right to admit foreigners into the City, and the Chinese Government being unable at present to coerce the people of Canton, the Plenipotentiaries agree it be postponed, though the claim is not yielded by Her Britannic Majesty."[28]

The Throne could not afford to ignore this rumbling in the South. On March 10, 1846, the Emperor received an alarming memorial from the censor of the Hu-kuang circuit, Ts'ao Lü-t'ai. Ts'ao insisted that popular xenophobia was more fervent than ever in Kwangtung. The foreigners' demands alienated the people more and more from their own officials, and local bandits were using the series of crises to further their own ends. Worst of all, local officials had lost all control over the militia movement, and the gentry no longer heeded their proclamations. In Ts'ao's opinion, foreign policy would have to be adapted to this new domestic crisis. A strong stand should be taken on the entry question, lest the coastal peoples of the South rise in rebellion.[29]

On May 28, 1846, the Emperor received Ch'i-ying's answer to the censor's charges.[30] The Governor-General divided the opposition in Kwangtung into two camps. There were the loyal and righteous gentry, and there were the troublemakers who would use any diplomatic crisis to foment riot and rebellion. In light of this, there were three steps that had to be taken. First, eliminate rumor mongers and mob leaders. Second, take a strong stand against the British. Third, win back the gentry's support. The first had already been partially executed: "We have instructed and ordered our local officials to secretly investigate and sternly punish [malefactors], devoting special attention to the ringleaders and sentencing them according to the strictest of laws. In this way, the followers of the bandits will be split up and scattered."[31] Unfortunately, the tragic abyss between the people and their officials would not be as easy to handle. Both really should be of one mind, for though the means differed, their aims were the same. "The officials want to use artifice to control the barbarians, while the people want to carry out their will without deviating. In reality, there is not the slightest disagreement between them."[32] Yet the two were like the snipe and the mussel: one hunting the other while the fisherman — Great Britain — caught them both. The Cantonese were too truculent, too antiforeign. "The city of Canton has had trade relations for one hundred years, and yet not a single foreigner has entered the city; and even though the people have had social intercourse with the barbarians, they still call them *fan-kuei*. They do not even consider them to be human beings."[33] Furthermore, their xenophobia had led to the creation of militia units which were sources of disorder and rebellion. "Such militia emerge at a summons, because they are robust and have leaders; but they are really unreliable vagabonds who make no attempt to keep from stirring up other members of the militia who frequently drift into banditry."[34] Not that all of the *t'uan-lien* should be condemned. Some, like the *Sheng-p'ing she-hsüeh*, were genuinely loyal and controllable.

If the militia are attached to local schools, then each one assembles the fathers and elders, the brothers and sons, of the villages for mutual defense. When there is no longer any reason [for mobilization], they scatter and dissolve, returning to their fields. And if something should happen, they always listen to official orders to move on. These local soldiers are regulated by laws, and their thoughts do not wander beyond the question of defending themselves. Even though when formerly assembled, they numbered several tens of thousands, yet by and large they are under the command of public-spirited and upright gentry.[35]

It was not they who had first opposed the prefectural officials. It was not they who had burned down the factories. The gentry and their militia were basically loyal. All the more serious, then, when they began to question official policy. During the recent crisis, they had refused to respond to the mandarins' orders for the first time. That was genuinely alarming. If the government continued to appease the barbarians at the expense of local patriots, "I sincerely fear that we shall be cutting off our own limbs." [36]

Yet the dilemma remained. If the barbarians were given a pretext for invasion before the unreliable militia and mob leaders had been singled out, Canton would suffer the same disorders that came in '41 and '42. This time, open rebellion might even ensue. On the other hand, if a moderate foreign policy were pursued, the barbarians might be appeased, but the gentry would grow restless.

There was only one course to follow. The barbarians would have to be soothed with token adjustments. That would give the Cantonese authorities a period of grace, during which they could use reliable local notables to weed out potential troublemakers. Artifice and flexibility was the key. "There has never yet existed a force which cannot be tamed; and so we can eventually use the barbarians to manage the barbarians." [37] But could Ch'i-ying appease the British and assuage the Cantonese at the same time? Could the circle be squared?

VIII

Huang-chu-ch'i: Time Runs Out

> Our cannibal mandarins have hitherto been the
> accomplices of the English robbers in all the
> acts that the latter have committed against or-
> der and justice. For five years to come our na-
> tion will mourn the humiliation it has been forced
> to undergo. — Placard cited in M. M. Callery
> and Yvan, *The History of the Insurrection in
> China* (London, 1854)

On July 8, 1846, a British merchant named Compton had an argument
with a Cantonese plum vendor. The enraged Englishman beat the huck-
ster and dragged him into Minqua's hong. A mob of shopkeepers,
laborers, and stall-owners collected on the street outside, and began to
clamor for their compatriot's release. When no official troops came to
break up the gathering, some of the hotter heads among the foreign
merchants armed themselves with fowling pieces and marched out of
the factories to disperse the Cantonese mob. In the confused struggle
that followed, three Chinese were shot to death.[1]

The tables had been turned. For the past five years the English had
righteously insisted on redress for each of the many attacks on their
own citizens in Canton. More often than not, the authorities had complied. Now, in a throwback to the days of the *Lady Hughes*,* the question
of guilt was reversed. Ch'i-ying was asking them to do what he himself
had done several times for Pottinger and Davis: punish the guilty parties.

As the affair stretched out, the news reached Great Britain. There

---

*When a Chinese was killed by a gun salute from the merchant ship, *Lady
Hughes*, in 1784, the Ch'ing authorities demanded that the culprit be handed over.
Naturally, it was impossible to determine which gunner was responsible for the
accident. Finally, in order to secure the release of the ship's supercargo, the *Lady
Hughes'* captain remanded one unfortunate seaman to the Hoppo, who promptly
had him strangled.

Palmerston swiftly deflected the thrust of the Chinese attack, and satisfied the Manchester lobby. In true *civis romanus sum* style, he categorically declared that "British residents are not to be attacked or insulted
with impunity." The deaths were ultimately the fault of the unruly mob,
not of the merchants who had fired on them, for the Chinese government
had neglected its own police duties. In fact, the Chinese should prosecute
the riot's leaders. And just to make sure that there would be no further
incidents, a British warship would be stationed off the foreign factories.[2]

This was Palmerston's public stand. In private he warned Davis not
to wantonly excite Chinese animosities. The merchants must not be
allowed to feel that Her Majesty's plenipotentiary condoned this sort of
vigilante behavior. Therefore, it was important to determine who was
responsible for arming the merchants.[3]

The only person to whom guilt could clearly be assigned was Compton.
According to the Chinese investigation, Compton had been involved in
a similar fight four days before the riot. Then, the apoplectic Englishman
had kicked a fruit-stall vendor on Old China Street, and used his cane
to beat up the police officer who intervened. Only the happy arrival of
a group of compradors had saved Compton from the hands of an enraged mob. On the actual day of the incident, July 8, it was really another
foreigner who had first gotten into an argument with the plum vendor.
Compton had been upstairs conducting business in Minqua's hong when
he heard the wrangle and had rushed downstairs to intervene. He had
tied up the Chinese, beaten him severely, and dragged him inside the
hong.[4]

The British never denied these facts. They only said that Compton
had dragged the vendor inside because he wished to bind him over
for delivery to the local authorities. In truth, even Palmerston was embarrassed by this local zealot who had involved the Chinese and British
in another, unwelcome confrontation.[5]

For the same pressures were at work. Behind Davis stood the cham-
bers of commerce, screaming for retribution and military protection.
Jardine, the English merchant-prince, particularly insisted that a man-
of-war be immediately stationed in front of the factories.[6]

Behind Ch'i-ying stood the local gentry, demanding retribution for
the three dead Cantonese. The inevitable placards appeared, all stating
the same indignant theme: the local officials were so afraid of offending
the barbarians that they could not even protect the populace from
assassination. The Emperor's *Sacred Edicts* "regard the lives of the
people as of the highest importance." If a man was killed anywhere in

the empire, and the local official there were to "evince the slightest insincerity" in punishing the culprit, the people had the right to indict the mandarin before the Emperor. This was the unalterable law of the land. Yet now, when mere barbarians murdered the sons of the Han, the officials were afraid to act: "The high authorities treat the matter as if they had not heard of it, regarding the outlandish devils as the god before whom nothing is obscure, but ranking the Chinese people as fish and flesh, and treating human lives as contemptuously as hairs in a cap." Therefore, proclaimed the gentry, the local *she-hsüeh* had taken it upon themselves to massacre the guilty foreigners.[7]

Ch'i-ying responded to such threats just as he told the Emperor he would. To restrain the urban mob, he had shopkeepers appoint one or two men as guards and informers in the more turbulent quarters of the city. The police were told to arrest any agitators on sight. To keep panic from spreading, all available information on the incident was publicly released as soon as it was received. Meanwhile the acting grain intendant of the province was charged with securing the cooperation of reliable local elders and gentry in the countryside. Finally, to prevent the affair from turning into a *casus belli*, Ch'i-ying decided to work closely with MacGregor in accord with treaty provisions, and to isolate the causes of the riot.[8]

The Emperor endorsed these plans: "Fairly handled. We must not permit the said barbarians to find a pretext for outrageous behaviour."[9]

However, Ch'i-ying was not as assured about the outcome as he would have liked to pretend. As he told John Davis, "The people are powerful by their numbers, whilst their superiors stand isolated."[10] On the British side, the residents' demands for protection seemed justified by the growing number of Chinese placards calling for the execution of the guilty merchants. MacGregor finally summoned the *Nemesis* on September 17, and the foreign merchants began to form their own self-defense groups just in case the plans of the "local schools" for a massacre materialized.[11] Matters looked ominous indeed.

But thanks to Davis's inclination to blame Compton for the entire situation, and Ch'i-ying's willingness to accept face-saving compromises, disaster was finally averted. On August 26, Davis had suggested that the Chinese punish the police officer who should have dispersed the mob; that Compton be fined for breaking down the fruit stall; and that the families of the three dead be compensated.[12] Ch'i-ying felt that Compton should be punished, not for breaking the stall, but for beating the plum vendor.[13] It might be impossible to single out the individuals who actually shot the three Chinese, but the English would have to offer Ch'i-ying something more than financial compensation. If a barbarian were punished for beating a Chinese, this would offer ample proof of Ch'i-ying's good will to his unmanageable Cantonese constituents.[14] Davis saw his point, and incurred the wrath of the mercantile community by levying a fine of two hundred dollars on Compton for attacking the vendor.[15]

Suddenly the diplomatic crisis was over. Ch'i-ying gave up all hopes of prosecuting the murderers, while the English relinquished their demand that the local police authorities be punished. But the social crisis endured. Sullenly, reluctantly, the "local schools" abandoned their overt campaign for retribution. Once again the Cantonese believed that they had been sold out.[16]

The Compton affair had primed the British for action. It was as if England were simply waiting for an opportunity to compensate for her earlier diplomatic embarrassment. A minor antiforeign incident in the fall of 1846 caused Palmerston angrily to tell Davis, "We shall lose all our vantage ground we have gained by our victories in China, if we take a low tone." [17] These instructions reached the British plenipotentiary just after a second incident: six hiking Englishmen had been stoned by a rural mob near Fatshan, in the heart of militia country.[18] On March 27, 1847, Davis peremptorily ordered Ch'i-ying to punish the assailants, or suffer the consequences. When the Governor-General failed to comply, General d'Aguilar led a sudden and slashing attack on the Bogue. On April 1, the forts were taken and 827 cannons spiked. An expeditionary force landed at the factories. Hog Lane was sealed off and preparations were made to enter the city. Ch'i-ying, astonished and frightened by this unpredictable display, yielded to *force majeure*. The three assailants were publicly flogged, and the British were promised that they could enter the city on April 6, 1849. The two-year interval would give the Governor-General time to calm the xenophobes and convince them of the government's good will.[19]

This hope was a delusion, for antiforeignism was even then spreading from the rural gentry and urban mobs to the "reliable" middle and upper classes of the city. After the April agreement was signed with Davis, a genuine panic swept through Canton. For a long time, the foreign merchants had been looking for land to rent in Honam or around the factories. New, British-owned warehouses were needed both to avoid onerous storage dues and to remove goods from the vulnerable factory area. In May, 1847, the Cantonese authorities began to clear away some of Hog Lane's firetraps and tenements, which housed most of the "vagabonds" the Chinese had promised to chase out of the factory area. Since at that moment the British were negotiating for land both in Hog Lane and Honam, the shopkeepers and householders of those two quarters became convinced that d'Aguilar's raid had frightened Ch'i-ying into secretly allowing the barbarians to annex their property. This panic was based on a misunderstanding, but it served to create the first urban militia that Canton had seen. On May 20, householders from the two areas held a meeting at the Consoo house. All voted to resist foreign expansion by hiring rural braves, supporting the families of any slain militiamen, and if necessary, erecting a temple to the heroic dead.[20] Other assemblies of shopkeepers contributed one month's rent for weapons and mercenaries, while the carpenters' and masons' associations pledged that they would never erect any buildings for the foreigners in Honam.[21]

The merchants and workmen who attended these assemblies derived great satisfaction from the decisions. It was almost as if they had collectively raised their "caste" status by going through the motions of recruiting militia, in emulation of the wealthy, honored, and envied gentry of the socially prominent "ninety-six villages." However, this new urban militia was quite different from the rural *t'uan-lien*. Its strength lay not in the braves, who were simply mercenaries hired when necessary, but in the leaders' ability to quickly organize the city into "control" wards. This was a police, not a defense, function that would prove of decisive importance in 1855.

For the time being, the militia were of no use at all, for the "real estate" crisis turned out to be a tempest in a teapot. By June 7, 1847, the Honam householders had finally understood that the British wished to rent, not purchase, land for their warehouses. However, some of the more obscurantist villages on the outskirts of the city continued to complain about the barbarian presence, and on August 3, the British Chamber of Commerce finally decided that whatever benefits might be had were not worth the public fuss.*

Canton City quickly settled down, but rural Kuang-chou saw one antiforeign incident after the other during the summer and fall of 1847. Time and time again, the surprisingly foolhardy English were cursed, stoned, robbed, and chased back to the city by peasants from Nan-hai and P'an-yü. In each case, Ch'i-ying did his very best to pacify Davis. The attackers were quickly punished while proclamations exhorting

*See Appendix III.

moderation were constantly being posted in the countryside. But try as he might, the Governor-General could not keep the English from growing annoyed, while his handling of each new incident made him appear to be more and more the appeaser in the eyes of the local gentry. Finally came an incident that could not be resolved by simple floggings or proclamations: the brutal murders of Huang-chu-ch'i.

Huang-chu-ch'i (the mountain path through the yellow bamboos) was a small farming village just south of En-chou in Nan-hai county, across the river from Canton. The village had joined the *Sheng-p'ing she-hsüeh*, and in August, 1847, groups of young men could be seen busily drilling and training. Once a group of the zealous braves even fired on a pleasure craft full of foreigners, but they failed to hit anyone.[22] On the morning of December 6, 1847, six young Englishmen disembarked near Huang-chu-ch'i to hunt for waterfowl. They had not returned by late afternoon. When the frightened native boatman heard shots and the clanging of the village's militia gong in the distance, he hurried back to the factories and reported their disappearance.[23] The following morning, rumors reached Canton that the villagers had murdered them. Those foreign merchants who had been lethargically participating in the self-defense corps were galvanized into activity. They had armed themselves and were about to leave *en masse* for the village when the consul, Mac-Gregor, heard of their plans and headed them off.[24]

On December 8, ominous placards began to appear. The *Sheng-p'ing* headquarters issued a proclamation attacking the British in the vilest of terms.[25] Something was clearly brewing. The next day, every rumor and suspicion was confirmed: the bodies of two of the young men had been found, cruelly mutilated by multiple sword wounds. The other four bodies were still said to be at Huang-chu-ch'i.[26]

Davis, shocked and irate, knew that he could not force matters too far. After General d'Aguilar's raid that spring, London had ordered him not to take any military action without prior clearance. On the other hand, Ch'i-ying could hardly know of this stricture, and might be bluffed into a corner. Davis could never have been more correct in an assessment, for just as soon as he threatened to remove the entire foreign community from Canton as a prelude to war, the Governor-General wilted.[27] Remembering the Bogue forts, Ch'i-ying decided to make an example of Huang-chu-ch'i. The village was occupied by banner troops and four men were immediately beheaded. Fifteen others were arrested and bound over for trial.[28] Three of the province's highest officials personally visited the major towns of Nan-hai and P'an-yü to warn the inhabitants that they would suffer the same fate if they molested foreigners,[29] and official placards were posted that read:

> Whereas, while a neighborhood is free from disturbance, the virtuous and well-conducted are enabled to dwell in comfort, when strife has once commenced, how is it possible for them to ensure the safety of each other's houses and families? To act on the anger of the moment is to press the foot unwittingly upon the spring of personal danger. . . . From the time that these commands reach the gentry and lower orders of the villages, the father must thenceforth exhort the son, and the elder brother persuade the younger, that, if foreigners are rambling to and fro, shooting or fishing upon the shore by the entrance of the villages, in no way molesting the inhabitants, they pay no attention to them.[30]

Ch'i-ying was still trying to drive a wedge between the gentry and "unreliable" rural elements. To him the most dangerous aspect of the antiforeign movement was the social threat that it posed. Fanaticism would lead to war, which in turn would produce banditry, pillage, and social rebellion. He firmly believed that the gentry could be awakened to that danger before it was too late; the forces of order in Kwangtung must see that a moderate foreign policy represented their best interests. Unfortunately, the Governor-General underestimated the unifying power of hostility. During the 1840's, the foreign threat helped hold the classes of the countryside together, in spite of increasing banditry and secret-society activity. Ch'i-ying simply could not understand this, because he was essentially a man of reason — confused, bewildered, and eventually destroyed by irrational forces. Now time had run out. The Emperor was growing weary of these troubles in the South.

The Governor-General's memorials to Peking during December and January recurrently stressed his fear of foreign invasion. He did pretend to a certain hard line in his reports to the Emperor,* but it was clear that he put the greatest emphasis on soothing the barbarians rather than the Cantonese.[31] The Emperor agreed that Ch'i-ying's three major policies were sound: ordering the British to calm their people; ordering local officials to calm the rural areas so as to give the foreigners no pretext for invasion; and secretly preparing for another British attack at the Bogue. But there remained the problem of redress.

In this matter, poor Ch'i-ying was left in suspense. On the one hand,

---

*"I ordered the barbarian headman to restrain the other barbarians," etc. See: *Ch'ou-pan i-wu shih-mo*, Tao-kuang 78:27-b.

the Tao-kuang Emperor agreed that local troublemakers should be
"firmly repressed." But at the end of his edict, he solemnly warned the
Grand Council that the Governor-General must be "firm in his management of affairs. Let him see that each side is meted out justice, but he must
not handle matters so as to lose the people's loyalty. This is the most
important of all." [32] On January 2, the Emperor learned of the executions
at Huang-chu-ch'i. Ch'i-ying assured him that an invasion did not appear
imminent. But once again, remembering Davis's unpredictable behavior
in April, 1847, he warned that the barbarians were like dogs: once
angered, they could not be restrained. New Year's was drawing near, and
the merchants would be clearing their debts, but the British still might let
their inexplicable fury get out of hand.* For, the barbarians behaved
according to the rules neither of decorum (*li*) nor of reason (*li*). They
simply reacted in unfathomable ways. [33]

This time the Emperor's response was much more ominous. Virtually
ignoring Ch'i-ying's warnings of war, he expressed alarm at the executions. The Governor-General's strictness might lose the loyalty of the
people. [34]

Although Ch'i-ying could not possibly have received the Emperor's
warning by the time he wrote his third report, which reached Peking
on January 12, he was already justifying his decision to execute the
four villagers on the spot. Hsü Kuang-chin's investigation had proved
that the six Englishmen had not incited the murders. Important local
officials, even the gentry militia leader, Hsü Hsiang-kuang, agreed that
only an immediate punishment could have forestalled a British attack
on the city. Besides, the government had not lost popular support. Local
officials were working hand-in-hand with responsible local gentry and
village elders to keep order and to weed out potential bandits. [35]

But, like Palmerston, the Emperor simply reversed the matter: what
were the British doing at Huang-chu-ch'i in the first place? Their presence, not the behavior of the peasants, was the real incitement. [36]

Ch'i-ying could not convince his ruler that he had acted correctly. On
February 3, 1848, the old Manchu was replaced by Hsü Kuang-chin as
governor-general of the Liang-kuang and Commissioner for Foreign
Affairs, while Yeh Ming-ch'en was named governor of the province. As
the Emperor confidentially explained to the Grand Council: "The only
important thing is to appease the people's emotions. If the people's loyal-

---

*Ch'i-ying was still operating in terms of cultural stereotypes. The city was
loaded with goods at this time of year, and the "profit-seeking" foreigners could
be expected to hesitate before launching an attack that would disrupt trade.

ties are not lost, then the foreign bandits can be handled. From now on, if there should be any incidents in Sino-barbarian relations, we must not be unduly lenient for fear of giving offense." [37] On March 1, Ch'i-ying received the imperial order. He immediately turned over his seals of office to Hsü, and left two weeks later for Peking, under the shadow of disgrace. Cantonese xenophobia and antiforeign feelings had cost him his job and eventually, one supposes, his life.

The die had been cast. The people's loyalty had to be retained, even if it meant risking war. Ch'i-ying's warnings of incipient rebellion, of an unrestrained militia movement that could wreck the province, were not heeded. Xenophobia was loosed, Hsü Kuang-chin would attempt to ride with it, and behind him one could see the flickering flames of the gutted Summer Palace.

IX

The Victory of 1849

The Viceroy secretly summoned the militia of the villages. Those who responded to the call were altogether more than a hundred thousand men. The Viceroy himself went in a small boat to the English ship and informed them that it was better not to incur public resentment. More than ten elders, one after another, called at the English consulate and expressed various opinions. The English chief then plotted to detain the Viceroy as hostage, and the shouts of the militia on the two shores shook the heavens. The English chief was frightened, requested restoration of the good old relations, and said nothing more of entry into the city. Hence, the Cantonese felt increasingly assured of themselves, claiming that unquestionably the foreigners could be easily controlled. — Hsüeh Fu-ch'eng*

On March 16, 1848, George Bonham, the cautious governor of Singapore, replaced Sir John Davis as plenipotentiary and governor of Hong Kong. During the spring and summer of that year, the new envoy gingerly raised the entry question with the new Chinese commissioner, Hsü Kuang-chin.[1] For, according to the Bocca Tigris Convention that Ch'i-ying and Davis had signed, the British would enter Canton that following spring: April, 1849. But the Chinese Governor-General cavalierly ignored the matter. Hsü Kuang-chin's appointment had erased his predecessor's diplomatic arrangements. Chinese unfamiliarity with international law or the concept of "full powers" meant that a given policy was regarded as the handiwork of a given man. If that man were dismissed, he took his policy with him. The Bocca Tigris Convention, as far as most Chinese were then concerned, had been disgraced along with its author, Ch'i-ying.

*Translated in Yen-yü Huang, "Viceroy Yeh Ming-ch'en and the Canton Episode (1858–1861)," *Harvard Journal of Asiatic Studies*, 6.1:49.

Oddly enough, Bonham himself was also inclined to dismiss the entry deadline, but for different reasons. He told Palmerston: "Your Lordship will be aware that, by orders from the Colonial Office, I am precluded from moving troops from Hong Kong; but without some military demonstration, I am satisfied that it will be useless to attempt an entrance into the City. Personally, I have not heretofore considered it a matter of much importance."[2] At that time there were two schools of thought among the British in China. The merchants at Canton, the residents of Hong Kong, and the older Chinese hands like Sir John Francis Davis, felt that Canton was the key to a rational China policy. If resistance were crushed there, the empire's arrogant foreign policy toward Great Britain would change. The other faction believed that such a view was myopic. Peking would shrug off a disaster in the South. The Emperor would disavow the disgraced commissioner, appoint a replacement, and continue to confine the barbarians to the far corner of the empire. Pottinger had felt this way. Alcock* and Bonham would have agreed with him, for Bonham wanted to bypass Canton altogether. Official opposition was too inflexible, and popular xenophobia too rabid, to allow the British peaceful entrance into the city. A large and brutal show of military force would be necessary, and that would disrupt the Canton trade. Instead, Bonham wanted to sail north to the Peiho, where he could submit his proposals for tariffs, entry, and so forth, directly to the Court. If necessary, he might threaten to blockade the Yangtze and cut off Peking's grain supplies.[3]

Palmerston, long under the influence of Davis's reports, vacillated. When Bonham's first dispatch concerning the question reached London in September, 1848, the Foreign Secretary ordered him to continue to press for entry. The plenipotentiary received these instructions in December, and obediently began to try to arrange a meeting with Hsü Kuang-chin.[4] By late January, the two had agreed to meet on February 17, 1849, at the Bogue office of the Chinese Admiralty.[5] There was just one problem: Palmerston, impressed by Bonham's pessimistic assessments, had changed his mind. Better to wait until there were more blatant treaty violations before taking steps which might lead to war. Bonham received these new instructions virtually on the eve of his meeting with the Chinese commissioner. And so, just as the home government had decided to drop the entry matter, the British plenipotentiary help-

---

*Then an up-and-coming young consul at Shanghai, and later (1865–1871) British plenipotentiary.

lessly began discussions designed to force Hsü to open the city's gates
to the English.

The modes of diplomacy practiced by the British and Chinese in 1849
were startlingly different. On the one hand, Bonham cleared every detail,
even to the amount of stationery purchased, with London, which was
months away. In contrast, Hsü acted almost independently, informing
Peking after the fact, engaging in flexible but risky diplomatic maneuvering. That is not to say that the Governor-General was impetuous, or
completely out of touch with the Emperor. On the contrary, the memorials he sent to the Court during the six months before the February
meeting outlined a lucid and rational foreign policy.

First of all, Hsü Kuang-chin realized that the British military position
was not as strong as Ch'i-ying had thought. Spies had reported from
Hong Kong that army supplies were low and that the English were
reducing their garrison. Nevertheless, he was certain that when April 6
arrived, the British would at least make a show of strength: "The nature
of these barbarians is such that they commonly love to brag and often
depend on force of arms. When their warships approach, then they issue
their demands. Such is their custom."[6] Entry was only a pretext. The
British would make use of it to extract more concessions, eventually
hoping to rescind the prohibition of opium. Appeasement was out of the
question. No matter what China did, the barbarians would continue to
demand more and more territory and resources. "The barbarian's nature
is to covet profit."[7]

Appeasement would also destroy the empire's ultimate defenses by
losing the people's loyalty. "Beyond [the territories] ruled by the
Heavenly Dynasty, rites should be stern. Within the boundaries of
the nourishing bosom [of the Emperor], tolerance should be permis-
sive."[8] How could one nurture the people "within," and still cherish
the barbarians come from afar? The two premises were contradictory,
and had already created an ominous situation in the South. Even though
Kwangtung's officials had never deliberately used the entry question
to arouse the people, the Cantonese themselves spontaneously exploded
whenever the barbarian presence made itself felt. Huang-chu-ch'i had
been an example of their ferocity. If thwarted, the people might even
rise in rebellion.[9] Not that the antiforeign movement in Kuang-chou
should be condoned. "These people use methods to coerce local officials
that absolutely should not be carried out. They force the masses to obey
them, causing the officials and the people to come to odds."[10] But the
fact was that the officials and people of Kwangtung were already mutually

alienated. Any foreign crisis was automatically blamed on the province's high officials. The major goal of the government in the South, then, should be to recover the people's loyalty. Local militia, even though potentially dangerous, should be encouraged but not allowed to run amok and provide the English with a *casus belli* (*hsin-tuan*).[11]

To a generation of treaty-port foreigners, Hsü Kuang-chin symbolized the rabid and irrational xenophobe. This simply was not true. He had watched Ch'i-ying fall, victim of the Canton mob. Now he resolved that the Governor-General should lead and not be led. The only way to regain control of events was to assume leadership of the antiforeign movement. This meant abandoning all of the cherished notions of the "barbarian management" experts. As a pragmatist, Hsü denied the tributary notion of nourishing the foreigners. The covetous English would never be content with minor concessions. China would have to gird itself for long-term combat, and that meant strengthening the "inner" against the "outer" by solidifying the dynasty's popular base. That in turn meant that Britain must categorically be refused entry. The only possible way to do this without having another war was to use Ch'i-ying's diplomatic argument of popular resistance. The means of certifying that argument, and preparing for war in the event it should fail, were the local militia.

On the seventeenth of February, 1849, Hsü and Bonham met aboard the flagship *Hastings* in Anson's Bay. Formalities were exchanged, and then Bonham invited the Governor-General into his personal cabin for a private talk with only the interpreters present.* Hsü was troubled, probably remembering how Ch'i-shan's private conferences with Elliot had been misinterpreted by the Emperor. He wanted his assistants with him, but Bonham insisted that he could call them in for consultation whenever necessary. Hsü finally agreed, and they went in together.† Bonham immediately raised the entry matter, and Hsü commenced a "harangue," which he excitedly repeated several times, to this effect:

> He had it not in his Power to carry out the Agreement entered into between Sir John Davis and Ch'i-ying, and that each of these officers was well aware of this fact when the arrangement was made, and, indeed, that Ch'i-ying had given the promise under constraint from fear that Canton would be bombarded, and that under the circumstances, he,

*Meadows and Gutzlaff.

†This was the incident that must have inspired later apocrypha to insist that the Governor-General was held as a "hostage" by Bonham, and was rescued by the militia. See: *Ch'ing-ch'ao yeh-shih ta-kuan* (A Review of the Apocryphal History of the Ch'ing Dynasty) (Taipei, 1959), Vol. 2, p. 176.

Ch'i-ying, should be compelled to return to Canton to carry into execution his own agreement; *that he would nevertheless write to Peking for the Emperor's instructions, and whatever they might be, would attempt to carry them out at any risk.*[12]

The following day, Bonham returned the visit at the Chinese Admiral's office at the Bogue. Hsü promised to have the Emperor's answer by the fifth of April.[13]

As soon as Hsü Kuang-chin returned to Canton, he alerted the garrison, and told Hsü Hsiang-kuang, who was intimately involved with the *Sheng-p'ing she-hsüeh*, to activate the militia. On no account, however, were the *t'uan-lien* to incite a British invasion.[14] "The barbarians are bent upon entering the city. If they are permitted to do so, then they will use their soldiers to force us [to yield]. First defend, then fight. That way, the fault will lie with them."[15]

Though laden with strictures, Hsü's order had reversed official policy toward the militia. For the first time since 1843, a governor-general had sanctioned *t'uan-lien*!

The militia had been chafing at the bit long before permission was granted to organize openly. All of Kuang-chou was aware of the brewing crisis. Some of the people panicked. Thousands made pilgrimages to a temple outside the city where they prayed for peace.[16] Others grew enraged. Inflammatory placards were posted around the city, urging the people to pour boiling congee from their rooftops onto the heads of the British troops.[17] Or the glorious victory of San-yuan-li was recalled: 100,000 braves were once again prepared to give up their lives to keep the barbarians from entering the city. "We must not leave one of this class of dogs and sheep able to eat; we must entirely destroy these spiteful and selfish vagabonds, so that not one of the sails of their ships will return."[18]

Once they had been given the Governor-General's mandate to resist the enemy, the gentry leaders began to plan with enthusiasm. Young men volunteered joyfully.[19] Others, with important fiscal powers delegated by Hsu Hsiang-kuang, began to levy taxes for the militia.* Details of financing were varied. In some areas, the "contributions" were scaled according to the estimated means of the individual household, which in turn were informally determined by a council of elders and notables. In other regions, a fixed rate was set according to amounts of land

---

*In Nan-hai: T'an Lu. In Hsiang-shan: T'an Chiu. In P'an-yü: Chin Ching-mao, Hsu Ying-jung, and P'an Cheng-wei. See, respectively: *Nan-hai hsien-chih*, 15:16-b. *Hsiang-shan hsien-chih*, 16:2-a. *P'an-yü hsien-chih*, 20:1-a; 19:30-b.

held.* The funds were almost always kept in the "local school." Before the crisis, the directors of the *she-hsüeh* had been allowed to lend out the money in any way that suited them. Now, since the funds might be needed at any moment, they could lend only to licensed pawnbrokers.[20]

The *Sheng-p'ing* headquarters issued a set of elaborate orders. Individual *t'uan-lien* were assigned to specific forts north of the city. Spike pitfalls and wooden barriers were built. Guards were posted at major intersections, behind walls, or in watchtowers. Weapons and fire-fighting equipment were numbered by each of the "local schools" and then distributed among the braves. Every man received a bamboo cap, a spear, and a double sword. The government provided some heavy muskets. Since most of the militia this time were genuine volunteers and continued to work their farms, they were promised rations only if they served overnight. A few of the more heavily armed units, however, were mobile, not assigned to any particular spot. Other twenty-man *tui* (brigades) were solely charged with fire prevention.[21]

Within the city, urban militia were created. The first such units, of course, dated back to the "real estate crisis" of 1847. In 1848, owing to the alarming increase in banditry around the city, the shopkeepers on the north side of town formed vigilante committees to arrest robbers and turn them over to the authorities.[22] But the city did not really engage in large-scale civil defense until after the Bogue meetings. Then, according to Hsü Kuang-chin's own description:

> After returning to the provincial capital, I met with Minister Yeh Ming-ch'en and aroused the merchants to mutually defend themselves: each person protected the other. Each household provided one adult, and no more, for the levy. Each household provided one month's rent, and no more, for operating funds. In the cities and suburbs, inside and out, the robust conscripts were able to amass several tens of thousands worth of public contributions, and to collect several hundreds of thousands [of recruits]. The merchants themselves controlled the masses, exerting their will to defend the city. By reputation, [the braves] were quite robust. In addition, each of the Cantonese guilds that had traded with the barbarians before, came to a joint agreement to stop trading for the time being. Whenever [the British] ceased raising the city entry [question], then the guilds would again trade as before. Those who, for fear of giving offense [to the British], broke the agreement were punished

*For every mou of rice paddies, one tael and two mace were levied; for every mou of gardens, seven mace; and for every mou of fish ponds, five mace. At that time, one tael was worth approximately $1.30, and one mace, about thirteen cents.

by the joint guilds [while] those who discovered this and informed [on
them] were publicly rewarded.[23]

On the surface, the *han-chien* (traitors) of yesteryear had become the
heroes of the day. The old security merchants, so suspected by the
moralistic Lin Tse-hsu, were the allies of the realistic Hsü Kuang-chin.
Had patriotism replaced commercial aims among the mercantile classes
of Canton?

The creation of the elaborate city militia would certainly indicate that
some kind of change had taken   place. By the fifth of March, the merchants had managed to organize a police force, using mercenary *yung*.
Five days later, placards invited the city's residents to enroll in a wide-
spread militia league. Large shops would provide three volunteers;
medium-sized shops, two men; and small shops, one man. In the event
of a crisis, a gong would be sounded, the city gates would be closed and
the militia assembled. Any wounded would receive fifty dollars for
medical expenses, while the families of the honored dead would receive
one hundred and fifty dollars. The most trustworthy shop-assistants and
artisans in the city went from door to door, registering these volunteers.
If a household could not provide a recruit, it paid for one to be hired
elsewhere. Weapons were made, and barriers erected within the city
walls. All of this was financed by Canton's shops, each of which —
regardless of size — was asked to contribute one month's rent. Some
of the hong, however, were unwilling to contribute to the central defense
headquarters because they believed that the funds donated during the
'47 crisis had been misused or embezzled. And so they formed their
own individual groups. Other wards on the outskirts of the city simply
hired special policemen from among the local "bare sticks." [24]

All of these efforts were urbocentric, not patriotic. These people were
protecting their homes, their shops, their streets — as much against
foreigners as against the domestic bandits, looters, and deserters that
were bound to follow in the wake of a barbarian invading force.[25] Hsü
Kuang-chin and Yeh Ming-ch'en were aware of this, because the prime
example they gave the Emperor of the merchants' patriotic zeal was not
the police units but the trade boycott. "Each of the merchant houses
that formerly traded with the foreigners were extremely rich in capital
and content with their businesses; but they were not willing to listen to
officials before. Yet now they have been stirred into righteous anger.
They were willing to fail financially, even go bankrupt, while cutting
off commerce." [26] If the officials' assessment were correct, then this

would have been impressive indeed: onetime "treacherous merchants" voluntarily boycotting the barbarians. But Hsü and Yeh were wrong when they spoke of the wealth and contentment of the mercantile houses of Canton. They failed to take account of the economic crisis that had struck Kwangtung shortly after the Opium War.

The Treaty of Nanking had abolished the Cohong and created a "new system" of free trading. Overnight the security merchants became "little better than brokers." [27] Unfortunately, the capital which they controlled still remained essential to the trade. Therefore, commerce was almost paralyzed during the first year after the war because the former members of the Cohong were themselves crippled by the five millions which had been levied on them to pay off the indemnity.[28] They also willfully refrained from trading in the hope that the "new system" would fail.[29] By September, 1843, five of the seven ships that left Canton were in ballast. However, as time went on, new Chinese traders began to step into the commercial vacuum. Shipments began to pick up again in the winter of 1843, and the hong merchants realized that unless they did play by the new laissez-faire rules they would find themselves squeezed out of commerce altogether. By January, 1844, they had accepted the "new system" and were trading as energetically as before.[30]

The British were jubilant. Public hostility had died down. The security merchants were buying as well as ever, and both black and green teas were still expected to come in via Canton. British woolen and cotton imports that year were higher than ever before, totaling almost eight million dollars. Tea, silk, and cassia were flowing out at about seventeen million dollars worth a year. And a record forty thousand chests of opium had been sold, bringing in almost twenty million dollars.[31]

Nevertheless, the hong merchants remained dissatisfied. They had traded too long and too well under the old monopoly system to appreciate the new free market. Constant attempts were made in 1844 and 1845 to reinstitute some form of tax-farming or monopoly capitalism. Some tried to form an iron monopoly. The cotton brokers attempted to impose a four-mace tax on their goods. The tea trade through Canton was artificially maintained by differential transit dues. A cassia monopoly was given to a single dealer in Canton, whose fee amounted to 50 percent more than the tariff. Ch'i-ying even asked for Davis's assent to the exclusive licensing of one hundred Cantonese merchants for international trade.[32] The old habits were hard to break, but the flourishing of the Canton trade in 1844 seemed to justify all of the British refusals to allow any resumption of the "old system." Then the boom dropped.

In 1845, a fever of industrial and railway speculation in England brought the inevitable crash. The following year, 1846, saw a disastrous autumn harvest; and in August of 1847, speculators in the corn market had their own crash. By October, 1847, British banks were stopping payments on their drafts.[33] The crisis was short-lived, but just as England was on the verge of recovery, the effects of the economic depression reached Canton.

Foreign merchants in Canton had overtraded during the heady days of 1844 and 1845. Pinched by the home market, the Manchester textile firms were growing tired of this excessive optimism. All too often their woolens, unsold and unwanted, had picked up warehouse fees in Canton. By 1847, Manchester refused to ship on speculation. Even the prestigious and reliable firm of Jardine and Matheson was forced to buy half of the British manufactures and staples in advance, and could take only 50 percent on consignment.[34] Gradually, British firms in Canton found all of their capital tied up. Money became tight. Newer Chinese trading houses which had borrowed heavily from the old security merchants or Shansi bankers during the boom suddenly had their notes called in and were forced to declare bankruptcy.[35] By the end of 1847, fewer and fewer British manufacturers were being imported, while tea and silk exports plummeted.

The tea trade quickly resumed once the credit crisis was over. Between 1838 and 1842 about 42 million pounds of leaves had been exported each year. But from 1844 to 1851 the average jumped to 64 million pounds. The alarmists who had predicted that the new treaty ports would ruin the Canton tea trade seemed proved wrong. However, the optimists overlooked one thing: Canton was separated from Central China by the Ta-yü-ling mountain range. All goods had to be carried along either one of two narrow routes through those high, axial scarps: the Che-ling or Mei-ling passes. This made the Cantonese trade a potential hostage to any rebel or bandit who could control those two passes. At first, this seemed unimportant. The Bohea, Chekiang, and Anhwei teas had naturally begun to move through Shanghai once the new treaty ports were opened. But the Kiangsi, Hupeh (Oopack), and Hunan (Oonam) leaves were still bought and sold in Canton. The market in these compensated for the loss of that other trade as far as Canton itself was concerned. This was nearsighted, for the tea trade was now geographically split: northern leaves going to Shanghai, southern to Canton. Boatmen and coolies along the upper stretch of the North River and at the Mei-ling pass suddenly found themselves out of work. Their confreres further

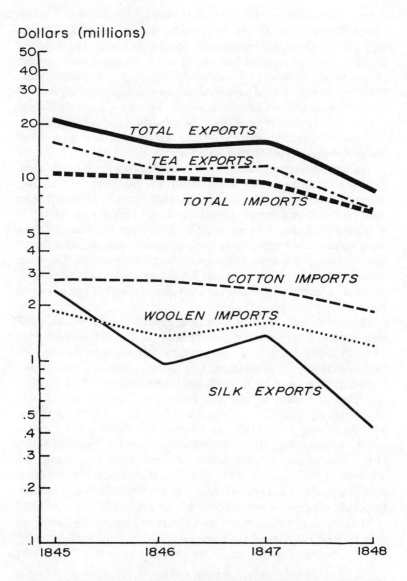

Fig. 1. Trend of imports and exports carried by British vessels, Canton, 1845–1848. These sums are derived from British consular reports: FO 228/61, Desp. 28; FO 228/72, Desp. 11; FO 228/85, Desp. 65; and FO 228/99, Desp. 25.

down the tea routes were transporting as much as ever; but they, essential intermediaries in the old haulage from the Yangtze region south, were unemployed. One hundred thousand jobless porters at Mei-ling, and ten thousand impoverished boatmen in the North River valley proved ready recruits for secret societies or bandit gangs. As disorder grew, fewer goods were hauled and unemployment increased. This cycle of unemployment and unrest was disastrous both for Central China and Canton. By the time the Taiping Rebels fought through these regions, sweeping up boatmen and coolies, the tea trade in Kuang-chou had dropped to almost half of what it had been.[36]

The shift in the tea trade had not been directly caused by the commercial crisis of the mid-forties. However, the change in the marketing of textiles was an immediate effect of the 1847 crash.* Fine-quality silks were produced in a narrow district about one hundred miles long, of which the northeastern corner was Shanghai. Since the Shanghai firms could quickly adapt their supplies to existing demand, Shanghai threatened to become the major exchange center for Chinese silk. The credit crisis simply realized this potential. While Canton, far from the centers of produce, overtraded, Shanghai leapt into the lead. Canton was no longer the greatest port in China.[37]

The first to feel the pinch were local porters, warehousemen, shroff merchants, and compradors who earned their livelihood from the foreign trade. Probably, much of the urban unrest that accompanied the antiforeign movement was an expression of this economic crisis.[38] But eventually even the great mercantile houses were affected. As silk trading fell, many of the old security merchants began to specialize solely in tea. Others engaged more and more heavily in usury. After the Opium War, funds were needed for reconstruction. The Cohong was happy to provide this capital at high rates of interest.[39] But the combined effects of the "new system" and the shift in trade could not be overcome. By 1900, all of the members of the Cohong, save Howqua's descendants, were impoverished and ignored. And even the Wu family's vast fortunes had declined to a mere one hundred thousand dollars.[40]

The Fu-ch'ao junk merchants were also ruined during this period, not so much by the Opium War as by the coming of the square-rigger. After the Thai state trading enterprises adopted square-riggers in 1835, junks

---

*As far as imports were concerned, the first hint that Shanghai was siphoning off commercial orders came early in '46, when large stocks of British woolens gathered dust in Cantonese warehouses. See: FO 228/61, Incl. 1, Desp. 28, Feb. 21, 1846.

were seen less and less on the high seas.[41] And after 1842, foreign ships were permitted to carry on the China coastal trade. Since foreign vessels were better armed and swifter than the pirates who arose after the Opium War, the junks were driven out of business. Finally, because the straits' trade was largely a luxury trade (*bêche-de-mer*, bird's nests), it was the first to fail during the hard times of the 1840's. At one time, the junk trade had netted fantastic profits of 200 to 400 percent. By 1852, it yielded only 20 to 40 percent.[42]

Finally, of course, those merchants who acted as brokers for British imports found that the native demand for foreign textiles responded to all of these pressures by dropping off to almost nothing. Little wonder, then, that it was only the textile hong which stopped trading with the English in 1849: the woolen dealers on February 26, the cotton traders on March 3.[43] One of their placards read:

> We constantly hear that "when people who are near are pleased, those in the distance will come,"* in which case commerce will go on favorably; and that when a country is in complete tranquility commodities will have free circulation. So we, the drapers, purchased from the barbarians and despatched our purchases to all the provinces, and always in mutual peace and concord. But from the twenty-first year of Tao-kuang (1841), since the troubles made by the English barbarians, the business of every firm has visibly decreased day by day. How many individuals are there, let it be enquired, in our guild who have during several years past obtained the smallest profits? . . . Can we not make our garments out of our own elegant silks and native cottons, and must we use the Camlets and Long Ells from abroad?[44]

Declining trade, not antiforeignism, inspired the boycott.† The city militia and the hong's economic resolutions did not represent a fundamental change of motives among the city's commercial classes. On April 2, for example, the city's notables wrote Bonham, begging him to abandon demands for entry. What use was this "irrational longing for glory"? If the city were attacked, everyone would suffer and trade would come to a halt. "If you lose one day's business, you lose one day's profit."[45]

In spite of the fear of invasion, and in spite of the economic resentment of Canton's drapers, the merchants still shared strong mutual interests with the English. Local, not national, concerns inspired them.

The English watched militia proliferate and public enthusiasm soar.

---

*Chin-che lo, yuan-che lai. See: *Analects*, 13.15:2.
†For a general discussion of the province's economy during this period, see Appendix IV.

There was no question that the people would oppose their entry. Bonham's only hope was that the Emperor's answer would be favorable, for by March 22, he had received Palmerston's rejection of his plan to go north should Hsü refuse entry.[46] His hopes did not seem entirely misplaced. Sanguine rumors emanating from Canton insisted that the Emperor favored admission.[47]

Hsü's report of the Bogue meetings had reached Peking on March 11. After describing his military preparations, but omitting all mention of the militia, the Governor-General warned that the British might bypass Canton and go north to Chekiang.[48] This effectively sabotaged Hsü's appeal for a rescript ordering the barbarians not to enter the city, because the Emperor was genuinely alarmed at the prospect of the English moving north. He therefore ordered Hsü Kuang-chin to back down and let the foreigners save face. "A date should be set for a temporary entrance into the city." [49]

The Governor-General must have received these instructions some time between March 25 and March 30, only a few days before Bonham expected to have his answer. Hsü was in a difficult situation. The popular resistance movement that he had sanctioned without Peking's knowledge was in full swing. To renege now might be disastrous. And so the Governor-General decided to tell the Emperor about the militia, masking his own role in their development. His memorial arrived by express messenger on April 14, and Peking finally learned that one hundred thousand men had "spontaneously" formed *t'uan-lien*. Naturally, "they sincerely obey Imperial precepts." But the garrison troops in Kwangtung numbered only a few thousand. "How can they oppose the embroiled mass of the people? . . . How can our local civil and military officials change [the minds of] these hundreds of thousands of people, and forbid them [the right to assemble]?" If the British were allowed to enter, it would mean "rebellion (*hung*) within and without." [50]

Yeh Ming-ch'en, Governor of Kwangtung, more than supported his friend's argument. The British were bluffing, mouthing "meaningless noises" (*hsu-sheng*). "They make a noise in the east and strike in the west. . . . They are all show and no force (*wai-ch'iang nei-kan*). . . . The words flow unceasingly from their mouths, but actually their strength poses no danger." [51] In the meantime, the local militia had been formed. "All are good and virtuous. They are not bandits. They come from those who care for their families and homes." [52] The Emperor was convinced. On that same day, April 14, 1849, he directed the governor-general and governor: "Do not let [the British] enter the city. . . . If they enter the city, there will be harm but no profit." [53]

This new imperial edict could not have reached Canton until April 29. During that interval, the matter remained in Hsü's hands. He may have been convinced that the news of the militia would force the Emperor to change his mind, but in the meantime he had to hold off the British. If he merely played for time, Bonham might realize that Hsü was hiding the truth and make that a pretext for invasion.* Therefore, completely on his own, Hsü Kuang-chin made the riskiest decision of his career. On April 1, Bonham was told that the imperial rescript had arrived, and that it read: "The Central Empire cannot oppose the People in order to yield to the men from a distance." [54] Hsü had "forged" a rescript! [55]

The implications of the gamble were frightening. Had the British ignored the false edict and attacked the city, Hsü would have been found guilty of official disobedience, if not treason. And oddly enough, the English had actually seen the genuine version. For even then, the British Chinese Secretary's office had a flourishing intelligence network in Canton's yamens: subclerks who smuggled copies of memorials and decrees out for a fee. At the very end of March, Gutzlaff† had managed to obtain and translate a copy of the imperial rescript permitting the foreigners to enter the city temporarily. But its authenticity was dubious. [56] So, when Bonham was handed the false edict, he never suspected duplicity. All that he could do was to shift the angle of his attack. How, he asked Hsü, could the inhabitants of one city prevent a great empire from fulfilling its treaty obligations? Was the Emperor's refusal a "positive refusal ever to fulfil the Treaty"? [57] Hsü parried the question deftly, for he had already begun to suspect that Bonham was going to back down. [58] The suspense lasted just over a week. On April 9, the British plenipotentiary abruptly and helplessly broke off the correspondence with the ludicrously mild warning: "I can but repeat my regret at the unsatisfactory report, which this evasion of the Treaty will compel me to make to my own Government." [59]

---

*However, Bowring later claimed that the American consul had told Howqua of Palmerston's willingness to drop the entry matter, and that Howqua in turn told Hsü. See: FO 17/188, Bowring–Granville, Desp. 1, April 19, 1852.

†A Pomeranian sent to Siam and China by the Netherlands Missionary Society, Gutzlaff was one of the first evangelists to master Chinese. While proselytizing energetically wherever he went, he also managed to interpret for both opium runners and western officials. Eventually, Gutzlaff became Chinese Secretary to the British plenipotentiary.

It had succeeded, the first great Chinese diplomatic coup of the nine-teenth century. Peking was jubilant.[60] The Emperor showered rewards on Hsü and Yeh* and on outstanding gentry leaders. Even the common people of the city were honored with votive tablets inscribed: "The people's will is as strong as a walled city." [61] The Cantonese themselves were euphoric. Above all, the gentry were grateful to Hsü Kuang-chin and Yeh Ming-ch'en for legitimizing the popular tradition of resistance and spiritually regenerating the province. When they erected monuments to the two heroes, they explained:

> From the time enmity was contracted in the war of 1840 and 1841 till now, during a space of more than ten years, they have, alas, trampled on our border country; seized and hunted after our men and women. Over the whole of the river and outer seas all have fallen in the same manner before them — except in our Kwangtung, where they were exterminated at San-yuan-li and slain at Huang-chu-ch'i, where even all the young boys of three feet high desire to eat their flesh and sleep on their skins. This arises indeed from the customs of the people; but if Their Graces had not constantly commiserated the secret troubles of the people, and roused them by encouragement, it would have been impossible for the public determination to become as strong and firm as a walled city.[62]

Hsü Kuang-chin was flushed with success. He even allowed himself the luxury of telling the Emperor that he had had this strategy in mind for a long time. "There are some [of us] who did not wait until the present moment to realize this." [63] But the Emperor ignored this slightly presumptuous tone, for he shared the Governor-General's optimism. Both, unfortunately, misjudged the permanency of the British assault on China. For the time being, though, the policy was indeed a brilliant success. Hsü Kuang-chin had squared the circle: "managed" the bar-barians and appeased the people. And so, on July 4, 1850, the Emperor decreed that Hsü Kuang-chin should be in sole charge of barbarian affairs for the empire.[64] From then until the *Arrow* war (1856–1860), the Governor-General at Canton was almost the sole architect of China's foreign policy, his recommendations accepted without dissent.

Hsü himself, jubilant and confident, felt that everything was within his reach. As an old friend of Lin Tse-hsu, he had long shared his senti-ments about opium suppression. Now he believed that he could call on the new unanimity of the community to finally stamp out addiction in Kwangtung. The vigorous disagreement of his subordinates forced him

---

*Hsü was made a viscount (*tzu*) and given a double-eyed peacock's feather; Yeh, a baron (*nan*) and given a single-eyed feather.

to abandon the scheme.[65] Then he turned, with more success, to foreign trade, perhaps because he wished to repay Howqua and the others for what they had done during the defense of the city. In January, 1850, he ordered a return to the old monopoly system by adding new taxes to tea, which could be stored only in the Cohong's warehouses.[66] Bonham managed to forestall that plan by appealing to the Hoppo.[67] The British heaved a collective sigh of relief and forgot all about the matter until June, when the Nan-hai and P'an-yü magistrates caught the English off guard by suddenly setting a two-mace tax on every picul of tea* and reinstating the old monopoly system. Before the British really realized what had happened, the Cohong alone had the power to select the Chinese merchants who would be allowed to sell tea to the foreigners. The additional tax that they collected was then sent to Hsü's yamen in exchange for the privilege of tax-farming the trade.[68] Two years earlier, British protests would have rocked the city. Now the English merely licked their burned fingers.

Hsü grew more and more arrogant. Some even said that he was so puffed up by his successes that he had turned over all of his official duties to his assistants, who sedulously "scraped the people's fat." [69] In addition to this kind of lore, the diplomatic victory of 1849 held some implications that were not so promising for China's future.

First, the encouragement of the militia helped polarize the society. The gentry really set themselves in control of local militia as the balance of power shifted more and more in their favor, while the mobilization had disrupted the countryside and encouraged "rowdy elements" (*hao-shih-che*).[70] The antiforeign crisis of 1849 thus set the seal to the social disorder that had been festering since 1841.

Second, Peking had tied itself to the decisions of the Governor-General's yamen in Canton. The tail wagged the dog.

Third, the British brooded resentfully over their defeat. It was no coincidence that shortly after the 1849 crisis, Palmerston came out with that famous swagger-stick remark of his: "These half-civilized Governments . . . all require a Dressing every eight or ten years to keep them in order." [71]

Peking had bought seven years of isolation. The price would be the Treaty of Tientsin.

*One-third of a cent per pound.

PART THREE

Rebellion and Reaction

THE POLITICS OF LOCALISM   1850–1856

X

Class and Clan

> In his village, Chiang Pen-chen founded a
> *Sheng-p'ing* public office, and built a shrine to
> the righteous braves in order to appease their
> noble spirits and inspire the people. — *P'an-yü
> Hsien-chih*, 19:9-a

The society of nineteenth-century Kwangtung was an intricate complex
of interlocking associations: militia groups, hong, secret societies, gentry
committees, pirate bands, "public offices," and — above all — lineage
groups. It was the last of these, manifested as the clan (*tsu*),* which
seemed to distinguish South China from the rest of the empire. This was
not because clans did not exist elsewhere; but in Kwangtung these huge,
exogamous lineages were a primary and ubiquitous form of mass organization. For one, they were the province's largest landowners.[1] Their
"clan fields" (*chi-t'ien* or *ch'ang-t'ien* †) provided an income which was
used by the clan elders to pay students' stipends, degree-holders' subsidies, examination expenses, relief for the poor or disabled, and care
for the ill.[2] Sometimes the rents were simply divided among the individual families within the clan. Just as often, those same families would
plough their shares back into the purchase of more clan fields. The
increment was staggering. In one Kuang-chou delta town of five thousand
families, for example, there were 130 clan temples supported by rents
totaling 900,000 dollars a year.‡

---

*Anthropologists usually divide the Chinese lineage system into four pro-
gressively larger units: the conjugal family, the stem family (*famille souche*), the
ancestral group (branch or moiety), and the clan or "sib." See: Daniel Kulp,
Country Life in South China, 121. Olga Lang, *Chinese Family and Society*, 19–21.

†Other forms of "public" (*kung*) land then held in the province were "educational fields," used to subsidize local schools but amounting to only 2 percent of
the arable land; "temple fields," which totaled 0.3 percent; and lands owned by
merchants' organizations (*hui-t'ien*). All of these were dwarfed by clan properties in Kwangtung, which stood in sharp contrast to the Yangtze provinces. This
was because the clan preempted most of the society's ritual and welfare needs.

‡This is an extreme example, of course. The large city of Fatshan (Fo-shan),
under the Manchus, had only 420 clan temples. These ritual lands were nominally

Such rich and influential sibs were each a "focus of economic and political power" in Kwangtung.[3] Clansmen who basked in the reflected glory of prestigious gentry leaders, or who welcomed the clan as a set of allies in case of local conflict, were naturally reluctant to leave its protective embrace.[4] The lands themselves symbolized this unity, this source of collective power and prestige. At the same time, however, other forces — also represented by clan fields — helped drive the lineage apart. The clan or *tsu* did not represent a set of either idyllic or static relationships. The very rents that paid for subsidies were often collected from poorer kinsmen, tenants of their own clan. These peasants could, and did, harbor deep resentments against the clan leaders who enforced high rents or usury.[5] Sometimes clan rules recognized this by forbidding

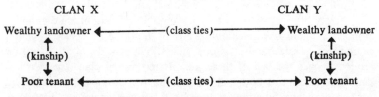

Fig. 2. Kin-class axes within the lineage group.

the rental of *chi-t'ien* to kinsmen.[6] But in regions where clan and village were one and the same, this kind of rule could not be enforced. Thus, there were constant forces pushing and pulling against each other, sometimes dissolving and sometimes uniting the clan. These forces can be represented in a number of ways. The starkest would assume that two axes existed within the lineage group, one representing class and the other kinship. Landowners and tenants* each shared potential, if not

---

held in stewardship by sublineage leaders, *chia-chang* (family heads), who had to concur in its sale. During the 1930's the percentages of clan fields in the delta region were the following: Hua-hsien, 50 percent; Ying-te, 20; Tung-kuan, 20; Hsiang-shan, 50; Nan-hai, 40; Shun-te, 60; Hsin-hui, 60; En-p'ing, 40; P'an-yü, 50. See: Makino Tatsumi, *Shina kazoku kenkyū* (A Study of the Chinese Clan; Tokyo, 1944), 573. Han-seng Ch'en, *Agrarian Problems in Southernmost China*, chap. 2. Kulp, *Country Life in South China*, 101–104.

* Poor tenants represent the lower levels of the peasant class in Kwangtung during this period. In 1852, some tenants only worked as temporary laborers at harvest time, while other landless farmers became year-round workers. The temporary laborer received from 2½ to 5 cents a day. The permanently hired hand received a daily ration of three meals and rice wine, and pay in kind at the end of the year amounting to ten "stone" of grain, or approximately 2,600 pounds, then worth about twenty silver dollars. It would be misleading, though, to conceive of the agricultural wage-workers of China as a totally separate economic class,

actual, class interests with their counterparts in other clans. At the same time, however, this horizontal solidarity was mollified by the vertical ties of kinship. Thus, the clans helped stabilize the countryside by mitigating class conflict. Unfortunately, one of the most powerful techniques of lineage unification — clan wars — also disrupted rural Kwangtung.

In 1766, the Ch'ien-lung Emperor became quite concerned over the large number of clan wars then being fought in Kwangtung.

> The ritual land attached to the ancestral halls in the eastern part of Kwangtung frequently caused armed feuds [between clans]. . . . If the land is used lawfully to consolidate and harmonize [kinship relations] . . . it is not a bad practice at all. But if [it induces people] to rely on the numerical strength or financial power of their clans to oppress their fellow villagers, or even worse, to assemble mobs and fight with weapons . . . [such a practice] surely should not be allowed to spread. This wicked custom is especially prevalent in Fukien and Kwangtung provinces.[7]

The Emperor then ordered that an investigation be carried out. What followed showed that some clans controlled many, many mou of *chi-t'ien*. The rents from these were collected each year in turn by one of the *chia* (family) within the clan. This family then paid whatever taxes were due and loaned out the rest on interest. Wealth begot wealth, and soon the countryside was divided into very rich and very poor *tsu*. The former easily oppressed the latter. But if two clans of equal strength and wealth were to quarrel over land or water rights, only warfare could decide the outcome. A battle was planned. Each clan assembled in its ancestral hall. The kinsmen were promised that the wounded would be paid rewards, the dead enshrined with honor, the bereaved guaranteed a lifetime stipend. If one of the enemy were to die, and the murder were to come to the attention of the local magistrate, then one of the clansmen who was wanted for another crime would volunteer to act as a "forfeit." By turning himself in, he satisfied the magistrate and ensured a steady future income for his family from clan funds.[8]

In sharp contrast, clan wars in a province like Kiangsi never involved gentry participation. It was the peasants themselves who secretly decided

---

sharply differentiated from the farmers for whom they worked. Like the rural wage-workers of France or southern Germany, they were "scattered up and down the interstices of a society based on a multitude of little properties." See: R. H. Tawney, *Land and Labour in China*, 34. My information on farm labor is drawn mainly from Harry Parkes' report on emigration, FO 17/192, Incl. 1, Desp. 132, Sept., 1852.

when to fight, and who chose leaders from among themselves. Only after the battle did they turn to clan notables for legal protection. Naturally, the wealthier members of the sib disapproved of all this and frequently tried to judge the peasant ringleaders themselves. But when the elders gathered in their own ancestral hall, they were apt to face a peasant mob of their kinsmen who would try to prevent the trial from taking place.[9] When this happened, of course, lineage conflict split the clan.

In Kwangtung, on the other hand, clan wars were openly backed and organized by clan leaders because this was one important way for them to increase their own power and the clan's control over ritual land. The ritual land in turn provided a means of payment for the struggle. Ultimately, the values that were invoked and the rewards that were promised strengthened clan solidarity and the hold of the wealthier sublineages.[10]

By the nineteenth century, clan warfare was endemic in Kwangtung. Parts of the province were in a state of "chronic anarchy," characterized by embattled villages, high walls, mud embankments, arms warehouses, semiprofessional fighters.[11] Around Whampoa, for example, two clans feuded almost continuously during 1835 and 1836, writing out vengeful scrolls with their own blood, defacing each other's graves, and employing the same "bands of devoted men" or "forfeits" described in the eighteenth century.[12] Most of these wars began as struggles over water rights or land. The clans preferred to fight rather than turn to the magistrate's court, where they would be subjected to extortion and the vagaries of Chinese justice. For each belligerent was fairly certain what his clan's military losses would be in advance. It was a calculated risk. Unfortunately, the area of violence tended to spread. Mercenaries were hired, or clans extended their network of alliances by calling on other, unrelated lineages of the same surname.[13] Even the militia offered means of extension. "Lineage members, for the purpose of common defense, banded together forming a *pao-chia* organization which raised local militia and posted sentries. All these matters were dealt with by the ancestral hall, which thus necessarily became a military headquarters and assembly point for the militia."[14] For clan and *t'uan-lien* were mutually intermingled in Kwangtung during the 1840's and '50's. The militia of a uni-clan village was nothing more nor less than a clan organization. Its leaders were clan leaders. The wounded or dead were rewarded with the clan's ritual land, and above all, honored by inclusion in the clan's ancestral hall.

The word for ancestral hall in that part of China is *tz'u-t'ang*. Because of the stress on geomancy, propitious sites were very desirable and therefore hard to acquire. Only wealthy lineages could afford the land for such a shrine.[15] The *tz'u*, therefore, was intimately related to the process of lineage segmentation and clan formation. Since ancestral tablets were removed from the domestic shrine once they were four generations away from the descendant who maintained them, "no segment higher than an extended family could find a focus in them."[16] However, they could be replaced by another sort of tablet which was placed, not in the household shrine, but in the special ancestral hall, the *tz'u-t'ang*. This, in turn, could lead to a more expanded kind of social grouping: intermediate lineage segments, one step above the regular extended family.[17] Then as the lineage formed around a *tz'u-t'ang*, and incorporated other intermediate segments, more economic resources were commanded, and a clan would emerge, growing geometrically. Thus, in a rural district with only one or two surnames, there might be one *tsu* containing over one thousand people with twenty or more *tz'u-t'ang*, and one main clan shrine called the *ta-tsung-tz'u*.[18]

However, the clan shrines, like the clan fields, both unified and divided the lineage.[19] For while the rich families built their temples and maintained extended families, the poor lineages, without ritual foci, remained divided and alone. In short, the shrine unified the expanding, aggressive lineage, and separated it from the less powerful households.

Since the tablets hung in the *tz'u-t'ang* had none of the immanent sanctity of the actual ancestral tablets in the domestic shrine, they represented ascribed social values, not personal religiosity. These tablets actually conferred genuine social status on those enshrined there, and on their descendants who came to pay ritual respect. No wonder, then, that inclusion in such an ancestral hall was so powerful an incentive to members of the local militia. In fact, some of the best descriptions of militia activities in the Kuang-chou gazetteers are to be found, not in the biographies (*lieh-chuan*), but in the sections on shrines.[20] Official sanction for such militia was even sought in the guise of laudatory tablets for the shrines. While the *t'uan-lien* may have attracted and abetted rebellious and heterodox forces of disorder, the basic values they invoked were conservative, familistic, and orthodox.

But what of lineage involvement in the gentry-inspired militia leagues that transcended village and clan? Even there lineage may have been just as important. Of the twenty-five leaders of the *Tung-p'ing kung-she*, 60 percent shared surnames. This does not necessarily prove kinship.

TABLE 2
LEADERS OF THE TUNG-P'ING MILITIA

Shared generational names: probable kinship	5	(20%)

Hsieh Cho-en
Hsieh Hsi-en
Hsieh Shih-en
Wang Shao-kuang
Wang Shao-kuei

Shared surnames: possible kinship	10	(40%)

Hsü Ta-hsiang
Hsü T'ien-po
Lin Ch'i-fa
Lin Hsiang-huai
Lin Shih-ch'eng
Wang Chen-tung
Wang Ch'ing-feng
Wang Hsi-ying
Yang Chin
Yang Li-ta

Others	10	(40%)

Ch'en Yü-hsien
Chiang Hung-yuan
Chou Ping-chün
Chung Chan-ch'i
Fan Jui-chao
Ho T'ing-kuang
Kao Liang-ts'ai
Lai Ting-sheng
Sung Ta-ch'ao
Tz'u Yang-chiu

SOURCES: Kuang-tung-sheng, "Kuang-tung jen-min," 292–293, and YPCC, 4:18.

But the high correlation, as well as the obvious relationship of the Hsieh and the Wang kin, who shared generational names,[21] suggest that the militia federations may have been successful in Kwangtung precisely because they were conglomerates of preexisting clan "banners." Could particular militia organizations even have existed in an early form as multiclan alliances? Perhaps. But the really large federations of *t'uan-lien*, such as the *Sheng-p'ing she-hsüeh*, transcended clan alignments. The gentry allied series of vertical lineage groups. Therefore, all of the potentially horizontal ties between the gentry and tenants of one clan and those of another were suddenly linked or strengthened. A peasant from one village discovered that he shared economic or social interests with a poor peasant from another town. Without the militia movement, the mutual hostility of the nucleated countryside, which favored the leaders' control of a clan, would have prevented this realization.*

Inevitably, this horizontal mobility pulled the two axes of the class-clan equilibrium against each other with a increased force. As long as the external enemy, the British, threatened Kuang-chou, lineage ties held. When that menace was apparently disposed of after 1849, class began to override clan. For the militia movement had also strengthened the gentry's control within each lineage segment. Ritual leadership among clansmen was not necessarily in the hands of local notables. A clan elder might be a relatively powerless creature, chosen for genealogical seniority and approved because he could not use his powerful position for selfish ends.[22] But because of the militia, it became necessary to elect politically acceptable gentry who then assumed leadership of the ancestral halls and "public offices." The disruption of the balance of control between the district magistrate and local notables eventually affected the clan. As the economic, political, and military roles allocated to the gentry increased, the functions of the clan-village multiplied. Sublineage leaders were drawn into compact political and ritual organizations: "public offices" (*kung-so* or *kung-she*), or "local schools" (*she-hsüeh*).[23] This process, which began in the mid-nineteenth century, was to culminate in almost a total congruence of ritual and political power in the twentieth century. By 1930, "in the present system of rural self-government (in Kwang-tung), the chiefs of sub-districts, and the chiefs of villages, as well as their subordinates, are for the most part recommended by the authorities of powerful clans."[24]

All of these changes disturbed the social balance maintained by the clan. By 1845, society began to polarize into wealthy and poor. Class interests were no longer "softened" by the lineage. These interests, though always present in Chinese society, emerged nakedly and boldly from the militia movement. They did not create the movement. Historians like Seiji Imabori have theorized that the gentry's militia were designed to

*It is hard to realize just how enclosed and hostile each clan-village might be. In the area around modern Swatow, for example, a marriage in which the man moved into the village (instead of the woman moving out) was almost socially unacceptable. Marriage was also tabooed between a widow and a man outside the village. Either of these betrothals would have introduced into the village males who were not of the same surname, thus threatening clan unity. This kind of social rigor was even a source of moral pride for the lineage that perpetuated it. See: Daniel Kulp, *Country Life in South China*, 81–82.

keep the hostile tenantry in economic subjection. Hence, the gentry militia of the Taiping period have been neatly defined as a "counter-revolutionary" force that suppressed the rebellious peasants. On the contrary, the militia originally unified landlord and peasant. Xenophobia and the clan held rural Kuang-chou together during the serious economic crises partially engendered by the Opium War. But the forces described above eventually polarized society, and then the militia changed their function. Instead of being devices of mass defense and popular consensus, they became organs of social control, putting enormous power in the hands of the wealthier notables. As this process went on, the peasantry became disaffected. Greater and greater numbers began to join secret societies that transcended the clan.[25]

This phenomenon was not peculiar to China. The same sort of polarization occurred in certain areas of southern Europe, notably in Sicily.

> The coming of the modern economy (whether or not it is combined with foreign conquest) may, and indeed probably will, disrupt the social balance of the kinship society, by turning some kins into "rich" families and others into "poor," or by disrupting the kin itself. The traditional system of blood-vengeance outlawry may — and indeed probably will — "get out of hand" and produce a multiplicity of unusually murderous feuds and embittered outlaws, into which an element of class struggle begins to enter.[26]

As with the Mafia, so with the Triads.

XI

The Secret Societies
of South China

> The sage Confucius handed down to us the ink
> and brush. For three successive years I have
> sat for examinations; some day Heaven will
> smile on me, and the names of the Sons of Hung
> shall appear on the list of successful candi-
> dates. — Triad initiation ceremony*

Students of the plot theory of history are prone to attribute enormous influence to secret societies. The thought of conspiracy is reassuring: man,
after all, is a creature of free will, not a tool of circumstances or a
product of social forces. Impersonal history is thus conveniently anthro-
pomorphized. Besides, secrecy as such holds its own fascinations: esoteric
passwords, hooded figures in the night, subtle handshakes of recognition,
a pervasive world brotherhood reaching into high places. It is tempting to
believe that history pivoted on the machinations of the eighteenth century's Illuminati, Italy's Carbonari, or the Third Republic's Freemasons.

Westerners in the nineteenth century succumbed to the same sort of
romantic notions about Chinese secret societies. After all, they were even
more shrouded in mystery than their European counterparts; and there
was no denying the fact that they were ubiquitous. Kwangtung, in particular, seemed filled with "Triads," a rubric that covered three similar but
separate societies: the *T'ien-ti-hui* (Heaven and Earth Society), which
was most prevalent in Fukien; the *San-tien-hui* (Triple Dot Society); and
the *San-ho-hui* (Triple Unity Society), which flourished in Kwangtung but
was also found in Kwangsi, Fukien, Kiangsi, and Hunan. Time and time
again, isolated revolts pulled aside the veils of secrecy to give the Europeans a tantalizing glimpse into this fascinating underworld. Early in the
nineteenth century, a Fukienese named Ch'en Li-nan had terrorized

*Translated in J. S. M. Ward and W. G. Stirling, *The Hung Society or the
Society of Heaven and Earth* (London, 1925), 1:49.

Tung-kuan with his chapter of the Heaven and Earth Society. Nan-hai and Hsiang-shan counties were often disturbed by local branches of the *San-ho-hui*, whose members were known familiarly as "brains" (*nao*), "old concubines" (*fang-chang*), "willow branches" (*liu-chih*), or "iron sticks" (*t'ieh-pan*). By 1838, even the Triple Dot Society had begun to recruit members openly in the delta area.[1]

Nomenclature hardly mattered. Regardless of chapter or branch, each society behaved in about the same way as far as the southern Chinese themselves were concerned. To the Cantonese the groups were collectively known as the societies of the "vast gate" (*Hung-men*), for these were individual, autocephalous bands, without central control, acting under different names at different times. This diffusion was at once the order's weakness and its strength. Because there was no ultimate headquarters, the societies found it difficult to sustain a large uprising for long. Over the years, the history of the Triads was a tale of futile, scattered rebellions, without any semblance of union or coherence. On the other hand, the cellular nature of the organisms made it almost impossible to break up the societies, unless one could wipe out all of the "dangerous classes" that joined the chapters in every market town of southeast China.[2]

The one thing that each society shared with the other was a common initiation rite and history, which was usually transmitted orally. For obvious reasons, there were differing versions of the Triads' origins, but most agreed on certain crucial details. During the initiation, the Grand Master told the neophytes how, in 1674, the monks of the Shao-lin temple in Fukien, all adepts in the martial arts, answered the K'ang-hsi Emperor's call for volunteers to help him drive off the Eleuths of Galdan. Thanks to divine help, the barbarians were defeated, and the Emperor rewarded the Abbot with a special seal. Sixty years later, the villainous prefect of Foochow coveted the precious seal still held by the nearby monastery. First, he managed to convince the Yung-cheng Emperor that the monks of the Shao-lin temple were planning a rebellion. Then, helped by a treacherous monk named A-ch'ieh, he fired the temple and killed all but five monks, who escaped with the seal to another temple high in the mountains of the province. There they discovered a porcelain censer floating on a stream and bearing the slogan, *Fan-ch'ing fu-ming* (Oppose the Ch'ing dynasty and restore the Ming dynasty). Out of the censer shot a red light,* which revealed a magic sword. After these discoveries, the five monks were suddenly and mysteriously joined by five new men, the

---

*"Red" (*hung*) is a homonym for "vast" (*hung*).

"Tiger Generals," and — some versions insist — the fourteen-year-old grandson of the last Ming emperor. All pledged a blood oath and raised the righteous banner of revolt. In their first encounter with the Manchus, however, they were defeated and routed. The brotherhood, hunted like dogs, split into five Grand Lodges, which spread across South and Central China, swearing to carry on the struggle against the nefarious Ch'ing.[3]

This legendary potpourri had little to do with the societies' real history. There was a Shao-lin temple, famous as the home of Chinese boxing; but it existed in Honan in the T'ang period. There were tales of thirteen warrior-monks helping an emperor; but the ruler was T'ang T'ai-tsung, the enemy Wang Shih-ch'ung, and the time the seventh century. There was a revolt in 1674; but the leader was Chu I-kuei, a Ming loyalist ensconced on Formosa. Still, some historical associations do emerge from the ritual myths. It seems clear that the Triads originated on Formosa, since the first verifiable historical reference associates them with Lin Shuang-wen's rebellion on that island in 1786. From there they moved to Fukien on the mainland, where the apocryphal temple was supposed to have existed. After the White Lotus revolts at the end of the eighteenth century, they spread throughout South China, periodically roiling the surface of society along with some of the other sects descended from the Buddhist societies of Yuan times: Green Lotus (*Ch'ing-lien*), Inactivity (*Wu-wei*), Eight Diagrams (*Pa-kua*). After 1800, every minor rebellion usually incited some Triad activity — always in the name of restoring the Ming: the *Pa-kua* revolt of 1813, Chu Mao-li in 1814, Chao Fu-ts'ai's *Yao* rebellion in 1832, and so on.[4]

The legendary accounts say nothing of this later history. Yet, in a way, the closely guarded ritual is much more revealing than a bald historical description of the Triads' activities. Its secrecy contrasted sharply with the openness of village life in China.* Like the walled yamen, or the Forbidden City, the secret society surrounded itself with a complex of awe-inspiring ritual forms. Within the rural confines of that agrarian empire, the Triads existed as a kind of counter-state, a political organism *within* society. More than that, the secret societies represented an artificial but complete social subsystem. To join the brotherhood was to be reborn, to enter a new set of eternal relationships. Social distinctions would be abolished. A great unity would emerge.

"We revere the heavenly doctrine of being united in one, and therefore desire to overthrow the Ch'ing and restore the Ming so that the will of

*This discussion is based on Simmel's discussion of secrecy. See: Kurt H. Wolff, transl., *The Sociology of George Simmel*, 330–376.

Heaven and that of Earth shall be once more united. . . . Tonight we
pledge ourselves before Heaven that the brethren in the whole universe
shall be as if from one womb, as if begotten by one father, as if nourished
by one mother, and as if they were of one stock and origin." [5] These were
ties that nothing could sunder, once the oaths had been sworn, each man's
blood drunk, and the special signs of identification learned.[6] "As thus I
strike off the head of this white cock, so may my head be struck off if I,
like A-ch'ieh, prove to be a traitor." [7] This was genuine blood brotherhood, an artificial sib functionally analogous to the family.[8]

The ideal Chinese social unit was the extended family. Usually, only
the stem family proved financially feasible. Extra sons had to create their
own conjugal units or become one of the loose, floating population known
as "dangerous classes" in Confucian social commentary.[9] This inner pro-
letariat automatically helped turn any minor social or economic crisis
into a disaster.[10] But so impregnated were they with the ideals of familism
that the very organizations of revolt sedulously copied kinship and guaranteed these artificial ties with elaborate rites of passage. The candidates
were always cleansed, then dressed in white clothes to symbolize the
purity of the new man — white, also, to symbolize the pure Ming against
the forces of darkness.* For the rebirth was total. The neophyte washed
off the dirt of the old order to enter a new age. "Wash the filth of Ch'ing
from off your faces with the water of the three rivers, that your true coun-
tenances may appear, and your mouths be closed. Divest yourselves of
the clothing of Ch'ing, an emblem of servitude, and in place thereof, don
the raiment of Ming." [11] This was restorationism: not revolutionary, but
revolutionist.[12] After all, not only did the Triads wish to restore the
Ming; they also derived their charismatic legitimacy from the K'ang-hsi
Emperor's seal. Their rebellions were always justified specifically because
local officials had let their avarice override Confucian duty, and generally
because the dynasty had violated the legitimate order represented by a
monarchical paradigm, the Ming. In fact, the only element in their ideology that distinguished the secret societies from sanctioned Confucian
protest was their anti-Manchuism; and even that was traditional. Ethnocentrism had been an ingredient in secret-society ideology since the days

---

*Again a play on words. Ming, the dynasty, is represented by a word which
also means "bright." Ch'ing, the Manchu dynasty, is usually written with the
ideogram for "clear." By omitting a portion of the word, a homonym is created
which means "dark green." Thus, the oral ritual creates a passion-play of Mani-
chean struggles: bright versus dark, good versus bad, Ming versus Ch'ing. Light,
the blazing glow of goodness and social redemption, is present in almost all the
imagery of the ceremony.

of the Southern Sung, when the regime insisted on the right of native Chinese to rule over foreign barbarians.[13] Whether Juchen, Kitai, Mongol, or Manchu, the barbarians became a target for the hatred of the "purer" Chinese. This was particularly true for Kwangtung. Who could forget the eleven-month siege of Canton in 1650, when the Tartar troops finally battered down the walls with cannon and killed over one hundred thousand people in a brutal bloodbath of revenge and fury? [14] These popular memories did not die early. In fact, anti-Manchu revolutionaries like Sun Yat-sen felt that hatred of the Ch'ing formed the essence of the Triads' ideology.

> By the era of K'ang-hsi, the Ch'ing dynasty had already consolidated itself, and the loyal remnants of the Ming were either dead or exhausted. The two or three remaining elders realized that their great forces had vanished and that there was nothing to return to, and so — wishing to keep nationalism (*min-tsu chu-i*) as their root and source — they passed it on to later generations. Thus, "Oppose the Ch'ing and restore the Ming" became their testament, leading to the organization of societies, so that later rebels could find future help awaiting them.[15]

Nevertheless, it is hard to believe that this ethnocentrism represented some form of "protonationalism." Even overseas, the secret societies were formed into rival speech groups, which split the Chinese communities vertically and hindered the development of nationalism. Their useless retention of the Ming ritual long after the Manchus were overthrown proved that ethnocentrism and restorationism served other purposes.[16]

First, the dispossessed could find pride and self-esteem in their own racial purity. Second, restorationism corresponded to a "rational perpetuative nativism" which looked back to the good old days when officials were just, food was in plenty, and society was not out of kilter.[17] Third, the Manchus diverted social anger from the native upper classes. Fourth, during periods of actual rebellion, restorationism permitted the Triad leaders to pretend to more than banditry — it gave them a sense of political significance. For there were really three levels of "rebellion" in South China: banditry, outlawry, and actual revolt.*

*Wolfram Eberhard has proposed a slightly different schedule of stages for an earlier period of Chinese history: juvenile bands, mountain gangs, gang warfare, emergence of a single regional band, attacks on cities, the enlistment of gentry support. He sees the members of these bands, not as familial rejects or uprooted members of society, but as younger men who live in symbiosis with the local peasants until they were proscribed by the gentry, or until they had coalesced into a larger band that broke off that symbiotic relationship. See: *Conquerors and Rulers*, 2nd edition, 100–106.

The bandits (*tao*) were *ad hoc* rural gangs which gathered in small bands to rob at random. Membership fluctuated. A peasant might join for one raid and abstain from the next. Only occasionally were larger confederations formed for temporary plundering. Seldom was secret-society membership claimed, as there was a clear distinction between mere robbers (*t'u-fei*) and dangerously rebellious societies (*hui-fei*). If there was any ideological consensus at all, it was the notion that these forces were limiting social oppression.[18]

The outlaws (*tsei*) were permanent brotherhoods living outside the villages in mountainous or wooded areas. There was little cooperation with the peasantry. In fact, villages often had to pay protection fees to keep the *tsei* away from their walls. The outlaws, in turn, lived in a state of permanent social insurrection, levying tolls, kidnapping travelers, collecting harvest taxes, and sometimes even attacking small administrative centers. Many of the outlaw bands of Kwangtung emerged from the irregular militia of the Opium War. One contemporary Chinese scholar wrote: "If righteous braves assemble, then they feed themselves from the rations of the militia. If they dissolve, they form secret societies, to lurk in the mountains and valleys, waiting to rob and plunder. The homes of the gentry are thus harmed. . . . The high officials have nourished a cancer." [19] Like the Mafia of Sicily, Chinese outlaws relied on secret-society ties to hold them together through good and bad times. Unlike the Mafia, their leaders were not rural landowners. Only in the districts around Ch'ao-chou, where the local notables were seldom officials, or else headed warring clans, did secret societies boast prestigious or weathy heads. In the richer and more settled Kuang-chou delta area, peasants opposed the *tsei* whenever possible.[20]

Finally, there were the secret societies in rebellion. When local economic conditions grew intolerable, increasingly larger numbers of normally peaceful peasants found themselves forced to steal for a living, and the line between *tao* and *tsei* was erased. Ineffable rumors hinted that the dynasty had run its term. A single outlaw band, acting in the name of the Ming, would unite multiple gangs of bandits and begin to recruit openly among the sedentary peasants. Government and justice had failed: the "Way of the Gods" was about to emerge. Political change, not gang enrichment, became the expressed goal.[21]

This political strain distinguishes Chinese secret societies from the Christian sects of medieval Europe. There the Church was universal. The sects, aiming at direct personal fellowship, renounced universalism and physically or spiritually fled from the City of Man.[22] They were not an alternative. They were an escape or a rejection. The secret societies, on the other hand, did not renounce a universal world-view, or compatibility with the greater society in which they existed. True, in the long history of China there have been "pure" sects whose adherents represented an ideological or social fringe: the vegetarians of the T'ang period, or the tantric followers of certain twelfth century White Lotus (*Pai-lien*) sects. But usually, no matter how bizarre the origins of a cult, its pretensions quickly became temporal and political. Chang Ling, leader of the *Wu-tou-mi-tao* (The Way of the Five Pecks of Rice) sects in the late second century A.D., may simply have created a faith-healing offshoot of Taoism. But his son, Chang Heng, quickly used the cult to carve out a satrapy for himself in Szechuan.[23] Even the most potentially revolutionary of Chinese secret societies, the antitax (*k'ang-liang*) movements of the Southern Sung, did not engage in utopianism. While the charitable Franciscans and communal Beguines had morally revolted against the very institution of property, the Chinese brotherhoods simply sought its redistribution.[24]

This distinction between utopian escape and perennial political engagement explains the continuing involvement of Chinese secret societies in dynastic change, as well as their perpetual inability to provide any alternative to the Confucian system. In that sense, Chinese social thought — whether part of the "Great" or "Little" tradition — was holistic. European Christianity, on the other hand, was only apparently integral, actually embodying two great currents of social thought. The first was conservative and best symbolized by Thomism, which used *lex naturae* and Aristotelian forms to explain the social system existing outside the City of God. The second was radical, characterized by chiliasm, "generous love," and a bent toward primitive communism. Rome tolerated this second, anti-institutional set of doctrines by creating the monastic orders. But the history of the Catholic Church from the ninth century to the sixteenth century can easily be viewed as a continuing failure to "enclose," disarm, or destroy the potentially revolutionary beliefs of the sects and heresies: Albigensian, Franciscan, or Taborite. The Church's ultimate defeat occurred with the Reformation. Both sects and secession were "pure" protests against the institutional and hierarchical nature of the temporal papacy, with its emphasis on order, law, and restraint. The history of the sects themselves was not a series of alternatives offered to that hierarchy, challenging the Church as a particular manifestation of accepted values and beliefs. Rather, the sects represented a series of alienations. The beliefs that inspired them were nurtured by emotions that the Church could never hope to meet, because of the fundamentals of the Thomistic social doctrine which lacked the necessary degree of "magic" to allow for shared belief.

Not so with traditional Chinese thought. The marvelous syncretism of Han Confucianism, with its "five agents," its cosmic trinity, its charismatic emperor-priest, its theory of omens, allowed it to absorb many potentially antinomian and rebellious strains of thought. Thanks also to Mencius' espousal of the right to revolt and the later Kung-yang thinkers' mystic *chün-tzu* (sage), there were enough safety valves to contain everything but new and powerful doctrines imported from outside the civilization. The really revolutionary element in the history of the secret societies and sects of China was the introduction of millennial Maitreyan Buddhism.

In times of famine or distress, the Buddhist theory of the three Kalpas brought hope and solace to the demoralized. Since the transition from one cycle to the next was supposed to be heralded by calamities, the doctrine corresponded perfectly to the real historical cycles of irrigation breakdown or invasion. The self-righteous were promised deliverance, and their tormentors, extermination. Spiritual power, in short, would triumph over temporal authority.[25] However, the Confucian political system was so arranged that no one doctrine could claim a monopoly of that spiritual power. Once a new emperor donned the dragon robes of state, he was endowed with magical control over the cosmos until fresh calamities should arise. Thus, this Buddhist belief in the intervention of Spirit in history ultimately allowed a ruler oriented to Confucianism to stabilize chaos. The world had not ended. The discontented, the alienated, the rebellious, were pulled back into the ever-renewing, never-ending whorls of Confucian history. Even Buddhism only predicted the Ultimate Void, Kunyata: not a solution to the world, but an issue from it. Amitabha's Buddhist Paradise was never secularized. History remained process, and never became progress.* In this context that was the most fundamental difference between Western and Chinese thought. When the Seventh Seal was opened, the secular world would vanish. But rationally with Vico and Condorcet, mystically with Joachim of Floris or Boehm, Paradise was secularized: Swedenborg's heaven emerged as a Big Rock Candy Mountain. This promise of rewards in this world was to prove the most explosive social force of the nineteenth century. Saint-

---

*I should add that Professor Eberhard has pointed out some exceptions to the account which I advance here. The messianic movements connected with Mi-lo in the fourth and fifth centuries A.D., or that of Wang Tse during the Sung period, imminently and concretely promised a better "new" society on earth.

Simon, Fourier, and Marx linked history as progress with the industrial revolution, and modern socialism was born. In China, this kind of historical view was not introduced until Hung Hsiu-ch'üan founded the *T'ai-p'ing* Heavenly Kingdom.* Only after that could K'ang Yu-wei change the "Great Unity" (*Ta-t'ung*) of Kung-yang Confucianism from Arcady to Utopia, from the halcyon past to the glowing future. By then, however, China wanted a Western, not a native, paradise. Marxism-Leninism emerged, and Confucianism gave its last gasp.

*Hung, like Fourier, brought heaven to earth. His personal annotation of the Gospel according to Matthew reads: "The Heavenly Kingdom is meant to include both Heaven and earth. The Heavenly Kingdom is in Heaven. The Heavenly Kingdom is equally on earth. Both in Heaven and on earth is the Heavenly Kingdom of the Divine Father. Do not imagine that it refers solely to the Heavenly Kingdom in Heaven. Thus the Great Elder Brother formerly issued an edict foretelling the coming of the Heavenly Kingdom soon, meaning that the Heavenly Kingdom would come into being on earth. Today the Heavenly Father and the Heavenly Elder Brother descend into the world to establish the Heavenly Kingdom." J. C. Cheng, *Chinese Sources for the Taiping Rebellion, 1850–1864*, 83.

XII

Kwangtung and the Taiping Rebellion

> Since the sacred traditions of our ancestors have
> fallen into oblivion, Heaven has abandoned us.
> Those who watch attentively the march and
> progress of events, those who observe how great
> is the selfishness of our magistrates, how pro-
> found the degradations of the people, feel a dark
> and wonderful presentiment. We are on the eve
> of an immense revolution. That is felt by num-
> bers. But will the impulse come from without
> or within? — A Chinese prefect, 1846*

The Opium War had about the same effect on the hill country of
Kwangtung and Kwangsi as the American Civil War had on the Middle
West and the Southwest. Like Younger and James, the secret-society
bands moved restlessly toward the frontier. As trade routes changed and
unemployment increased, displaced adventurers and desperadoes who
found the pickings too slim, or control too rigid, around Canton moved
west into the mountains.[1] In the spring of 1841, the Governor of Hunan
worriedly reported that the coolies in the mountain passes were becoming involved in the opium racket, and joining secret societies originally
from Kwangtung.[2] After 1846, these were joined by pirates from the
Pearl River delta who had migrated up the river network to the high
mountain country.[3] By the late 1840's, there were five major bands
operating in the border area between the three provinces of Kwangtung,
Kwangsi, and Hunan: Jen Wen-ping's ten thousand Cantonese river
pirates near P'ing-nan; T'ien Fang's band at Wu-chou; the "cudgel
gang" (*pang-pang-hui*) on the Hunan border; T'ao Pa's forest bandits
in Kwangsi; and Ling Shih-pa around Lo-ting.[4] These groups moved back

*From a conversation cited by R. P. Huc, *A Journey through the Chinese Em-
pire* (New York, 1856), 1:372.

and forth across the borders of the three provinces, robbing here, levying tolls there. Out of the disorder they helped to create emerged the Taiping rebels, and when that happened, the bands fought first with them, and then with Ch'ing troops, shifting sides as often as they shifted bases. Clever enough to survive, the outlaws often earned the tolerance of local officials by simply living off the rural areas and leaving the cities alone.[5] When the polity weakened, they increased in numbers and descended from the hills. When it strengthened, they receded — a barometer of the empire's military fortunes. Most of all, they provided a backdrop of violence for all of South China. The constant financial and manpower drain that they imposed on Kuang-chou colored the history of Kwangtung during those years. And their presence on the Kwangsi border turned the surrounding countryside into armed encampments.

The disturbances around Canton during the 1840's had diverted much of the opium distribution network to Kwangsi. That in itself attracted secret societies and Cantonese ladrones. Moreover, many of the province's silver mines had been closed down two years after the war, creating an army of unemployed. Finally, a series of droughts in 1848, 1849, and 1850, rice riots in Kuei-p'ing, and terrible inflation, all coincided with the banditry that had spread from Canton. Disorder became so serious that militia were created in 1850 and 1851.[6] Once formed, the *t'uan-lien* were used by the Punti (original settlers) landlords against their Hakka (guest families) tenants, who began to join an obscure sect called the Society of God Worshippers.[7] The society of the province quickly polarized: Punti landlord militia against Hakka tenants' "God Worshippers." And so the communal brethren of obscure iconoclasts became the militant brotherhood of the *T'ai-p'ing t'ien-kuo*.

Given the similar situations in the two provinces, how could the God-worshipping brethren of Kwangsi have been transformed into a revolutionary movement, while the secret societies of Kwangtung remained restorationist and ideologically innocuous? Was the introduction of Christian theodicy, as a socially disassociated myth, enough to invest certain strains of Confucian thought with imminence and revolutionary potential?

Christian eschatology has acted as a powerful catalyst in a number of non-European millenarian movements.[8] But utopian thinking can never become situationally transcendent unless the existing order is prepared to receive it. A charismatic leader must be attuned to collective dreams and fears around him if he wishes to harmonize his inner fantasies with outer reality.[9] In fact, he cannot sanely accept his own delusions unless they seem to be confirmed externally. This was certainly true of the future Taiping Emperor, Hung Hsiu-ch'üan. His moment of "illumination" preceded his discovery of Christian doctrine. In the mystic dream that accompanied his nervous breakdown, he was symbolically reborn: cleansed by an old woman, every part of his body surgically replaced by a council of sages.* Then, as the Chosen One, he was presented with a divine sword by a mysterious old man who told Hung of the true doctrine.[10] Shaken and changed, Hung nevertheless forgot all about the experience until the day he ran across Leang A-fa's Christian pamphlet. Suddenly, the meaning of the dream became clear. The old man was God, the "Heavenly Father." Hung Hsiu-ch'üan was his son, and the brother of Jesus Christ. He would transform the world.

> These books are certainly sent purposely by Heaven to me, to confirm the truth of my former experiences; if I had received the books without having gone through the sickness, I should not have dared to believe in them, and on my own account to oppose the customs of the whole world; if I had merely been sick, but had not also received the books, I should have had no further evidence as to the truth of my visions, which might also have been considered as the mere productions of a diseased imagination.[11]

The transvaluation of values had to occur before Hung could accept millennial Christianity.† In a similar way, others had to experience some of the psychic pressures in order to believe the doctrines that Hung himself propagated. Those most likely to feel this alienation were members of that "social transitional" group which hovered on the edges of the gentry world without real honor or wealth: small-town schoolteachers, tutors to large country families, or unemployed intellectuals. These people had tried again and again to win a place in the Confucian state system: like Hung himself, always first in village scholarship, yet never a *hsiu-ts'ai*. Resentment, even mild paranoia, turned many against that

---

*This rebirth, common to most mystical experiences, recalls the Triad initiation ceremony. That ritual and Hung's version also shared the theme of spiritual cleanliness. As the Heavenly Mother told Hung: "Son of mine, you are filthy after your descent on earth. Let me wash you in the river before you are permitted to see your father." Wang Chung-min, *et al.*, eds., *T'ai-p'ing t'ien-kuo* (The Taiping Heavenly Kingdom) (Shanghai, 1952), 2:632.

†In the later, apostolic version of the hallucination, Taiping scribes had God tell Hung: "After your return to earth it will be several years before you awake, but do not worry about that. Later a book will be given to you to explain this, and when you learn the truth you will act immediately in accordance with the book so as to avoid mistakes." J. C. Cheng, *Chinese Sources for the Taiping Rebellion, 1850–1864*, 9–10.

system. Once, the future rebel Emperor was beaten by his elder brother for having dared to throw the Confucian tablets out of his classroom. The iconoclast answered: "Am I not the teacher? How is Confucius able to teach, after being dead so long? Why do you force me to worship him?"[12] Normally, such alienated individuals would turn to the secret societies: mystical Taoism, popular magic, dreams of the restored Ming. But now this *lumpenintelligentsia* suddenly discovered another charismatic source of power: the West.

Meadows has made the point that Hung Hsiu-ch'üan studied alien Christianity every time the British were militarily successful in South China. For example, he started reading at Issachar Roberts' Baptist Mission in Canton just after d'Aguilar spiked the Bogue's guns.[13] The Taiping leaders were thus victims of the same sense of cultural inferiority that the xenophobes felt in the face of the British onslaught. But even xenophobia was fraught with ambivalence. Just as the Cantonese hated the foreigners, so did they secretly admire their military prowess. Hung's ideology represented the pole of attraction. As a Chinese, however, he still had to retain his self-respect. He could not simply become a "slave" to foreign doctrines. Therefore, he appropriated Christianity for himself and claimed doctrinal originality in a new world of universal values where the barbarians functioned better than the Chinese. China was keyed into that world by fusing some of its own postmillennial themes with Christian doctrines of imminence.

Hung, nurtured on the Kung-yang texts, took the "great peace" of the *ta-t'ung* (loosely, "one world") and created an original utopia of his and China's own: "The Great God, the heavenly Father, the Supreme Lord, in the beginning created, in six days, heaven and earth, land and sea, man and all things; and from that time till this the whole world has been one house, and all within the four seas have been brethren; there can be no difference between man and man, between high and low born."[14] During this era of equality between all, China had received the original doctrine of the Heavenly Father. Thus, the Central Kingdom was still the source of all culture, but historical villains had subverted the true doctrine. The original truth that China had shared with the One World had been corrupted and denied by "devilish" Central Asian barbarians who had assailed China after the fall of the Han dynasty: "According to Chinese and barbarian historical chronicles, the road [which led to] worshipping God was the same great road which both China and the barbarians followed during the first several thousand years [of history]. But the western barbarian countries continue to

follow this road down to the present. China only followed the great
road down to the time of the Ch'in and Han dynasties, when it diverged
into the devils' road." [15] The Tartars, as agents of deviation and impurity,
thus came to symbolize history itself. For, like all believers in the mil-
lenium, the Taipings took change as such to be an agent of corruption,
moving man farther and farther away from original ideological purity.

This theme was not solely Hung Hsiu-ch'üan's invention. During
the early Ch'ing period, Ming loyalists like Ku Yen-wu or Yen Yuan
believed that the original texts of the Sage had been corrupted by the
Sung Neo-Confucianists. To these Ch'ing empiricists, born into an age
of barbarian conquest, the Chou period had been a social paradigm. But
they had lost the relatively "naïve" view of earlier Confucianists who
thought that the ideal institutions of the Chou could be restored whenever
morality was regenerated. In other words, history had become a limiting
factor. Huang Tsung-hsi, another one of this school, believed that the
only good "laws" were "natural," and had to emerge from a "good"
social order. In another time and another place, the identical "law" would
be unjust or impossible to introduce. Historicism was thus born, and
some, like Wang Fu-chih, began their first hesitant gropings toward the
discovery of a "national" tradition. Wang simply could not believe that
whoever accepted Confucianism automatically became Chinese. His
Yellow Book (*Huang-shu*) introduced the theory that what was
barbarian was not historically Chinese, because Confucius himself had
opposed the barbarians. This was still illogical, of course, because no
matter what Wang said, the Manchus remained good Confucians. Therefore, a new organic tradition of the Han people would have to be created.
This was Hung Hsiu-ch'üan's contribution, albeit fantastic, visionary,
and intellectually distasteful to an upper-class Chinese of the time. But
it was quite attractive to those anti-Manchu Southerners who had no
vested interest in the Confucian social order. "God has divided the
kingdoms of the world, and made the ocean to be a boundary for them,
just as the father divides his estates among his sons; every one of whom
ought to reverence the will of his father, and quietly manage his own
property. Why should these Manchus now forcibly enter China and rob
their brothers of their estate?" [16]

Nevertheless, Hung's hatred for the Manchus was relatively muted.
It was really Yang Hsiu-ch'ing, a leader of miners and charcoal-burners,
who introduced fanaticism. Yang added the "practical" element of emotional racism, essential to the creation of a revolutionary movement.[17]
The Manchu Tartars came to stand for all that was evil, all that had

sucked China dry of its vital essences. "The world belongs to China, not to the Tartars. Clothes and food belong to China, not to the Tartars. Sons, daughters and people belong to China, not to the Tartars. Unfortunately, the rulers of the Ming failed in their duties, and the Manchus took advantage of this chaos to defile China, steal its territory, injure its sons and rape its daughters." [18] When those Tartar "devils" were exterminated, China would return to itself, and the Kingdom of God on Earth would be established. Here, finally, was the millennium, the promised land — and the mechanics of deliverance was to be the massacre of the Manchus. Thus did the recessive brethren of "God Worshippers" become the aggressive brotherhood of Taiping revolutionaries. Past suddenly became future. China could be itself only by destroying Confucian history.

The economic and social crisis around Canton after the Opium War directly caused the Taipings to form. However, the real seedbed of discontent and zone of recruitment for the *T'ai-p'ing t'ien-kuo* was Hunan and Kiangsi, full of unemployed boatmen and coolies; and the Yangtze valley, with its impoverished peasants and "propertyless vagabonds." [19] Because of that, and because the Heavenly Kingdom centered on Nanking, the Taiping rebellion as such bypassed Kuang-chou. But, like hyenas at the kill, other traditional secret societies watched the mandate as it seemed to change, and moved in from the hinterlands to feast on the great city of Canton.

XIII

The Circle Tightens

All the neighboring country was in a state of chronic anarchy; the villages, towns and hamlets were all walled, and each seemed prepared to fight with its neighbor. There were villages, certainly not a quarter of a mile distant from each other, both surrounded with distinct walls about sixteen to twenty feet high — the house tops inside were just visible; the walls generally formed a square; there were no buttresses or places from which a flanking fire could be directed along the walls, nothing but architectural fortification in its most primitive form. — J. Scarth, *Twelve Years in China (1860)*

In the summer of 1850, the Kwangsi rebels made their first great foray into Kwangtung. Fifty thousand outlaws, enrolled under a Ming banner, swept down from the hill country and captured the city of Ch'ing-yuan, one hundred miles up the North River from Canton and ninety miles from the Kwangsi border. By January, 1851, they had consolidated their control of the county and began to move slowly downstream. Their approach gave other secret-society groups the courage to revolt at Tsung-hua, only forty miles northeast of the provincial capital. And that was not all. During the summer, revolt spread to the West River districts, where all along the Kwangsi border new bands of rebels arose under the Taiping adherent, Ling Shih-pa. Instead of merely looting villages and farms, these outlaws began to levy moderately scaled taxes, hoping to win the allegiance of the peasantry in order to increase their own numbers and attack the delta cities. This was rebellion, not banditry, and the authorities grew alarmed. Hsü Kuang-chin's friends and colleagues in Peking began to send warnings that the new Hsien-feng Emperor had heard of the revolt and was growing more and more upset. If the area was not quickly pacified, the Governor-General would be held personally responsible. And so, Hsü began to send braves to the border, men who had been recruited from the counties around Canton. Unfortunately, the "volunteers" more often than not simply deserted to swell the rebel ranks. Increasingly worried, the Governor-General decided that he personally would take a picked group of banner troops to Kaochou, three hundred miles west of the capital. Once there, he began to clear a *cordon sanitaire* between the major city of Lo-ting and the Kwangsi border, hoping to keep the bandits from moving down the West River and linking up with the Ming pretenders at Ch'ing-yuan. But his forces were unable to contain the rebels. In September, 1851, Ling Shih-pa broke through the perimeter and captured Lo-ting. Hsü Kuang-chin quickly sent for two thousand "volunteers" from Shun-te, and dropped back to Hsin-i, fifty miles from Lo-ting, where he spent the winter of 1851. With spring, he hoped to renew the offensive. But at that moment, T'ien Fang's armies attacked Wu-chou, just across the Kwangsi border.[1]

The Governor-General could not pacify both areas. Sending for even more militiamen, he begged Governor Yeh to relieve him at Lo-ting so that he could move on into Kwangsi. On June 1, 1852, Yeh handed over the seals of Commissioner of Foreign Affairs to the acting Governor, Po Kuei, and left for the mountains. Three weeks later, his troops reached Lo-Ting and immediately met Ling Shih-pa's troops in battle. The banner men and volunteers lost. Yeh Ming-ch'en realized that he could not hope to defeat Ling as long as most of the secret societies around the city of Lo-ting continued to help the Kwangsi rebels. And so he began to subvert the rebel movement by offering money or rank to the local bandits in exchange for their allegiance. The policy succeeded. On August 2, 1852, when he once again challenged Ling Shih-pa, the rebel's forces were crushed, and Ling himself reportedly committed suicide to avoid capture. The outbreak, which had lasted for exactly twelve months, had been put down.[2]

But the Wu-chou revolt continued. True to his word, the Emperor finally replaced Hsü Kuang-chin as Governor-General with the successful Yeh, and ordered Hsü, now operating under a shadow, to continue the pacification campaign in Kwangsi. Yeh, on the other hand, decided to apply the same tactics to some of the other rebellious areas in the fall of 1852. But by November, Kuang-chou itself was growing restless, and he hastily returned to find revolt brewing around the provincial capital.[3]

As soon as the Taiping rebels burst out of Kwangsi and into Central China, it became evident that Hunan and Kiangsi would have to depend on relatively undisturbed Kwangtung for military supplies and specie. As far as Peking was concerned, Yeh Ming-ch'en's major duty was to keep the province under control so that Canton's revenues could be used to pacify the rebels.[4] But the initial cost of the Kwangsi campaigns had already overburdened Kuang-chou. By July, 1852, a total of four million taels in military expenses alone had been spent in the Liang-kuang. This huge deficit (roughly equivalent to $5,250,000) was partially covered by drafts on the provincial treasury at Canton, proceeds from the sale of offices,* and 500,000 taels destined for Peking but taken from the Hoppo's customs revenue. A year later, when the government was even considering paying banner troops with promissory notes, the provincial treasurer had to order Kwangtung's magistrates to subscribe ten thousand taels apiece to the province's coffers. But that was only a stopgap. Other sources had to be found. In the fall of 1851, the Emperor, remembering how generous the gentry and merchants of Kwangtung had been during the entry crisis, asked Hsü and Yeh to explore the possibility of gentry-financing of military costs in the Liang-kuang. Sixteen months later, in March of 1853, the notables of the region were asked to contribute one month's rent on all of their property to the provincial treasury. The gentry sullenly assented. This kind of assessment gradually became almost an accepted source of official revenue. From 1852 to 1855, the landlords of Shun-te county alone volunteered 352,000 taels, and were assessed an additional 200,000 taels.[5]

Inevitably the gentry of the delta grew restless, for the entire costs of the two provinces were coming to rest entirely on their shoulders, and the burden was staggering.† The authorities realized this, but what could they do? Militia and troops had to be paid if the province were to be defended. On the other hand, if the Cantonese were squeezed too hard, they themselves might rebel. The Emperor had added to the dilemma in late 1850 when he ordered the land taxes of Kwangtung and Kwangsi remitted the following year. For he, too, wanted both popular support and revenue. To ensure the latter, and their own continued "squeeze," Kwangtung's local magistrates had kept the edict secret and continued to collect taxes. Sooner or later, the news was bound to get out.

In late March, 1851, the gentry of P'an-yü and Nan-hai discovered the deception, and immediately wrote to their friends throughout the

---

*By August, 1852, the pecuniary value of rank had dropped to almost nothing. See: FO 17/192, Bowring–Malmesbury, Desp. 106, Aug. 23, 1852.

†From 1854 to 1857, the inhabitants of the single county of Shun-te supplied a grand total of 668,682 taels to the provincial government, or 14 percent of its *total* military revenue. See Appendix V.

province, announcing that the provincial treasurer was liable to impeachment for failing to publish the remission. The ensuing scandal rocked the province. The district magistrate at Hsin-hui apologized publicly and promised to return twice the amount of money collected. Some suggested that all the literary candidates should refuse to attend the prefectural exams that year. The worst repercussions were in Tung-kuan, where a gentry mob blockaded the local yamen, demanding their taxes returned on the spot.* The magistrate luckily escaped by the back door, taking his funds and seals with him to Canton, where he promptly filed a countersuit against the local notables of the county. Hsü Kuang-chin decided to back the magistrate and make an example of the gentry. First, he wrote Peking, asking that the literati of Tung-kuan be forbidden to participate in the local examinations. Then he had one of the mob's leaders, a military *hsiu-ts'ai* named Li, imprisoned on charges of sedition. Thereupon, Li cut his throat in jail as a protest, and the Tung-kuan gentry vowed never to pay a tael of taxes until they had obtained redress. When Hsü was transferred out of the area in the fall of 1852, they then began to put pressure on Po Kuei, demanding that the dead man's family be compensated. Po Kuei refused to answer their petition. In October, the military graduates assembled for their triennial exams at Canton, and Li's old *t'ung-nien* (classmates) demanded to see the acting Governor. He again refused them. This time they declared that they would boycott the examinations and thus bring the matter to the Emperor's attention. Frightened, Po Kuei grudgingly conceded and hoped that the county would finally calm down.[6]

But already the tax protest movement was spreading. In Hsin-an and in other areas around Canton, the gentry refused to pay any land taxes at all. The year 1852 had been a bad one: summer floods had destroyed many villages between Hua-hsien and Canton and almost completely ruined the rice harvest. Now the government wanted more taxes, more levies, more contributions. Disorder began to spread. In P'an-yü serious clan wars broke out, involving secret societies which were paid bounties by warring lineages.[7] All of this — the tax protest movement, the fiscal drain, the forced assessments — was merely an added load to the already suffering province. The rampant militia movement, urban disorder, rural impoverishment, the polarization of society — all of these piled on each

---

*Similar gentry tax riots occurred around Ningpo in 1851 and 1852. See: Sasaki Masaya, "Hsien-feng ninen Yin-hsien no kōryō bōdō" (The Anti-tax Uprisings in Yin-hsien in the Second Year of the Hsien-feng Reign), *Kindai Chūgoku kenkyū* (Research on Modern China), 5:185–300 (1963).

other as the hill bandits and the brooding gentry were joined by a re-
surgence of secret-society activity.

As early as 1843, the Triads had once again come into the open around
Canton. First, to levy illegal tolls and to rob; second, to carry on gang
wars with the rival Sleeping Dragon Society (*Wo-lung-hui*).[8] Although
they were reported throughout the prefecture, they operated in greatest
strength on the east coast of Hsiang-shan county, near Macao.[9] There,
bandits from the poorer counties of Hsin-hui and Hsin-ning began to
hold daylight meetings during the winter of 1843. Several hundred would
gather at a crossroad, post guards with guns, and encourage the local
peasants to join their society: the *San-ho-hui*. Some farmers, believing
that they could avoid onerous extractions by belonging to the society,
pledged membership for a fee of three hundred cash. Occasionally, entire
villages would join for their own protection, because the society maintained itself by attacking unprotected hamlets. Eventually, the subclerks,
yamen runners, and policemen of the local magistrate's office even
became members and helped keep the society's activities from being
discovered. Throughout 1844, matters worsened, until it seemed that
nothing could prevent the Triple Unity Society from taking over the
county. In the winter of 1844, the brotherhood's leaders decided they
were strong enough to attack the county seat itself. There they made
their great mistake. When the armed bands moved into the city and
began to enter home after home, demanding protection money, a local
notable named Cheng K'uei-hung and a magistrate home on mourning
leave rallied the gentry and organized militia that drove out the *San-
ho-hui* and pacified the county.[10]

The Triads did not disappear after 1845. They were either held in
check locally by the vigorous militia movement, or driven away from
Canton to Kwangsi. Now and again there would be isolated reports of
local activities, but not until 1853 did the dormant societies around the
city begin to emerge into the open again.

If 1852 was a bad year for agriculture, 1853 was a bad year for the
city's trade. Canton was having its worst financial recession since 1848.[11]
More porters, coolies, and compradors lost their jobs, just when the
marginal peasants of the countryside were feeling the tax squeeze tighter
than ever. Urban unemployed and rural tenants began to drift together
into the Triads, waiting and watching, for something was in the air. At
Amoy, at Shanghai, and around Canton, the Triads slowly began to

believe that this was the time, that the political universe was about to undergo another great dynastic readjustment.

Sensing this, Yeh's government attempted to spread unfounded rumors during the early spring of 1853 that the British were planning to reopen the entry question. The authorities were apparently trying to use the specter of foreign invasion both as an excuse to maintain security precautions during the New Year's festivities and to help draw the classes of the countryside together. But it was too late. On April 26, 1853, the first of many antiofficial placards began to appear in the streets of Canton. By June, the Triads had begun several small uprisings in the hamlets around the delta, even going so far as to levy taxes. Daylight robberies and kidnappings became commonplace. As disorder spread, collisions between the officials and the people occurred almost daily. Bands of freebooters, overrunning most of Tung-kuan, Hsin-hui, Shun-te, and Hsiang-shan counties, moved closer and closer to the city. Within Canton itself, panic spread. Rice was so hard to get and hoarding so prevalent that the provincial government had to forbid rice dealers to raise their prices any higher. By October, hundreds of Triads roamed through the suburbs of the city, plundering and looting. The provincial capital seemed defenseless, for Yeh had been so afraid that the Taiping rebels would plunge down from Kiangsi and Fukien into Kwangtung that he had transferred a large part of Canton's garrison to the Che-ling and Mei-ling passes. Thanks, however, to the reconstitution of the urban "control" and militia units, most of the bands were driven off. But the suburbs began to assume the aspect of an armed camp with heavy barriers, paid police patrols, armed householders.[12]

That same month, the first large-scale uprising occurred near the city. The professional gamblers and casino owners at the Bogue had been having trouble with the police, who were extorting more than their usual bribes, and so decided to ally themselves with an offshoot of the Small Sword (*Hsiao-tao*) Society that had captured Shanghai and Amoy. After a series of inconclusive struggles with the police, the society members finally went into open opposition and struck out across the countryside toward Hui-chou, seventy-five miles away from Canton on the East River.[13]

Before Yeh Ming-ch'en knew what was happening, his line of communications with Hui-chou had been cut. Attempts to crush the rebels failed miserably; but at least by November, they seemed contained in the Hui-chou area. Order might have been restored had not the presence of the Small Sword rebels in their vicinity inspired the bellicose clans of

Tung-kuan to renew the tax protest movement. This time, however, the poorer lineages were allying with secret societies. Yeh decided that an example would have to be made, if the county were not to inspire tax delinquency throughout the province. In January, 1854, he ordered the prefect of Canton to make a special trip to Tung-kuan and report on the increasingly dangerous situation there. The prefect recommended strictness and proceeded to arrest and execute members of the dissident clans. As usual, the situation got out of hand. Unleashed banner troops wiped out entire villages: men, women, and children were killed, houses razed. Suffering, discontent, popular anger swelled and grew.[14]

The tinder was fired by a smuggler and secret-society member named Ho Liu, whose brother had been murdered during the prefect's purge at Shih-lung, halfway between Hui-chou and the capital. Mad with grief, he styled himself "Avenger of Sorrow" and began to raise a band of other malcontents and vengeance seekers. In June, 1854, helped by a friend named Liu Ying-ts'ai, Ho Liu massed his men for an attack on the county seat of Tung-kuan itself. As if on signal, every other secret-society leader in the delta raised the banner of revolt. The Red Turban rebellion had begun.[15]

XIV

The Red Turban Revolt

> The ancient books tell us that once in five cen-
> turies some man of talent beyond his fellows
> will appear, on whom the hope of the nation will
> depend. That period has elapsed since the fall of
> the Ming dynasty, and it is full time that a hero
> should come forward and save the nation. —
> Red Turban proclamation*

To the authorities, the simultaneity of the risings proved that the revolt
had been planned in advance — a huge and secret conspiracy against
the forces of order.[1]

> In the fourth month of the fourth year of the Hsien-feng Emperor (April
> 27 to May 26, 1854), the Red Turbans (*hung-chin*) arose. Before that
> time, all of the disloyal subjects of Kwangtung had met in [secret] society
> conclaves, divided into groups in each *chou* and *hsien*. They fixed a date
> for a general uprising. . . . Others assembled at the sound of a whistle,
> joining them as partisans [in such numbers] as cannot be recorded here.
> They followed the rebels, wearing red turbans and uniforms, founding
> armies and official ranks, all with usurped titles. The Imperial soldiers
> all wore white headgear, and so the bandits came to call them the "White
> Soldiers." [2]

In truth, there was no plotted conspiracy, no coordinated plan. Rather,
rebellion engendered rebellion, in a distinct crescendo of disorder after
Ho Liu's revolt. First, the warring clans around Whampoa combined
with six thousand secret-society marauders to throw Honam into chaos.[3]
Then, seven thousand members of the *San-ho-hui*, led by a man named
Ch'en K'ai, made a surprise attack on Fatshan and, to the dismay of the
entire province, captured the great city† on July 4, 1854. There, Ch'en
declared that a new reign had been ushered in: the Great Peace (*ta-ning*).

---

*Translated in FO 17/226, Incl. 1, Desp. 18, Jan. 9, 1855.

†At Fatshan, fifteen miles southwest of Canton, a population of two or three
hundred thousand processed textiles, rattan, brassware, ironwork, cassia, grain,
and oil. See: FO 17/30, Gutzlaff's report, Incl. 1, Desp. 4, Jan. 10, 1839.

He and his cohorts changed their clothing and let their hair grow long, symbolically calling their troops the *hung-ping* (vast soldiers). The Ming restorationists were amazingly lenient at first. Only the very wealthy were taxed, which heartened some but dismayed the Governor-General and the Governor, who feared not only that Ch'en might gain popular support but that he might learn how to use Fatshan's famous foundries and arsenals. Imperial troops were immediately stationed off the city in war junks, advancing and retreating with the tide, cannonading the rebel fortifications whenever they could. But Fatshan was only the beginning. From as far away as Wu-chou, the hill bandits smelled opportunity and began to descend from the mountains, racing toward Canton. On July 12, Kan Hsien started a rebellion at Hua-hsien, twenty-five miles directly north of the provincial capital. Three days later, a secret-society leader named Ch'ü Ch'iu raised the Ming banner at San-shui, an equal distance to the west. Nan-hai burst into warfare. The country yamen of the district magistrate was completely destroyed. A column of banner troops was ambushed and massacred.[4] Canton was rapidly being surrounded.*

On July 13, the first assaults were launched by Kan Hsien's band on the north gate. If all of the rebels north of the city could coordinate their attacks, then the walls might fall. A week later, the government's major fear was realized: the three rebel forces converged under the general leadership of Kan Hsien himself. From then until the siege ended with the New Year, the city would be under constant attack. Now, with tens of thousands of bandits encamped at the northern base of the White Cloud Mountains, Yeh Ming-ch'en had to draw in the government troops that had been blockading Fatshan. He could only hope for three things: that Canton could defend itself, that Ch'en K'ai's Fatshan rebels would not be able to link forces with the bands north of the city, and that the key clans and militia of the rural counties would remain loyal to the government.

The city's defenses came first. While skirmishes occurred daily at the city walls, banner troops burned down the northern suburbs, destroying any cover for the rebels.[5] Within the city, the official garrison was supplemented by popular militia.† Self-defense corps were formed and

---

*See Appendix VI.

†At that time, there were five thousand banner troops, four thousand green standard troops, two thousand braves from Ch'ao-chou, and four thousand braves from the delta, all attached to the Canton garrison. The braves were considered the elite of the defensive forces. While imperial troops received only five dollars a month, the mercenaries were paid anywhere from seven to ten dollars. Most of the delta braves were from Tung-kuan county, led by a military *chü-jen* named

placed under the control of ward committees, which ensured that each householder contributed a fixed amount of money. The merchants outdid themselves: Howqua and Kingqua (Liang Lun-shu) collected and subscribed half a million taels. The ward committees were in turn "managed" by four directorates — one for each quarter of the city — composed of influential residents and presided over by the provincial treasurer, the provincial judge, the grain intendant, and the circuit intendant.[6]

Meanwhile, the Fatshan rebels, reinforced by a large contingent of Kwangsi outlaws, prepared to join Kan Hsien north of Canton. Banner troops could never hope to bar their advance. However, between Fatshan and Canton lay the old militia area of the *Sheng-p'ing she-hsüeh*. The *t'uan-lien* there were defunct and their headquarters, the *Sheng-p'ing* "public office" at Niu-lan-kang near En-chou, had been taken over as a rebel command post. But if the Nan-hai gentry and peasantry could be inspired to reactivate their militia, then Yeh Ming-ch'en might hope to contain the Fatshan rebels and keep Canton's communications open with the outside. Therefore, the Governor-General made every effort to capture the peasantry's loyalty in that area. While promising a general amnesty for all who laid down their arms, Yeh also invoked the "righteousness" of the entry crisis, when peasants and officials acted in unison against the British. The appeals seemed to work. On July 29, 1854, a rebel column that tried to fight its way through to Kan Hsien was repulsed by banner troops and small groups of local militiamen. But could the gentry leaders retain the loyalty of the rural masses while the balance of power seemed to favor the Red Turbans?[7]

There was no doubt that the rebel victories were impressive. By August 5, Shun-te's county seat had been captured by Ch'en Chi's band; Ch'ing-yuan and Shao-ch'ing were completely under rebel control; most of Hsiang-shan county was overrun by Li Hung-ying's men; and the forts north of the city, deluged by heavy rains, suffered daily assaults. Matters only worsened during the following two weeks: Ch'en Sung-nien attacked the county seat of Hsin-hui; a Triad named Hsü Chao-piao started a revolt near K'ai-p'ing, sixty miles southwest of Canton; the first rebel gangs began to show up in Honam; and Ho Liu, the "Avenger of Sorrow," captured Ts'eng-ch'eng and marched on to join Kan Hsien at the White Cloud Mountains.

Chu Kuo-hsiung. This contingent participated in most of the major encounters of the civil war: the parade grounds battle, the recapture of Fo-ling-shih, and the assault on Shih-ching. Later, Chu led this militia group against the British during the *Arrow* war. See: *Tung-kuan hsien-chih*, 72:4-a. J. Scarth, *Twelve Years in China: The People, the Rebels, and the Mandarins*, 229.

The pincers were tightening around the city. Now there were thirty thousand men outside the north gate, and people began fleeing to the even more dangerous countryside. An Englishman described the terror that gripped the city:

> What misery have these cities not endured! Capture and recapture, fire, rapine, and destruction. . . . The people of Canton were governed by terror. Justice was left out of the question. Lies were not only spoken, but acted. If prisoners could not be taken in battle, innocent people were brought in for execution. . . . For months the gates were closed, and only opened at certain places, with vast precautions. The people were made to wear badges, bearing their name, age and residence. . . . The panic was very great — shops closed, trade suspended; there was scarcely any communication with places in the neighbourhood.[8]

From Hui-chou, Red Turbans were filtering through P'an-yü county to camp on the Manchu parade grounds just outside the east gate. If the twenty thousand Fatshan rebels, armed now with thirty cannon and one hundred and ten river craft, ever joined Kan Hsien, the city would be doomed. Could the militia of the *Sheng-p'ing* districts prevent that juncture?

Suddenly, during the last days of August, the tide began to turn. A series of minor local victories seemed to justify Yeh's hope that the Nan-hai *t'uan-lien* dared to oppose the rebels. On August 11, militia from San-yuan-li had supported banner troops in an attack on the "public office" headquarters at Niu-lan-kang. By then, Ch'en K'ai himself had realized that the major obstacle between his forces and Canton was the league of village militia, which a local notable named Ou-yang Ch'üan had organized at Ta-li, five miles north of Fatshan. On August 19, and again on August 24, Ch'en's Red Turbans tried to crush the *t'uan-lien*. Each time they were driven off. Enraged, the bandits finally captured one of the resisting villages near Ta-li and burned it to the ground, but already the Canton authorities were supplying the militia headquarters there with arms, supplies, and a small reinforcement of official troops.[9]

Hopelessly waiting for Ch'en K'ai to arrive, the rebels at the White Cloud Mountains began to grow restless. For one, there was the problem of central control. The Red Turbans definitely claimed to be restoring the Ming dynasty:

> Lo, Administrator of the affairs of Government, Exterminator of Villains, Great Dignity Displaying General for Cutting off the Ch'ing Dynasty, and Generalissimo of the Army;

Yung, Administrator of the Affairs of the Empire, Chancellor of the Inner Council, promoted three ranks, recorded five times:

To make manifest that whereas the population of the Dominion of China is dense, it is difficult to distinguish between the good and the bad. When Hung-wu, the first Emperor of our Ming dynasty, was on the throne, ten thousand countries opened trade, the Superiors and Inferiors harmonized, and there was no war, no imposition with the neighbouring countries.[10]

The only trouble was, they had no pretender around whom they could rally. When one secret-society leader declared himself commander-in-chief in the name of the Ming, the others refused to serve him, and he disgustedly offered his six thousand men to the government. Some of the leaders argued over the distribution of booty or taxing rights, even engaging in gang wars. And, as time wore on, the large groups that were assembled north of the city exhausted the resources of Nan-hai and P'an-yü, where most of the villages were burned or deserted. Many left for wealthier regions. By September 5, even Ho Liu had decided to pull out of the confederated force.[11]

Unaware of this, but emboldened by the success of the militia, the military authorities in Canton decided to make a dangerous foray to try to relieve the pressure on the east side of the city. On September 7, 1854, troops commanded by Wei Tso-pang* rushed out from the gates and attacked the large rebel encampment at the Manchu parade grounds. The Red Turbans fled in surprise, leaving Ming seals, arms, and supplies behind as they rushed back around the city to Kan Hsien's headquarters at Niu-lan-kang. For the first time, imperial troops had defeated a large group of rebels in open battle. Now the city had gained some military security, but the siege had already taken a heavy toll. The merchants simply could not believe that the government would be able to hold out. They themselves were financially exhausted by the constant levies. While antiofficial talk was heard more and more openly in the city's streets, many merchants secretly transferred large sums on private account to Hong Kong. International commerce came to a stop as the regular tea shipments were rerouted to Foochow. Canton's shopkeepers even began trying to undersell each other so that they could clear their inventories before the city fell. On the other hand, rice was exorbitantly expensive

---

*Wei, a native of Tung-kuan, had been named first captain of the Left Brigade of the Green Banner battalion attached to Shun-te county. He became famous during the Red Turban revolt as a major antibandit fighter. See: *Shun-te hsien-chih*, 16:5-b.

as the city's provisions began to give out.[12] To survive, the government would have to recover its lost sources of revenue by restoring administrative and fiscal links with the countryside. And so the civil war entered a new and protracted phase of rural recovery. Town by town, district by district, the gentry-led *t'uan-lien*, with whatever logistic support Canton could offer, would have to re-establish order and exterminate the secret societies. Militia centers were founded. In Nan-hai county, the Ta-li league and the "Bureau for Nurturing Humaneness" contained the Fatshan rebels. In P'an-yü, the "North Road Pacification Bureau" was charged with attacking one of the major rebel headquarters in the "local school" at Fo-ling-shih, while the militia network of the Wu clan fought the Whampoa Red Turbans around Blenheim Reach. The district magistrate, Hua T'ing-chieh, led the resistance in Tung-kuan county, finally defeating Ho Liu on December 26, 1854. And in Shun-te, the "Tungkuan" militia bureau financed and trained local *t'uan-lien* to recover the county seat.

In many cases, militia bureaus were run by men who had led the antiBritish movement in the 1840's.* This time, however, the techniques of defense differed. Vast areas of the countryside had to be pacified instead of defended. This was not a matter of static control, as in *pao-chia*, but of wiping out rebel bands within a given district. Gradually, a technique of pacification was developed. A group of twenty or more villages would form a "span" (*wei*). Then that area would be cleared of all disorderly elements: armed bandits, secret-society members, or those considered by their clan leaders to be troublemakers. Once a safe area had been created, an alliance would be made with another *wei*. This was arranged by means of a "covenant" (*yueh*). Since the "covenanted" area could muster relatively large bodies of armed militiamen, the regions between the "spans" would be cleared. At the same time — and this was crucial to the later development of localism — the *yueh* would try to ensure that disorder would not recur by controlling food prices, supplying relief grain, and distributing the income of ritual lands. All of this was managed by "public offices" (*kung-chü*), which were ancillaries to the militia bureaus, thrusting political, judicial, and fiscal powers into the hands of important local gentry.

Slowly and gradually, the forces of order recovered their control of rural Kuang-chou during the fall and winter of 1854. In September,

---

*There was no question that Kuang-chou's history of self-defense, the existence of large clans, and the long shadow of the provincial capital, held the countryside together and finally enabled the forces of order to triumph.

Ts'eng-ch'eng was recovered. In October, militia reconquered the county seats of Hsiang-shan and Hsin-hui, and razed the old *Sheng-p'ing kung-so* at Niu-lan-kang where Kan Hsien had made his headquarters. The following month, Lung-men was retaken, and the Red Turban center at Fo-ling-shih was destroyed. In December, Hua-hsien was under imperial control, while the rebels in both Hsin-ning and Hsin-hui were dispersed and scattered. And by January, 1855, the area around San-yuan-li had been cleared.

This rural pacification went almost unnoticed as public attention focused on the city itself. After the victory at the Manchu parade grounds on September 7, 1854, there were three major matters of concern to the authorities: the area just north of the city, the rebels at Fatshan, and the increasingly active band of Triads at Hsin-tsao (Blenheim Reach) near Whampoa.

In September, the band at the north gate had moved six miles back from the walls; but they remained there, continuing to menace the city. The following month, some of the semiliterate yamen employees were detected in a conspiracy to admit their secret-society brethren through the north gate, and Yeh Ming-ch'en decided that the threat would have to be removed. The banner troops were promised thirty thousand dollars if they cleared the area north of Canton. In a series of engagements on November 3 and 4, the garrison complied and drove the rebels from the walls. For the first time in many months the north gates of the city were opened.[13]

Now the authorities could turn their attention to Fatshan. On November 10, imperial troops disembarked from their junks, joined a large body of Ta-li militia, and advanced on the city. The attack was inconclusive. A week later, they decided to try again. This time, though, the rebels had learned a lesson from the previous assault. As the banner troops landed from their junks and started up toward the city, some of the Red Turbans slipped behind them and quickly captured three lorchas, seven guard boats, and sixteen war junks. Then they turned the cannons of the fleet on the men between them and the city. When the smoke from the crossfire cleared, fifteen hundred official troops were missing or dead.[14]

The attack on Fatshan was a miserable failure. It was abandoned just as Canton found its southern exposure threatened by a Red Turban fleet from Blenheim Reach. This contingent of rebels was an urban group, a *lumpenproletariat* of shopkeepers' assistants, sailors, coolies, and men who had worked as compradors for the hong merchants. There were even some foreigners working with the outlaws, mainly American and Dutch seamen who were hired to make ammunition and explosive missiles. In keeping with the group's character, the titles used were drawn not from China but from the West: the society leaders were called "consuls." [15]

The elected leader was named Ch'en Hsien-liang. He had taken over the yamen of the local assistant district magistrate. There, as "Commander of the Patriotic Volunteers of the Province of Kwangtung," his avowed aim was to "destroy the extortionate and oppressive officials and their myrmidons, and to reestablish the ancient sovereignty of the Great Ming." [16] Ch'en had been a petty shopkeeper in Honam. When Kan Hsien revolted, he had joined the rebels at Fo-ling-shih. Then he had moved down to Whampoa, and had joined forces with some of the Red Turbans from Shun-te.* His band financed itself by levying tolls on the chopboats that ran between Canton and Whampoa, and by seizing the crops of any peasants in their area. In spite of his dynastic pretensions, Ch'en Hsien-liang's only consistent goal was to conquer and loot Canton. [17]

The Blenheim Reach bandits forced the British to mull over the question of their own role in the civil war. When the rebellion first broke out in July, 1854, the consul, Robertson, had written the British plenipotentiary, Sir John Bowring: "I deem our policy to be simply neutral, to confine ourselves to the factories, and await the results now pending without getting into communication with one side or the other." [18] The plenipotentiary himself did not quite know how to feel about the matter. On the one hand, England's commercial interests realistically favored the forces of order in Canton. Conversely, however, Bowring was just a little pleased to see the haughty Chinese authorities in such desperate straits. Also, as a close friend of the English Utilitarian James Mill, he tended to view the rebels as bona fide resistants, engaging in the right of free men to revolt. Ch'en Hsien-liang appealed to these sentiments on October 1, when he respectfully invited the British plenipotentiary to visit the rebel camp at Whampoa. [19] By the time this note reached Bowring many weeks later, however, there had been so many clashes between the rebel junk fleet and British merchant vessels, that the English were losing all natural sympathy for Ch'en and his rebels. The

---

*Ch'en may have led an insurrection in Kwangsi in April, 1854. British reports spoke of "red-girdled rebels," led by "a man who was a small shopkeeper in Canton." See: FO 17/213, Bowring–Clarendon, Desp. 14, April 20, 1854.

Red Turbans themselves correctly believed that British merchants were secretly selling arms to the Cantonese authorities. On February 10, therefore, Ch'en angrily accused the foreigners of sneaking powder into the city and imperiously ordered all barbarians to leave Canton immediately.[20] Bowring was infuriated by the note ("I deem it a piece of experimental impertinence") and began to lose patience with the rebels.[21] Besides, since Ch'en was running out of fields to loot and merchants to kidnap, his only means of supply was to raid vessels along the river under the guise of a blockade. In late February, scarcely a day passed without another British or American ship being boarded and plundered. Rebellion was turning into piracy. By then Bowring had decided that the Blenheim Reach "rebels" were no more than ladrones. "The small element of patriotism and insurrection entitled to the slightest respect and consideration is sunk in the great object of subjecting the opulent city of Canton to be sacked by hordes of vagabonds."[22] Did this mean that the English would actively support the provincial authorities?

Yeh Ming-ch'en had been angling for British help since the beginning of December, 1854, when the Whampoa fleet cleared Macao passage of imperial junks and began to fire on Canton. The British mercantile community, angered by the shipping incidents, had been trying to think of ways to destroy the Blenheim Reach group since November. An American named Drinker had assembled a group of foreigners, intending to recapture Hsin-tsao in exchange for a cash reward of twenty-five thousand dollars, which had been promised by the Governor-General. But before they could leave, Drinker was dissuaded by Robertson, who feared rebel reprisals. Although the "Drinker Expedition" came to naught, it symbolized a new phenomenon of the 1850's: the forces of order, which now included both merchants and gentry, were coming to view the British as natural allies rather than as racial enemies. As early as May, 1853, Howqua had asked Harry Parkes — then serving as the Canton consulate's interpreter — to arrange for British intervention against the Taiping rebels.[23] Now, after the rebel fleet attack on December 2, the commander of the garrison of Canton, Shen Ti-hui, himself was urging Yeh to use the security merchants to request British naval support.[24] Bowring's answer to this informal approach was to insist that Britain would have to observe strict neutrality. Only if the rebels won would England step in to avert a general massacre. However, he added, if Yeh Ming-ch'en really wanted the British to help, he would have to apply personally.[25] This last was sheer malice, for when Yeh finally swallowed his pride on

December 7 and desperately asked for British naval intervention, Bowring gleefully responded that it was not his country's policy to interfere in the domestic affairs of another sovereign nation.[26]

As the rebel fleet of two hundred junks sailed with impunity back and forth from Fatshan to Whampoa, there seemed precious little that Canton could do to protect herself without getting outside help. Fierce mercenaries, imported from Ch'ao-chou to defend the waterfront, only added to the disorder by getting out of control and looting. Robertson, the British consul, was convinced that the city would be assaulted at any moment.[27] Yet, as week after week passed, the rebels did nothing. Robertson saw only the rebels' mastery of the river. While the junks bombarded Canton at will, the local gentry around Hsin-tsao, led by the prestigious Wu clan, were organizing "public offices" and "covenants" that eventually put thirty-five thousand militiamen in the field against Ch'en Hsien-liang's rebels. The Red Turbans monopolized the river, but they were losing control of their land base. On March 7, 1855, while imperial junks offered what support they could, the braves of Whampoa completely wiped out the Hsin-tsao headquarters, scattering the Red Turbans in every possible direction.[28]

Long before that, Ch'en K'ai's relatively moderate regime had worn out its welcome in Fatshan. In early January, the rebels had demanded contributions from an obdurate quarter of the city. When one of the rebel lieutenants went there in person to collect the taxes, he was captured and held by the citizens until he promised to lower the levies. As soon as he was released, he returned to headquarters, gathered a large body of men, and returned to set fire to that part of the town, killing all who emerged from the holocaust. The fire raged for two days, and when it was over, the inhabitants of Fatshan were solidly progovernment. Thus, when the Ta-li braves and banner soldiers (reinforced with two thousand fresh troops from Fukien) attacked on January 18, 1855, the city was easily retaken. The official forces marched in to find deserted and smoking ruins, but the twenty thousand Red Turbans had scattered and Canton was now thoroughly safe.[29] The most dangerous phase of the civil war had passed.

XV

The Purge

> After the execution of such immense numbers as were decapitated last year, the Police Authorities are embarrassed to carry out the orders of the Viceroy (probably based upon good information) for the apprehension of many more suspected rebels in various parts of the country. In most instances, the responsibility of surrendering them is laid upon the inhabitants with the alternative of destruction of their villages in cases of disobedience. — Morrison's report, FO 17/245, Incl. 1, Desp. 62, Feb. 12, 1856

The reaction, the White Terror, set in. There had been three sorts of rebels. The large bands marched back into the mountainous borderlands and resumed their outlaw existence. The pirates and river bandits sailed downstream to the sea, where they would plague British and Chinese alike for years to come. But the smaller bands of secret-society discontents simply dissolved and remained where they were. Yeh Ming-ch'en was determined that these "dangerous classes" would never threaten the delta again. A hunt began for known secret-society members, then for "vagabonds," and finally, for all who had "collaborated" with the rebels: poor lineages, even hapless villages that had paid taxes to the Red Turbans. Old enmities were resolved. Opportunists and informers seized what they could: land, water rights, burial sites. The death toll climbed higher and higher. Normally Peking would have had to review every judicial execution. But Yeh had been given a general warrant to exterminate the rebels.* From the very beginning, therefore, he had insisted

---

*Yeh was not particularly anxious to let the court know of the extent of disaffection in his jurisdiction, nor of the great debt he owed to the gentry-led militia. When his military aide, Shen Ti-hui, presented him with an honors list of loyalists and militiamen, Yeh shelved it. Not that he failed to reward the loyal gentry with the usual tablets: he simply made it an honor granted by him and not by the Emperor. Moreover, when describing even so important a victory as the Blenheim Reach (Hsin-tsao) encounter, the Governor-General made no official mention

on mass executions. During the early days of the Tung-kuan revolt, for example, his military commanders presented him with three large boxes filled with right ears, in lieu of heads. By the summer of 1855, his soldiers had standing orders to take no prisoners, and Canton City alone had seen over seventy thousand decapitations. The rivers were clotted with corpses.[1] Although officially acknowledged executions totaled only forty-seven thousand, some claimed that as many as one million were killed throughout the province.[2] Yeh Ming-ch'en himself boasted of personally ordering the death of one hundred thousand "rebels." His only regret was that he had not managed to "extirpate the whole class." [3] But he had not missed by far. The purge of 1855 put the gentry and wealthy lineages of Kwangtung in complete and undisputed control of the countryside. The balance of local administration, which had begun tilting in 1839, had now fallen all the way over to the side of the rural notables. Even the focus of political activity had shifted to the rural *hsien*, for the cities were ruined or bankrupt.[4] Yet this was not the political "localization" of the 1840's. The leading county notables were no longer simple *sheng-yuan* or clan elders. Rural affairs were now being managed by a new generation of specialists, sanctioned and approved by the Emperor himself. Peking had changed its attitude toward local defense.

The militia had received a powerful shot in the arm when Hsü Kuang-chin used the *t'uan-lien* in 1849 to keep the British out of Canton. In fact, the standard manual for rural militia, based upon this experience, was written by the man who had been Kwangtung director of studies during the crisis: Hsü Nai-chao. But even though local braves were successfully used against Hunanese Triads in the summer of 1850, the Court remained wary of sanctioning unrestrained militia. Ultimately, the failure of banner troops during the early Taiping campaigns forced the government's hand. If the rebels had to be stopped, it would be better to use a multitude of civilian leaders than to permit a Count Belisarius to arise. Therefore, early in 1853, the Court selected former high officials and commissioned them to return to their native districts as *t'uan-lien ta-ch'en* (militia ministers).[5]

By breaking the "law of avoidance," the dynasty was taking a great risk. The "old boy" network of *t'ung-nien* (classmates) and *t'ung-hsiang*

---

whatsoever to Peking of the braves' crucial role. See: *Ta-ch'ing li-ch'ao shih-lu* (Veritable Records of Successive Reigns of the Ch'ing Dynasty), Hsien-feng, 167:1-b to 2-b. *Nan-hai hsien-chih*, chüan 5. Hsieh Fu-ch'eng's account, cited in, Huang Yen-yü, "Viceroy Yeh Ming-ch'en and the Canton Episode (1858–1861)," *Harvard Journal of Asiatic Studies*, 6.1:52, n. 4 (March, 1941).

(hometown friends) might mobilize local resistance to the rebels, but would the victorious gentry then willingly restore power to Peking? Or would the empire break up into fiefs and satrapies? The Manchus gambled that high officials, who had conducted brilliant bureaucratic careers, would feel more loyalty toward the official system than they would toward clan or village. This was immediately true, and made the T'ung-chih "restoration" possible. But ultimately, the regional military and political machines created by these men decentralized the empire and helped bring about the downfall of the ruling house.

On the other hand, these high-ranking specialists helped centralize local politics. Pure localism gave way to regionalism as semi-independent provincial leaders like Tseng Kuo-fan or Li Hung-chang linked gentry, militia armies, and financing in a personalistic complex of tightened loyalties and obligations. But this was not generally true for Kwangtung. Provinces like Hunan or Chekiang had to create entire armies, mobile enough to be used against the Taiping rebels. In Kuang-chou, on the other hand, defense was purely local; and in spite of attempts at regionalization, power remained locally centered. Nevertheless, the *t'uan-lien* of 1855 did differ from the *t'uan-lien* of 1841. The militia of 1841 had represented the change from "mass" to "communal" action. Those of 1855 represented the change to "class" action.[6] The Red Turban revolt had not only turned the *t'uan-lien* into instruments of social order: it had also indirectly elevated their political standing. Suddenly, a magistrate found himself dealing with gentry whose status and prestige were far higher than his own.[7] Instead of simply appropriating some of his functions piecemeal, these notables were actually constructing parallel organs of local government, creating coordinated county political systems that superseded his own functions and incidentally favored the economic and social interests of the gentry. The best example of this took place in Shun-te county.

Shun-te *hsien* was hard hit by the Red Turbans. Not only was there the usual village-by-village devastation of Hsü Chao-piao's "native" rebels; there were also the ruinous raids of Ch'en Chi's outlaws from K'ai-p'ing. On August 1, 1854, Ch'en Chi began three long days of rapine and plunder around the county seat at Ta-liang, fifteen miles south of Canton. Virtually all of the regular military leaders there were killed, the houses outside the city walls were looted, and most of the shops and homes inside the city were burned. By the time the town was taken, the magistrate, Ma Ying-chieh, had fled.[8] Civil government had dissolved; and the countryside was distinguished, not by embattled villages, but by large households scattered in indefensible positions throughout the rich delta lands. Only concerted and aggressive gentry defense efforts could restore peace and order.

Of course, there were the familiar *t'uan-lien* organized by lower gentry, working through local schools and academies.* But the really large-scale defense efforts were organized by higher ranking *t'ung-hsiang* who remained in Canton until the county seat, Ta-liang, was retaken in May, 1855. Men like Ch'en Sung and Ch'en Yuan-k'ai coordinated militia, amassed huge sums of money, and helped win the loyalty of indecisive clan and rural leaders.[9] The most famous of these prestigious literati was a man named Lung Yuan-hsi, who was to become virtual overlord of the county and a key figure in the antiforeign movement during the British occupation. Scion of an old and wealthy Ta-liang family, he was considered one of the best scholars of the realm. During the palace examinations of 1835, he ranked among the top three candidates, and went on to become an expositor of the Hanlin Academy, a libationer of the National Academy, and a director of the Court of Sacrificial Worship. In 1853, after supervising the palace examinations, he was promoted to the second rank, and appointed a *t'uan-lien ta-ch'en* for his native Shun-te. Returning to Kwangtung, he helped direct militia affairs until Ta-liang was recaptured. Then he returned in triumph to his birthplace, where the people "were delirious with joy," showering gifts and contributions upon him and his militia office.[10]

Lung did not operate independently of the Governor-General, Yeh Ming-ch'en. On the contrary, Yeh felt that men like Lung Yuan-hsi and Ch'en Sung could help Canton establish some sort of formal relationship with the autocephalous militia units scattered at random throughout the countryside. If the government was to restore its links with rural Kuang-chou, it would have to get these higher gentry to form encompassing militia bureaus that would be theoretically answerable to, and appointed by, Canton. On May 7, 1855, Yeh therefore ordered Lung Yuan-hsi to open up the Shun-te Central Militia Bureau (*Shun-te t'uan-lien tsung-chü*) in a local shrine on the south side of Ta-liang. There, eighteen members of the local gentry, under Lung's control, took charge of rural reconstruction and defense.[11]

The Central Bureau did, indeed, reunify and rebuild the county, partly because of the prestige of men like Lung Yuan-hsi, and partly because

---

*The most renowned of these were the militia leagues organized by the P'an clan at Ch'ung-ho; Tso Meng-heng at Lung-shan: Ch'en Hsüan at Hsiao-wan-pao; and Yang K'ang around Ta-liang. See: *Shun-te hsien-chih*, 17:3-a, 9-b, 10-a; 18:6-a, 10-a, 11-b, 14-b; 19:3-a; 22:18-b.

the gentry absorbed and used preexisting institutions. Some of these institutions were simple *t'uan-lien*. Others were of a slightly different sort: the "sand offices" (*sha-so* or *sha-chü*).

These "sand offices" were originally used to reclaim the alluvial soil in the delta area southeast of Ta-liang, known as the *Tung-hai shih-liu sha* (sixteen delta lands of the eastern sea). There, the large clans had been wresting land from the river for centuries. Once the *sha-t'ien* had been diked and the water drained, the incredibly fertile fields had to be protected against neighboring clans. Therefore, each lineage's "sand office" used rents from the ritual fields to hire guards (*sha-fu*). Occasionally, some of the individual "sand offices" would unite into larger bureaus to fight boundary wars or disperse bandits. The most famous of these was the *Kung-t'ung-t'i* (joint organization), founded during the K'ang-hsi period. Under a variety of names, this league continued down into the nineteenth century, when Lung Yuan-hsi's uncle, Lung T'ing-k'uei, used it against Chang Pao's pirates in 1809. In that sense, it was a gentry organization. As an agent of boundary wars, however, it represented an alliance of clans.[12]

Naturally, the district magistrates had always tried to control both the reclamation and defense activities of the local "sand offices" and *Kung-*

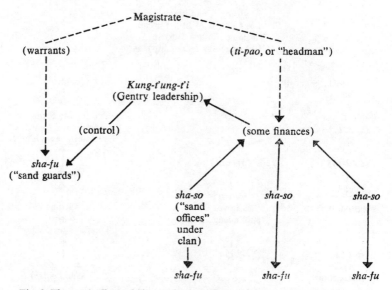

Fig. 3. The sand offices of Shun-te in the seventeenth and eighteenth centuries.

t'ung-t'i. All reclamation had to be reported within one month of completion, and the *sha-so* were always under the supervision of an officially appointed *ti-pao.* If either the "sand offices" or the gentry league wished to collect funds to hire *sha-fu,* they had to possess a warrant from the local magistrate.

Now, all this had changed. The new Shun-te Central Militia Bureau, which was locally known as the Ta-liang Public Office (*kung-chü*), absorbed the *t'uan-lien* and turned the "sand offices" into mere financing organizations, which funneled the rents from the lineages' *sha-t'ien* into the Central Bureau.[13] As the gentry thus gained control of the clans' ritual resources, they also developed a new method of financing which made them partially independent of the lower *sha-so.* This new source of revenue was "likin": transit tolls levied on articles of commerce. Each bureau (*chü*) under the Ta-liang Public Office was functionally charged with the management of funds: the hiring of militia, distribution of relief,

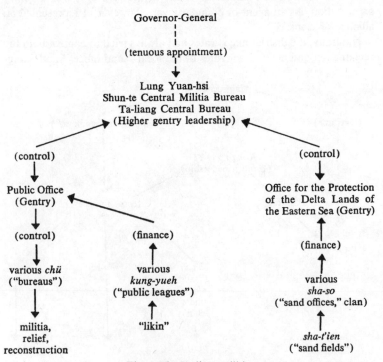

Fig. 4. The Ta-liang militia.

reconstruction of local schools, and so forth. And for each bureau, there was a corresponding "public league" (*kung-yueh*), which provided the finances used by the *chü*. The "league" got these funds by erecting customs barriers around the *hsien* capital and major market towns.[14] Unused income was reinvested in "sand fields" (*sha-t'ien*), as the wealthier gentry added more and more fertile bottomland to their sublineages' ritual property, which was held in the name of the local bureau. The Central Bureau itself accumulated an annual rental income of twenty thousand taels. There was no question that these moneys, ostensibly used for public purposes, were actually appropriated by the gentry who managed the bureaus. In 1889, an official secretly told the Governor-General — then Chang Chih-tung — what a similar public bureau attached to the Confucian temple of Tung-kuan was doing with its properties: "I have investigated the fields and property of the Confucian temple of Tung-kuan county. Although [these assets] are owned by the gentry's public office in the county, they are not exclusively used for local schools. Many [of the assets] are covertly usurped by the gentry and officials of the great local families."[15] By then, however, it was too late to curb these excesses. Whereas the magistrates had exercised direct control over the "sand offices" of the seventeenth century, now the Governor-General only appointed the heads of the militia bureaus, relying too heavily on their social support to restrain their appropriations. And whereas the traditional thirst of the wealthy for more power had been balanced by the fear of peasant revolt, now that the "dangerous classes" had virtually been wiped out by Yeh Ming-ch'en's purge, the gentry of Kuang-chou were socially unopposed. Besides, how could a local magistrate dare to object when men like Lung Yuan-hsi took land off the tax rolls, or illegally tried criminals and bandits?[16]

Eventually, the officials even turned over the collection of taxes to the gentry, willing to let them squeeze the peasants as long as they received their official share. Rent and taxes thus became confused. By 1900, what had begun as tithes, paid to the magistrate's proxy, had become a form of crop sharing. Freeholding began to disappear because excess commercial capital also upset the traditional systems of tenure around Canton. Landholding was so socially prestigious and seemed such a stable form of investment that city merchants paid much more for a plot of land than its normal agricultural return warranted. Sometimes, they would rent delta land *en bloc* from rural clans, and in turn lease it to a third set of landlords, who used laborers or tenants to cultivate cash crops. By the 1930's, Kwangtung had developed a ruinous system of rack rents, which equalled as much as 71 percent of the harvest.[17] Communal and clan resources had also fallen completely under the control of local notables. "Contractors" (*pao-shang*) agreed to pay fixed sums to corrupt local officials in exchange for the privilege of taking over all of the school land in a county. They in turn sublet the school land to smaller "contractors," and so on, down to the tenant, through as many as five stages of progressively higher rents.[18] With no official local power to counterbalance the control of the gentry, there came to be no communal need for the local elite to protect the peasantry and to mediate power. The gentry, bereft of degrees and functions, had become parasitic. All of these inequities were the direct result of the disbalances of the mid-nineteenth century. Militia, antiforeignism, and rebellion had sundered the polity and riven the society. Revolution was almost inevitable.

PART FOUR

Canton Conquered

THE POLITICS OF COLLABORATION
1857–1861

XVI

The Capture of the City

> Its striking element was that impressive silence, that absence of all movement on the part of a population of a million and a half, that lay as though entombed with the city walls, whose very pulsation seemed arrested by the terrors of the night before, and whose only desire, if they could think at all, appeared to be, that the bare fact of their existence should be forgotten by the conquerors. — George Wingrove Cooke, *China: Being the Times' Special Correspondence* (1858)

The second Anglo-Chinese war began in October, 1856, with the famous *Arrow* incident.* Three months of intermittent British naval warfare followed. Then Bowring and Admiral Seymour stopped to await London's final decision: the mounting of a joint Anglo-French expedition against the Chinese empire.

The *Arrow* war piled a terrible economic burden on an already impoverished Kwangtung:† even during the quiescent period, the costs of defense ran over 1,200 taels (approximately $1,700) per day.[1] Yeh Ming-ch'en declared: "I look entirely to the subscriptions of the gentry and people for supplies." Shun-te would have to furnish 200,000 taels; Hsin-hui, 120,000; and Hsiang-shan, 100,000. While subscribers were prom-

---

*On October 8, 1856, a member of the Cantonese gentry reported to local officials that he had recognized a pirate among the crew of a lorcha (a Western schooner with Chinese rigging) anchored at Whampoa. Four mandarins and sixty soldiers boarded the Chinese-owned vessel, which was illegally registered under British sailing papers as the *Arrow*. When they hauled down the masthead flag and arrested twelve Chinese sailors, the bellicose consul, Harry Parkes, claimed that the British flag had been insulted. His demands for a public apology from the Governor-General, Yeh Ming-ch'en, were fully backed by Bowring and Admiral Sir Michael Seymour. Yeh could not, of course, accede to such an ultimatum, and war resulted.

†During the summer of 1857, a dearth of rice carried prices to three times their normal level. Whatever rice Canton could get had to be imported from Siam. See: FO 17/271, Parkes' report, Incl. 1, Desp. 355, Aug. 20, 1857.

ised that their names would be sent in to the Emperor for rewards, the Governor-General also warned that there must be no deficits. The moneys had to be obtained.[2]

This was not collection. It was extortion. In October, 1857, for example, the son of Samqua,* one of the hong merchants, was tortured and had his property confiscated because he had not contributed enough.[3] Usually, however, local notables or clan elders were issued subscription booklets. At the same time, the authorities assured them that "If any be contumacious, the gentry of their village committee are authorized to apply privily to have them arrested and brought to trial."[4] This may have given the local notables innumerable chances to "squeeze" the peasantry, but Canton was assured of keeping its fiscally desperate administration functioning.

Yet, even the "righteous" gentry eventually tired. As tael after tael poured into Canton's coffers, they began to demand a reckoning of the immense funds that they had contributed: 1.5 million taels (about $2.1 million) from P'an-yü, Nan-hai, Hsin-hui, Shun-te, and Hsiang-shan counties alone. Some, like the proud notables of the "ninety-six villages," refused to turn any funds over at all, assuring the Governor-General that when the call came, every male over sixteen could assemble in trained and armed *t'uan-lien*. Other areas, particularly eastern P'an-yü, simply disbanded their village braves. Canton City, which had prepared, as in 1849, by forming defense committees, allowed the inhabitants of each ward to decide whether they wanted to maintain militia. Most chose not to.[5]

It looked as though the British were never going to attack. True, the barbarians continued the sporadic naval war.[6] But the Cantonese began to believe that the English had given up any idea of actually taking Canton because of the Sepoy Mutiny in India.[7]

While the Chinese were confidently removing the fortifications they had built in front of Canton's gates, Lord Elgin† was deciding to assault the city and chasten Yeh Ming-ch'en before proceeding north to the Peiho.[8] Fifteen months after the initial *Arrow* incident, French and British forces began to shell Canton. By then, the waiting war had crippled the official militia movement. Only Lieutenant Teng An-pang's one

---

*Samqua is usually identified as Wu Chien-chang, who took charge of foreign relations at Shanghai in 1851 after making a fortune in foreign trade. See: Arthur Hummel, ed., *Eminent Chinese of the Ch'ing Period* (1944), 865.

†Lord Elgin, one of the most distinguished peers of the realm, had brilliantly served his Queen as governor of Jamaica and governor-general of Canada. In 1857, he was Palmerston's first choice as leader of the expeditionary force to China.

thousand Tung-kuan braves offered any real resistance. The rest of the *yung* vanished out of the north gate under the withering artillery barrage.[9]

By 2 P.M. on December 29, 1857, Canton was completely at the mercy of the allied forces. For a week the conquerors looked down on the city, wondering how the Cantonese would react when European troops first entered the rabbit warren of streets. They waited, too, for the Governor-General's final surrender.[10]

It never came. It was as though Yeh Ming-ch'en were trying to will the barbarians out of existence.[11] His colleagues, his subordinates, even those who knew him well, were genuinely puzzled by his refusal to deal with the British as the walls fell before Admiral Seymour's cannons. To some he epitomized the supremely self-confident individual: a Governor-General before the age of forty, notoriously successful in suppressing the Red Turbans, gloriously incapable of realizing how dangerous the British could be. To others he appeared a poseur, resorting to ridiculous postures, as if his inner calm and grandioseness could compensate for military weakness. In this light he seemed a tool of the Cantonese mob, a last embodiment of Ch'i-ying.[12] Then there were the darker rumors about his character: suggestions that he had been brutalized by the purge, or that he was a Taoist adept, turning to magic during those last fateful days of his official career.[13] One thing was certain: concession, moderation, compromise, he viewed as weakness. Time and time again, he rejected the advice of his colleagues to deal with the barbarians, as if diplomacy were a game of cards in which the opponent had to be bluffed into submission.[14] And so he continued to ignore the British presence during that week of watchful waiting. Finally, on January 5, 1858, allied troops entered the city. They quickly took Kuan-yin Hill at the north edge of the city, where the provincial officials had withdrawn to make their last stand and shortly afterwards captured Yeh Ming-ch'en as he tried to escape in disguise over the back wall of a friend's house.[15]

As soon as it became obvious that the British were going to capture the city, the Cantonese authorities had secretly begun to negotiate with the allies. As early as December 29, the governor, Po Keui, sent Howqua and Kinqua to plead for moderation. By December 31, the Tartar general, Mu-k'o-te-na, and the Governor were both publicly trying to calm the populace, for their greatest fear was that the unruly mob might use the invasion to burn and loot.[16] Thus, when Yeh was finally captured, the other Chinese civil and military authorities offered no resistance and generally helped the allies preserve law and order.

Order was the major concern of the British and French. With only five thousand troops and two Chinese interpreters, the allies had to have the cooperation of the existing authorities if they hoped to rule a hostile and turbulent population of one million.[17] Two plans were considered. Po Kuei and Mu-k'o-te-na could return to their yamens, while the allies simply kept their troops in the city. Or, Po Kuei could be made a prisoner of war aboard a British ship, whence he could "govern" Canton. A compromise was finally chosen. Po Kuei would be installed in his yamen, "in a manner calculated to increase rather than impair the prestige of that authority upon which the tranquility, and indeed, the very existence of the city, at that critical moment, depended."[18] However, he would be told privately that all of his administrative decisions were subject to the approval of the allies.

Po Kuei thought over the proposal for twenty-four hours, while many of the city's gentry pleaded with him to acquiesce in the interest of trade and social order.[19] Cautious and conservative, he was hardly the sort to "take to the hills" and lead a popular militia movement against the English. On January 8, he accepted the allies' conditions.* The following day, the British and French installed him with pomp and circumstance in his yamen, because his prestige and his administrative "aura" were to be the real instruments of allied government. In fact, however, he was the creature of French and British rule. He was physically confined to the innermost part of the yamen, guarded by British sentries, while the outer part was turned over to the allied commissioners: Colonel Thomas Holloway, Captain F. Martinez de Chenez, and Harry Parkes.[20] In practice, Parkes wielded most of the power and personally conducted the daily administration of the province's affairs.[21] Although the Tartar general voluntarily disbanded his garrison and turned over all arms to the allies, Parkes either drafted or approved all of the official communications from the Governor's yamen.[22]

In addition to that, and to the creation of an allied tribunal, Parkes also supervised the policing of the city. At first, the corps of one hundred British and thirty French policemen patrolled alone. But the fearsome *fan-kuei* produced such consternation wherever they went that robbers shoplifted in their wake as merchants and householders scurried for cover. Eventually, each patrol comprised a file of foreign marines and a file of Chinese police.[23]

As the city slowly revived, the allies began to wonder how China

---

*Many of his countrymen believed that he had been forced to take this decision. "They coerced the Governor, Po Kuei, into ruling the Cantonese." See: *Nan-hai hsien-chih*, 14:35-b.

would react to this new departure. Would the Emperor allow Po Kuei to continue in office?

When the news of the disaster reached Peking on January 26, 1858, Yeh Ming-ch'en was belatedly removed from office for being "stubborn and presumptuous." He was replaced as Governor-General of the Liang-kuang and Imperial Commissioner for Foreign Affairs by Huang Tsung-han. But pending Huang's arrival, Po Kuei was made temporary tenant of both offices, even though the Emperor was fully aware of the allied commission.[24]

Nevertheless, Po Kuei had compromised himself as far as local affairs were concerned. While the allied commission was being set up in Canton, the provincial judge, prefect, and grain intendant were creating a shadow government in Fatshan to offer a loyalist alternative to the rural gentry.[25] And other, high-ranking *t'uan-lien ta-ch'en* were setting plans for a coordinated resistance movement to drive the British and French out of Kwangtung.

XVII

The Kwangtung Militia Bureau

> Order Po Kuei, and the gentry leader, Lo Tun-yen, and others, to secretly announce Our will to the militia of each village. . . . If the barbarians are still stupidly disobedient and hold the city for long, the only thing to do is to gather together the troops and irregulars of each town, unite them into one, and expel the said barbarians out of the city so as to make them dare not look down upon China. — Imperial edict*

The rural *t'uan-lien* were too transitory, too undisciplined to offer any real opposition to the invading force. However, the British and French were now in occupation, subject to the kind of harassment any resistance movement can devise. The village militiamen might have felt reluctant to oppose an officially appointed governor, but it quickly became known that three of the higher ranking gentry of the province had the Emperor's secret approval to oust the enemy. Drawn home by the Red Turban rebellion, these patriots had decided to try to create the same kind of regional militia that other gentry were forming elsewhere.

The first of these was Lung Yuan-hsi, creator of the Shun-te Central Militia Bureau. The second was Lung's classmate and fellow townsman, Lo Tun-yen. Lo, like Lung, came from a prominent Ta-liang family. His father, Chia-cheng, had passed his *chü-jen* examinations in 1813, headed the famous Yueh-hsiu Academy, been promoted to the fifth rank for his role during the entry crisis, and headed the bureau that revised Shun-te's local history. When his son Tun-yen was born, "a red glow filled the room," foreshadowing the brilliant and distinguished career the boy was destined to follow: compiler of the Hanlin Academy; director of studies for Szechuan and Anhwei provinces; assistant-reader

*Ch'ou-pan i-wu shih-mo, Hsien-feng 17:44-b.

of the Grand Secretariat; deputy-commissioner and finally full commissioner of the Transmission Office. With the accession of the Hsien-feng Emperor, whose own beliefs coincided with Lo's conservative fiscal and political views, his standing soared. That year he submitted a famous memorial, warning that traditional morality was being vitiated by official corruption and maladministration. The Emperor approved. The following year, Lo Tun-yen became vice-president of the Board of Civil Appointments, then senior vice-president of the Censorate. By late 1853, he was vice-president of the Board of Punishments, and a famed proponent of local militia.[1]

Su T'ing-k'uei, the third of the three leaders, shared Lo Tun-yen's moralism. But unlike Lo, Su was a hothead, repeatedly involved in policy disputes. Also from Kwangtung, he was a *t'ung-nien* of Lo and Lung, and joined the two of them at the Hanlin Academy in 1835. By the time the Opium War ended, Su was known as one of the most vociferous critics of the moderates' "barbarian management" policy. In 1843, he had the effrontery to accuse Mu-chang-a of negligence. Defeated, Su spent eight years in semi-retirement until the Hsien-feng Emperor acceded. Then the Emperor rewarded Su for his long years of opposition by precipitately promoting him to the Grand Council. Even then, T'ing-k'uei managed to get involved in a fight with Sai-shang-a, but once the old Manchu was disgraced for his military failure in Kwangsi, Su recovered his high status.

Like Lo Tun-yen and Lung Yuan-hsi, Su was an ardent advocate of the local militia. After the court decided to support the *t'uan-lien*, T'ing-k'uei returned to Kwangtung to manage local defense. There, during 1854 and 1855, he worked closely with the Ta-liang bureau, becoming something of a specialist at supplying corps of braves, which were sent to Kiangsi against the Taiping rebels.[2] Thus, four years before the anti-British resistance movement, two of the three leaders had already developed a coordinated system of local defense.

Lo, highest ranking of the three, was terminating a three-year mourning period just as the allies entered Canton City. He, Lung, and Su promptly sent a memorial to the Emperor, asking to be allowed to coordinate militia activities against the British. On February 8, 1858, a secret edict was issued, giving them that permission.[3] As soon as they received the dispatch, the three men opened the Kwangtung Central Militia Bureau (*Kuang-tung t'uan-lien tsung-chü*) in Hua-hsien, twenty-five miles north of Canton. There they hung a tablet over their gate, inscribed: "Imperial

Commissioners for Managing the Barbarian Affairs and Coastal Defenses of Kwangtung."[4]

The Kwangtung Militia Bureau derived its strength from the counties to the south of Canton City: brawn from Tung-kuan and Hsin-an; funds from Shun-te.[5] Tung-kuan, with its fierce fighters and excellent marksmen, was a traditional recruiting area for braves. Hsin-an, not so noted, had organized local *t'uan-lien* in 1856 at the behest of Su T'ing-k'uei. Ch'en Kuei-chi, head of Hsin-an's most influential clan, was a brother of one of Su's pupils. Kuei-chi himself was a *chin-shih* who had worked for the Board of Revenue in Peking before returning to Kwangtung to look after his family's properties during the Red Turban troubles.[6] When the *Arrow* war began, Su T'ing-k'uei asked the two Ch'en brothers to form militia and organize a boycott against the British, since Hsin-an was a major supplier of farm produce and labor for Hong Kong.[7] Su was to be their link with Yeh Ming-ch'en's yamen in Canton. However, the Governor-General discovered that this militia, which had been given twenty-four thousand taels by the Central Militia Committee in Canton, was really a clan instrument, used by the Ch'en family to settle old scores with some of the coastal villages in Hsin-an. When, during the Wu-chou outbreak, the Ch'en brothers convinced Po Kuei that they could organize three thousand braves to stop the rebel advance if only they had more funds, Yeh Ming-ch'en exploded. Naturally, the brothers retracted their offer, but they retained control of the county militia. When Su T'ing-k'uei adopted the title of "Imperial Commissioner" in 1858, they promptly pledged whatever men they could spare to the Kwangtung Militia Bureau.[8]

Funds and supplies came from Shun-te's militia headquarters. As soon as the Hua-hsien office was opened, Lung Yuan-hsi turned over some of the workings of the Ta-liang bureau to trusted members of the gentry committee.* A special fund-gathering and liaison organization was formed under the management of Yuan-hsi's kinsman, Lung Pao-hsien. This was called the *Hsin ch'ing-yün wen-she* (the New Empyrean Literary Association), and funneled 150,000 taels of loans, *sha-t'ien* rents, likin, and contributions to the Kwangtung Militia Bureau.[9] There the money was turned over to the "commissioners'" quartermaster, an ex-

---

*Particularly P'an Nien-tsu, of the powerful P'an clan at Ch'ung-ho; and Lai Tzu-yu, a *chin-shih* who had served in the Grand Secretariat. See: *Shun-te hsien-chih*, 18:4-a, 19:3-a.

magistrate from Shun-te named Ho Ta-chang, who bought boats or rations, and hired braves.[10]

Relying as they did on Shun-te *hsien*, the "commissioners" decided to move their headquarters there in early 1859.[11] For even though the northern counties were anti-British, they had not tendered the support the Kwangtung Militia Bureau needed in that area. This was particularly true of Nan-hai. There, the "ninety-six villages," congruent with the old *Sheng-p'ing she-hsüeh*, had possessed self-sufficient militia since 1841. During every crisis, they had consistently refused to turn over men or funds to any of the central militia bureaus. This was still true. They fought bravely and fiercely; they even coordinated their activities with directives issued by the "commissioners." But they were ultimately controlled by their own central committee at Shih-ching (Shektsing), which was headed by Liang Ch'i-p'eng, a lower-degree holder of the famous Liang clan.[12] If they recognized any source of political legitimacy, it was the militia organization created by the shadow government of the provincial judge at Fatshan.

Lo Tun-yen had immediately secured the allegiance of the Fatshan loyalists, but for a long time the government there retained its own defense command: the United Defense Bureau of the Silk Markets (*ssu-hsü lien-fang chü*), which had a recruiting office in every silk market in Nan-hai and P'an-yü,[13] and headquarters at Fatshan. In 1859, the "silk market" offices were finally absorbed by the Kwangtung Militia Bureau.

The political disintegration of the Red Turban period helped make the Kwangtung Militia Bureau possible. However, that same decentralization also kept Lo, Lung, and Su from creating a genuine regional organization. For a brief period, it seemed as though the "commissioners" had formed a new provincial political center. But even an imperial mandate and the collective drive to oust the foreigners could not undo twenty years of accumulated localism.

XVIII

The Resistance Movement

> Although the county seats adjoining the provincial capital have trained militia, they have yet to be set in order; while, after the bandit troubles of the past four years, the people's strength has never returned to what it was before. To assemble a mob is easy, but you cannot order the people to become filled with righteousness. — Mu-k'o-te-na and Po Kuei*

The rural militia terrorized the city during the first six months of 1858. Policemen and soldiers were seized whenever they wandered near the gates. Bounties were put on the heads of all foreigners. Booby traps were set. Incendiary rockets and arsonists fired buildings every night. The wealthier classes fled the city. The suburbs, depopulated and ruined, gave cover to predatory bands.[1] The foreigners, whether in the provincial capital or in Hong Kong, even found it difficult to buy food or hire help: the district magistrates ordered shopkeepers to leave Canton, and twenty thousand laborers returned to their homes from Victoria.[2]

Parkes vainly tried to use Po Kuei to quiet the local gentry and loyalist officials. The Governor agreed, writing to ask the shadow government at Fatshan to end their useless opposition.[3] But his intercession had no effect. The imperial mandate that the "commissioners" possessed seemed to cancel Po Kuei's powers.[4] Besides, everyone believed that the Governor was just Parkes' mouthpiece. Even the Grand Council felt that "since Po Kuei has proscribed the righteous militia, it is obvious that he is under coercion. He must be transferred, and then [the barbarians] can be haltered. . . . As soon as the said Governor-General [Huang Tsung-han] arrives in Kwangtung, then he can lean upon the strength of the gentry and the people."[5] Po Kuei realized that the three "commissioners" would continue to speak for the province until a figure endowed with higher powers, Huang Tsung-han, arrived to supersede them.[6]

*Ch'ou-pan i-wu shih-mo, Hsien-feng 21:45-b.

Nonetheless, he tried to let Peking know that the rosy pictures Lo Tun-yen painted of a vigorous militia movement were distorted. The people were actually impoverished. Bandits were once again active throughout the province. Most of the Cantonese were fundamentally unconcerned about the occupation.[7]

The doubts which Po Kuei raised in the Emperor's mind were partly confirmed by reports which were being received from Huang Tsung-han, at that time on his way south.[8] The new Governor-General had been trying to collect military reinforcements in Kiangsi, Kiangnan, and Fukien; but none of these provinces could spare troops for the South. The Kwangtung Militia Bureau seemed to offer the only hope for the recovery of Canton.[9] But there were already indications that popular zeal was not as intense as Lo, Lung, and Su pretended: "The militia of each *hsiang* no longer have any desire to cope with the barbarians, so I am told."[10]

Was Lo Tun-yen, then, not to be believed? Judging from what he wrote the Emperor, the entire province was ready to drive the barbarians into the sea. Guns were loaded, recruits trained, supplies prepared, spies and terrorists smuggled into Canton. All that was needed was Peking's order to attack the city in force.[11]

The Emperor hesitated. Obviously, no final decision could be made until Huang Tsung-han reached Kwangtung and sent back an unbiased and reliable report.[12] Besides, too much depended upon the state of China's diplomatic bargaining with Elgin and Gros,* now at the Peiho. If the Russians and Americans could be used to "manage" the British and French, then there would be no need for an attack. But if diplomacy failed, the Cantonese could be used to strike a blow at the allies' flank. "It is inextricably involved with the nature of the negotiations at Tientsin. I have already ordered Vice-President [Lo] and the rest to secretly prepare their inner [defenses] and await the Imperial command to act."[13] But by May 19, 1858, the day before Elgin and Gros forced their way through the Taku barrier forts, the Emperor had lost all hopes of Russian or American intercession. Lo's *t'uan-lien* might not be as zealous as the Kwangtung Militia Bureau pretended, but at least they existed.[14] Huang should plan to assume control of this militia movement as soon as he arrived in Kwangtung, and warn the English and French that if they had not left the city within four months, they would be forcibly expelled.[15]

Then the allies assaulted the Taku forts. Enraged, the Hsien-feng

*Baron Gros, leader of the French expedition, was Lord Elgin's counterpart.

Emperor shortened the timetable. The barbarians would have to leave Canton by June 25.[16] Huang and Lo Tun-yen should plan the offensive together: first recapture Canton, then attack Hong Kong. But the affair had to be kept secret. Huang must not be publicly involved with the militia, because he would have to step in and "mediate" (*tiao-t'ing*) when the barbarians frantically sought to protect the foreign goods they had stored in the two cities. For the time being, though, the Governor-General was not to order an attack without clearance from Peking, because a diplomatic solution still might end the war.[17]

By June 11, 1858, Huang Tsung-han had finally arrived in Kwangtung and established his official yamen far from Canton at Hui-chou. The British promptly warned him not to countenance the *t'uan-lien*; but the Governor-General ignored them and met with the three "commissioners" to carry out the Emperor's orders.[18] While publicly announcing his approval of the "righteous zeal" of the Cantonese, he had posters put up warning the allies that they would have to leave and promising rewards for the loyal militia.[19]

Immediately the tempo of the resistance movement picked up; it looked as though the rural *t'uan-lien* would finally be allowed to attack the provincial capital. Anonymous antiforeign placards appeared everywhere. Squads of terrorists, disguised as coolies, slipped into the city. Chinese policemen grew afraid to be seen in the streets with foreigners. Cantonese servants left their foreign employers.[20]

The allied commission did its best to police Canton. Patrols were increased, traffic restricted, some of the gates closed. Suspected terrorists had their queues cut off for identification, and were expelled from the city.[21] But the enemy was too elusive; and Lord Elgin, afraid of needlessly inciting the rural gentry, had forbade the British to patrol more than a mile from the city gates.[22] Only once did the allies break that rule. On June 1, a patrol discovered a large contingent of braves (including one thousand Hsin-an men led by Ch'en Kuei-chi) gathered six miles from the city in the foothills of the White Cloud Mountains. On June 3, eight hundred allied soldiers attacked and scattered the encampment: a minor but heartening victory.[23]

At this juncture, the Court was engaged in a major foreign policy debate. The warhawks, mainly indigenous Chinese in the Censorate or National Academy, were clamoring for an end to negotiations and a return to armed conflict with the barbarians.[24] On June 23, the censors were argued down, and three days later, Kuei-liang signed the Treaty of Tientsin.[25] Less than twenty-four hours later, the Emperor received a memorial from Lo, Lung, and Su describing the battle of White Cloud Mountains as a glorious victory for the militia.[26] Somehow, news of this secret memorial was leaked to a few of the more bellicose members of the central government: Chu Feng-piao, president of the Board of Revenue; K'uang Yuan, vice-president of the Board of Civil Appointments; and Ch'en Chao-lin, vice-president of the Board of Revenue. These three officials tried to use the news of the "victory" to reopen the barbarian policy debate, asking the Emperor to encourage Lo's attempts to recapture Canton. "The Cantonese have already struck. Their enmity has ripened. Their power cannot be established a second time. . . . If these people are forbidden to enter the city, then they will become the enemies of the officials. . . . The foundation of the nation rests entirely on the people's loyalty. This is precisely what the English barbarians fear." [27] It was the same argument that Yeh Ming-ch'en had forwarded, and the Emperor agreed that the people would have to be appeased. But now that the treaty had been signed, the British and French would certainly end their occupation. The matter was closed.[28]

The Emperor was wrong: the British and French did not intend to pull out of Canton. The Governor-General reported that the English were building a permanent set of barracks, and Parkes was creating a staff of over one hundred native *mu-yu* (private secretaries) to rule the city; and Lo Tun-yen repeatedly stressed that the barbarians were there to stay.[29] The Emperor was naturally concerned to hear this, but China now owed a large indemnity to the British and French. Some of these funds would have to come from Canton's customs receipts. Even if the British were actually ruling the city, the empire could not afford to jeopardize that revenue. The *t'uan-lien* would have to adopt a strict defensive posture, and Huang would have to publicly disassociate himself from the Kwangtung Militia Bureau.[30]

On July 21, 1858, before the Emperor's go-slow decision reached Lo Tun-yen, the long-awaited assault on Canton finally took place. Seven thousand braves confidently attacked and climbed the city walls. But they had forgotten about the English cannons mounted on Kuan-yin Hill. The artillery fire drove them off with severe injuries, and the dispirited militia retreated.[31]

Even worse, the arrival of Peking's new instructions meant that the Militia Bureau could not "legally" order another attack. One last time, the three "commissioners" pleaded with their ruler to change his mind.[32] The Emperor was adamant: "At present the barbarians occupy the provincial capital. Since they have had no trouble with the officials and gentry, for the time being there is peace. The fact that the people and the barbarians are opposed to each other and kill each other has nothing to do with the larger matter." [33]

The failure of the July attack broke the back of the loyalist movement. Rumors of the Emperor's veto circulated, and suddenly the "wealthy households harbored doubt" of the Kwangtung Militia Bureau's mandate. The sources of funds began to dry up. Even the San-yuan-li bureaus, still antiforeign, were running one month behind on *t'uan-lien* rations. [34] Without food or pay, the hired militiamen degenerated into bandits. [35] The cycle of disorder began again. The officials fled to the city. Even the yamen staffs were dissolved.

> The private secretaries (*mu-yu*) all scattered like so many stars and returned to their homes, each to his own *chou* and *hsien*, to await orders from the higher officials asking them to return. For six months they have not been able to return. The provincial capital was the best place for officials to be since law and government elsewhere were in a state of disturbance. Bandits and robbers arose in all four directions, and the peasants were one day drowning, one day burning. [36]

The coordinated militia movement had temporarily ended, but for the time being, antiforeignism did not lessen. Local units, under no central control, continued to harass the allies. Elgin even brought the matter up during his negotiations with Kuei-liang at Shanghai in September, 1858, but to no avail. [37] The British would personally have to make their presence felt in the countryside, personally wipe out or frighten the centers of opposition. By December, daily patrols were leaving the city gates to march through the towns and hamlets around Canton. These columns of soldiers were unmolested until January 4, 1859, when seven hundred marines drew near the Nan-hai militia headquarters at Shih-ching. Some of the braves there courageously fired at the British, who withdrew to await orders from the allied commission. Parkes decided that other districts would remain intractable unless the Shih-ching headquarters was chastised. On January 8, thirteen hundred troops, supported by six gunboats, attacked the militia base. After three days of intense fighting, the braves were defeated, the bureau captured, and the village burned to the ground.

This was rapidly followed by three other expeditions. On January 20, a flotilla of gunboats approached Fatshan, expecting a fight from the shadow government. To their surprise, they were received peacefully by the authorities there. On February 8, 1859, over one thousand British and French soldiers, supported by a force of coolies, attacked the Kwangtung Central Militia Bureau at Hua-hsien, helping drive the "commissioners" to Shun-te county. Finally, on February 19, a large expedition sailed up the West River through the silk growing districts all the way to Shao-ch'ing, where Su T'ing-k'uei had been organizing *t'uan-lien*.[38]

The effect of these forays was dramatic. Among papers captured at the Shih-ching militia center, Parkes found a copy of one of the secret edicts that the Emperor had sent to Lo when he was encouraging the militia. This incriminating document was rushed to Elgin, who showed it to Kuei-liang and Hua-sha-na, pretending to disbelieve that the Emperor could have treacherously sanctioned the resistance movement.[39] He coupled this with a demand that the Kwangtung Militia Bureau be dissolved and that Huang Tsung-han, who had ended by compromising himself, be dismissed as Commissioner for Foreign Affairs. Its clandestine involvement revealed, the Court acted quickly. On January 29, Ho Kuei-ch'ing, one of the foremost leaders of the "peace party" that included Kuei-liang, replaced Huang as Imperial Commissioner for Foreign Affairs. At the same time, the secret edict was disavowed: "We now therefore command Huang Tsung-han to take strict measures for the seizure of the lawless fabricators, and to punish them with the utmost rigor of the law." [40]

"Loyalism" was now ideologically disloyal: the Emperor had accepted the dual system of government in Canton. Most important, the forays into Kuang-chou had cast the foreigners' political shadow across the province. As soon as the Shih-ching militia bureau was destroyed, for example, antiforeignism began to die out in the "ninety-six villages" area. Whenever a British patrol appeared, the *hsiang* elders would all line up at the edge of their town to greet the soldiers with effusive politeness.[41] The gentry now saw the allies as genuine political and social rivals, but the peasants of the delta accepted the foreigners as the established rulers of Kwangtung.

XIX

Departure

> In the suburbs, the idlers indulge as of old in abuse of foreigners, but on the whole there is a decided change for the better even in that region. There seems to me to exist a sort of confidence in the foreigner who has ventured to face the late disturbances, and a growing desire to be informed of foreign matters, and to be acquainted, especially, with the English language.
> — Thomas Wade, Acting Chinese Secretary*

The allies, political overlords of Canton, slowly developed a cordial working relationship with the Chinese authorities.[1] Soon it became almost natural for a Ch'ing official to turn to the British for authority or help.[2] Besides that, the allied commission created a kind of social protectorate over the delta. By breaking up the vicious "pig trade" in coolies, and keeping city officials from levying a 3 percent "chowle" tax on Canton's shopkeepers, Parkes and Alcock earned the undying gratitude of thousands of peasants and merchants.[3] Soon the inhabitants of the delta were turning to the allied commission as they would have appealed to traditional Chinese authorities, seeking redress from local corruption and injustice. In fact, the people were even resentful when the British and French did not intercede in local affairs:

> In the early portion of the past year, a willingness to redress wrongs was evinced at the yamen of the Allies, but during the later part of the year, from the time that the conclusion of hostilities was announced, they have in most cases refused to receive petitions from the Chinese; and thus the poor people have been deprived of a means of making their complaints known. This, we presume, is not because the Allies are inattentive to what is going on around them, but because they are unable to thoroughly inform themselves of all that relates to China.[4]

*FO 17/244, Incl. 1, Desp. 23, Jan., 1856.

After the Opium War, the English had been identified with the forces of disorder: bandits, pirates, "traitors." Now that the Red Turban revolt had destroyed local government, the Cantonese began to look to the barbarians as a force of political stabilization. This was a source of great consolation to Kuang-chou in 1859, when revolt broke out once again at Shao-ch'ing, Chia-ying, and around the Mei-ling pass. Only the allied armies seemed capable of keeping the bandits from reaching Canton.[5] "It is indeed already reported that the local banditti desire to effect a combination with those of the outer Provinces, in which case the moment they see their opportunity, they will enter on extensive hostile operations. Our dependance would in that case rest on the Allies, who now hold Canton, and trusting in them, we may hope that those banditti would not dare to trouble us."[6] The Western barbarians were no longer strangers to China; they were political rivals for its control. Kwangtung showed in microcosm what would later occur throughout China during the apogee of European imperialism.

When war broke out again in the North in 1859 and 1860, the three "commissioners" vaguely thought of reviving the resistance movement.[7] It was too late for that. The Kwangtung Militia Bureau had exhausted its sources of funds. The rural gentry did not even seem to care about the Taku incident. Lo Tun-yen harried the local magistrates, complained bitterly that the notables were refusing to pay their assessments, even drew up lists of defaulters: all to no avail. The clans and villages would not cooperate. The "commissioners" were spoken of with hatred and contempt; and villages armed themselves whenever the Militia Bureau's tax collectors appeared.[8]

Naturally, there were some among the local gentry who still opposed the barbarians, who still wanted to drive the British and French out of Kwangtung. But the Emperor had told the "commissioners" that "disturbances at Tientsin at the present time cannot be helped, but affairs at Canton are to be carried on in accordance with former orders. You must not cause disturbances or originate troubles."[9] Knowing full well that inaction would lose him the support of any remaining local xenophobes, Lo Tun-yen still had to tell the gentry to call off their attacks.[10] The militia withered and died. British patrols that probed the old rural centers of antiforeignism found only friendly farmers who refused to pay defense assessments to their gentry bureaus. One group of English soldiers even spent the night in the very *kung-chü* that Lo, Lung, and Su had once used as a *t'uan-lien* headquarters. There the local assistant magistrate "feelingly deplored the increasing power of the gentry of the neighbourhood who had already, he said, reduced his position almost to a nullity." Nothing but tattered antiforeign placards, blowing in the wind, remained to remind the British of the Kwangtung resistance movement.[11]

For the first time in three years, the Governor-General celebrated the New Year of 1860 by appearing in full court regalia, symbolizing that the old order had been restored.[12] The British continued to prosecute kidnappers, patrol the countryside, and keep the border rebels from venturing near the delta.[13] Even the gentry of Nan-hai and P'an-yü began to accept the allied presence. Once they petitioned the allied commissioners, asking "for a document in the writing of their honorable nations" permitting them to form militia at Shih-ching against local bandits.[14] How could they possibly ignore the fact of foreign rule? Their own district magistrate had been peremptorily thrown in jail by Parkes for having used judicial torture on two captured criminals.[15]

The irony of all this was lost on the British. They had almost forgotten how far they had come in twenty-five years. And they could not, of course, know that within another sixty years they themselves would be identified with the official classes that they had fought and curbed. They could not foresee that they, the English, would be viewed as imperialistic oppressors of a new China that they had unwittingly helped create.

It was too sweet, this ease of rule. Parkes himself sensed it and told his wife: "We have long ago attained all the objects we originally had in taking the place, and now the sooner we get out of it the better, before fresh complications arise."[16] And so, on October 21, 1861, on the very heights that Gough had occupied during these hot May days twenty years before, the allied commanders assembled their troops one last time. So much had changed below: the thick walls breached and broken, the fabulous summer houses of Honam in ruins, their ponds full of duckweed.[17] Now, martial salutes were fired, flags exchanged with the Chinese authorities. With a last triumphant flourish, the allies left Kwangtung.[18] Canton, exhausted, humbled, irrevocably changed, was finally left to herself. Without relief, without anger, without protest or even hope, the city watched them go.

Appendixes

Appendix I

POPULATION PRESSURE*

Kwangtung's census figures have always been notoriously far from fact. Nevertheless, what is available shows that the province experienced the same population explosion as the rest of China after the sixteenth century, when sweet potatoes and peanuts were introduced by Europeans and used to cultivate the normally barren hillsides. In 1787, however, Kwangtung was still relatively underpopulated, comparable to a province such as Shansi. By 1812, it had become much denser than Shansi, but nowhere nearly as heavily populated as Kiangsu or Chekiang. Thirty years later, it still ranked below Kiangsu and Chekiang, but had moved far beyond Shansi and could be compared with Hunan.

The crucial factor in population pressure is the ratio of cultivable land to population. A general estimate based on land figures for 1812, which allotted approximately 32 million mou of fields for the entire province, would give a ratio of only 1.67 mou (or about one-fourth of an acre) per person. This was considerably below the national average at that time of 2.19 mou per person. We can assume that this disparity continued and may well have increased; for although there was some reclamation of delta land, it could not possibly have matched the increase in population. This put Kwangtung among the most land-hungry provinces of the empire. According to the 1812 figures, for example, it had less cultivable land per person than all but Kweichow, Kwangsi, Kansu, Fukien, and Anhwei. Remember, too, that these were provincial averages. The Canton basin itself, though quite fertile, was much more densely populated than the rest of Kwangtung.

*This description is primarily based on the following sources: Lo Erh-kang, "T'ai-p'ing t'ien-kuo ke-ming ch'ien te jen-k'ou ya-p'o wen-t'i" (The Problem of Population Pressure Prior to the Taiping Rebellion), in *Chung-kuo chin-tai shih lun-ts'ung* (Collection of Articles on Modern Chinese History) (Taipei, 1958), 2nd ts'e, 32–43. *Shina shōbetsu zenshi* (Gazetteer of China by Provinces) (Tokyo, 1917), 1:19–20. Harry Parkes's report on emigration, in FO 17/193, Incl. 1, Desp. 132, Sept., 1852.

Conceivably, emigration might have helped drain off some of the population. In 1852, however, the major centers of emigration for the province were considered to be Ch'ao-chou and Chia-ying, both impoverished areas where many of the peasants were itinerant laborers. At that time, only three to four thousand Cantonese emigrated every year. Much later in the century, about 120,000 residents of the province left each year, but 90,000 returned. In spite of emigration and the fertility of the basin, the Kuang-chou region experienced a constant pressure on land and food resources during the period under study.

APPENDIX TABLE 1
POPULATION OF KWANGTUNG, 1787–1850

	1787	1812	1842	1850
Millions of people	16	19	26	28
Percentage increase		19%	36%	8%
Density per square mile	160	192	264	284
National median density per square mile	419	509	631	n.f.
National mean density per square mile	256	278	349	n.f.

Appendix II

ACADEMIES AND LOCAL SCHOOLS*

Canton, though far from the political and social excitement of the Court, was a lively intellectual center in the 1820's and '30's. Nothing symbolized this better than the empire-famous *Hsüeh-hai-t'ang*, the academy that was founded by Juan Yuan, governor-general of the Liang-kuang from 1817 to 1826. Synonymous with academic and scholastic excellence, the academy is best known to posterity for its superb gloss of the Classics, the *Huang-ch'ing ching-chieh*, first published in 1829. On the academy's board of directors were some of the best classicists of the realm, and the intellectual luminaries of the province: Lin Po-t'ung, Ma Fu-an, Chang Wei-p'ing, Huang P'ei-fang, Ch'en Li, Liang T'ing-nan.

The Canton basin was one of the most academically prestigious areas of the country. During the Ch'ing period, Kuang-chou *fu* ranked fifth among the nation's prefectures in numbers of *chin-shih*. And the combined districts of P'an-yü and Nan-hai were considered the eighth most outstanding region of the empire, producing 248 *chin-shih* during the dynasty's reign.

One of the reasons for this intellectual preeminence was the elaborate network of local academies that clustered around Canton. These, like the rest of China's academies, were patterned after Chu Hsi's famous "Academy of White Stag Grotto" (*Po-lu-tung shu-yuan*). From 1506 to 1649, during the latter days of the Ming, fervent philosophical disputes stimulated local scholars to establish academies. As havens of free thought and philosophical speculation, however, the *shu-yuan* began to decline during the last despotic and chaotic years of the Ming.

When the Manchus acceded, they first forbade the founding of any new academies, in fear of the "empty talk" of the loyalist cliques of local scholars. In 1657, however, the Prime Minister, Yuan K'uo-yü, lifted

*This discussion is primarily based on Liu Po-chi, *Kuang-tung shu-yuan chih-tu* (The System of Academies in Kwangtung) (Taipei, 1958).

the ban by personally restoring Heng-yang's famous "Stone Drum Academy" (*Shih-ku shu-yuan*). This new policy was designed to win the support of the many literati who had remained loyal to the old regime. It was continued by the K'ang-hsi Emperor. When the Yung-cheng Emperor took the throne, however, the pendulum swung back. To bring the academies under strict control once more, the government declared them all to be semiofficial "charity schools" (*i-hsüeh*). The Ch'ien-lung Emperor initiated another period of relaxed controls. But even though the reinstated academies were given a great deal of apparent freedom, a fundamental change had occurred in 1744. The freewheeling philosophical courses of the old curriculum had been replaced by a standardized course designed to prepare the student for the examination system's *pa-ku* (eight-legged essay). To ensure compliance, the Board of Rites administered a monthly examination in each academy. Thus, even though the number of private academies increased, they were incorporated into the official system as conformist preparatory schools. Carelessness, disinterest, even corruption, crept into the administration of local academies. By 1817, they had finally lost the great reputation that they had held over the centuries.

This was the background to Juan Yuan's foundation of the *Hsüeh-hai-t'ang* in 1826, for he was consciously attempting to restore the great centers of learning of the past. By doing away with cramming for examinations and by insisting that the directors be capable scholars, he set a pattern for the rest of Kwangtung. Almost immediately, the other established academies revived the untrammeled study of the Classics, while a spate of new and distinguished academies were founded around the capital. Suddenly, the post of director of an academy began to carry with it immense social and intellectual prestige. During the Ming period, heads of academies had been very influential. After the reform of 1744, the directors had a great deal of indirect power because of their role in the selection of examination candidates, but their intellectual influence was nil. Juan Yuan changed that. The *Hsüeh-hai-t'ang* and *Yueh-hua shu-yuan* became brain trusts for Kwangtung's high officials. The scholar-gentry of Canton's academies operated at a relatively high social level, associating with important officials and wealthy merchants. Thus, a clear distinction must be made between their activities and those of the heads of the lower-level "local schools" (*she-hsüeh*). For example, the higher level, with a few exceptions, was not intimately involved in local self-defense during this period, even though there were channels of communication between it and the local gentry of the *she-hsüeh*. The only Cantonese academy which I have been able to find that founded a *t'uan-lien* organization during this early period was the *Shih-kang shu-yuan*.

The academies were called *shu-yuan* because they were storehouses of books when they were founded under T'ang T'ai-tsung. This remained one of their functions even later. The Ch'ien-lung Emperor had sets of Classics distributed to the local academies, and many of the *shu-yuan* acquired their own sets of wood blocks so that they would be able to print additional copies.

During the Ming period, there were three ways for a scholar to rise to official rank: Attend a local academy, attend the national Academy (*Kuo-tzu-chien*, or *T'ai-hsüeh*), or pass the provincial examinations. But even though the first two were equivalent to holding a degree, the academies had no real, official status. When the Manchus tried to win the allegiance of the literati by opening more offices to them, they made sure that mere attendance at an academy conferred semiofficial status on the student. Theoretically, they also incorporated the academies into the administrative system by trying to make the rise from studenthood to official rank more automatic. In practice, the term *shu-yuan* covered three sorts of institutions: meeting places for scholars; schools for village elders or illiterate local notables; and shrines that had enough rental income to support a small teaching staff. In size they ranged from large, provincially run schools down to *chou* or *hsien* academies, which were often no different from genuine "local" or "charity" schools. In any case, any academy during the Ch'ing period was legally under the supervision of the local educational authorities. The director of a local academy was often simultaneously a county or prefectural director of schools.

The academy's internal organization depended on its size. Attendance varied, although the total number of students rose enormously under the Manchus because the new dynasty assumed the cost-of-living stipends, which amounted to one or two taels per month per student. This might be increased if the student did exceptionally well. A student was limited to an academy in his native region: a provincial academy could recruit only from within its own province, a prefectural school from within its own *fu*, and so forth. Entrance examinations were held once a year, supplemented by investigation of the applicant's moral character. Once accepted, the full-time scholars fell into one of two semiofficial categories: *chien-sheng*, who were all licentiates; or *t'ung-sheng*, non-degree-holders. The average Cantonese academy had twenty-three of each. In addition there would be about thirty-five part-time or day students. The course of study usually lasted three years, with an examination given either at the end of each year or at the end of the three-year period.

During the Ming period, the academies' costs — publishing, salaries, construction — were financed by rents from donated lands. Under the Ch'ing dynasty, other types of private endowment were made. In spite of the state stipend system, more and more private citizens founded academies after the eighteenth century.

Under the Ming, only *sheng-yuan* could attend academies and state schools. In 1375, therefore, the Emperor urged that "local schools" (*she-hsüeh*) be created for those without degrees. During the fifteenth century an enormous number of these local schools were founded. In Kwangtung, there were eleven schools for every one academy. Some failed for lack of local support, for the late Ming saw a general negligence of the *she-hsüeh* in favor of the more prestigious academies. Yet many survived, particularly in the South. During the 1850's, Shun-te county still had twenty-one of these community schools dating from the Ming.

The Ch'ing dynasty officially revived the *she-hsüeh* in 1725, during the Yung-Cheng Emperor's ideological purge. Each *hsien* was ordered to replace its potentially subversive academies with *she-hsüeh* or *i-hsüeh*. In Kwangtung, as elsewhere, many of the academies simply changed their name to pose as "charity schools." Since their curriculum was politically innocuous, they were tolerated. When the Ch'ien-lung Emperor dropped the strictures against academies, many resumed their old titles. But these switches resulted in permanent confusion at the local level between village academies and community schools. Both filled the same function, the only major differences being their size and the fact that local schools were more apt to cater to "youths of mean circumstances." However, as a local school's endowment grew, allowing it to service more pupils, it often renamed itself as a *shu-yuan*. Juan Yuan's revival of the old, prestigious system of academies helped dispel this confusion. Yet, like so many Chinese political institutions operating at the local level, the academies, local schools, and charity schools had all blurred and merged by the nineteenth century. During the 1840's and '50's however, local gentry organization was almost synonymous with the word *she-hsüeh*. One reason for this phenomenon in Kwangtung was the identification of local schools and clan schools. If a clan was well integrated in a particular area, the local *she-hsüeh* was financed by the clan's "scholars' fields" (*hsüeh-t'ien*), and became — for all practical purposes — the clan's school. During the late Ch'ing, local schools began to disappear in the rest of China. But because the clans were so powerful in Kwangtung, they continued to flourish there.

APPENDIX TABLE 2

PREFECTURAL DISTRIBUTIONS OF ACADEMIES AND LOCAL
SCHOOLS IN KWANGTUNG DURING THE CH'ING PERIOD

Prefecture	Academies	Local Schools
Kuang-chou fu	152	317
Shao-ch'ing fu	43	77
Hui-chou fu	31	50
Ch'ao-chou fu	42	46
Kao-chou fu	34	38
Chia-ying chou	14	32
Lo-ting chou	2	5
Lien-chou	9	9
Shao-chou fu	23	60
Ch'iung-chou fu	39	67
Lien-chou fu	15	30
Lei-chou fu	7	17

Appendix III

THE "REAL ESTATE CRISIS" *

June 4, 1847:	Howqua sold three shops on Hog Lane to the British, who wished to build a church. However, they still needed the land under three more shops. MacGregor requested Ch'i-ying to ask the proprietors of the three buildings to sell them to the English.
June 5, 1847:	The British merchants bought one of the remaining three shops, but the other two were owned by one of the local temples.
June 7, 1847:	The Honam householders realized that the British only wished to rent land and buildings.
June 23, 1847:	One Chinese landlord agreed to rent warehouses in Honam to the British, but he refused to allow foreigners to reside there.
June 25, 1847:	The three thousand inhabitants of Shih-wei-tang in Honam warned the family that was planning to rent to the British that this would endanger the area. At the same time, they petitioned the Governor-General, asking him to halt the transaction.
July 6, 1847:	Ch'i-ying told the petitioners that the imperial rescript of 1846 gave the foreigners the right to trade. Therefore, if a landowner wished to rent his property, others had no right to stop him.
August 3, 1847:	The owner now wanted a higher rent to compensate for the added risk. The British Chamber of Commerce thus formally gave up its plan to acquire warehouse space in Honam. On the other hand, the Hog Lane negotiations were successfully concluded.

*FO 228/73.

Appendix IV

CERTAIN ECONOMIC CONSIDERATIONS*

Some of the textiles that Canton sold to other parts of China were produced by home weaving, which was a welcome source of extra funds for the marginal peasant family. As more and more British manufactured textiles were imported, some of these families found themselves losing that extra income. In 1830, this led to riots in two of the counties around Canton; and in 1834, many weavers refused to stock foreign textiles in their shops. Much later, in 1853, it was reported that half of the women in Shun-te county had given up weaving because of the low price of foreign cloths. A similar report was given for P'an-yü county in 1870. However, in spite of the wish of some historians to find concrete proof of rural impoverishment in Kwangtung owing to the decline of cottage industry, most evidence consists solely of import statistics of foreign cloth and these few scattered references to the decline of home weaving. The matter has been grossly overemphasized as an important economic factor in the history of this region. The most important thing that can be said is that the rural areas in which the decline of cottage industry seemed to be most marked were precisely those areas which were the

*This discussion is largely based on the following: Wang Ying, "T'ai-p'ing t'ien-kuo ke-ming ch'ien tuo t'u-ti wen-t'i te i p'ien" (A Glance at Several Land Problems Before the Taiping Rebellion), *Shih-huo*, 2.3:39–44 (July, 1935). Yen Chung-p'ing, "Chung-kuo mien-yeh chih fa-chan" (The Development of the Chinese Cotton Industry), in *Chung-kuo chin-tai shih lun-ts'ung* (Collected Essays on Modern Chinese History) (Taipei, 1958), 2nd ts'e, pp. 245–271. Li ·Wen-chih, *et al.*, comp., *Chung-kuo chin-tai nung-yeh shih tzu-liao* (Materials on the History of Modern Chinese Agriculture) (Peking, 1957), vol. 1, 1840–1911. Hatano Yoshihiro, "Taihei Tengoku ni kansuru nisan no mondai ni tsuite" (On Certain Problems Relating to the Taiping Heavenly Kingdom), *Rekishigaku kenkyū* (Historical Research), 150:32–42 (Mar., 1951). R. H. Tawney, *Land and Labour in China* (London, 1964). Robert Fortune, *A Residence Among the Chinese* (London, 1857). G. William Skinner, "Marketing and Social Structure in Rural China," *Journal of Asian Studies*, 24.2:195–228 (Feb., 1965). Liu Po-chi, *Kuang-tung shu-yuan chih-tu* (The System of Academies in Kwangtung) (Taipei, 1958).

most antiforeign. It was almost as if the peasantry rationally blamed their plight on foreign imports.

This, in turn, raises a larger problem. How dependent was the Kuang-chou peasant on external markets? By the twentieth century, South China unquestionably had a consumer economy: about one-fourth of the goods used by agricultural families in Fukien and Kwangtung were purchased. The decline of rural self-sufficiency coincided with an increase in cash crops, in turn creating a monoculture economy which put the peasant at the mercy of national, or even international, price fluctuations. As early as the Tao-kuang period, Kwangtung's hillsides were being planted with tea by Hakkas. Cantonese leaves were never highly prized, but they were found more and more frequently in London's marketplaces in the 1850's, usually artificially colored to resemble the famous green teas. However, the best available evidence indicates that large-scale conversion to cash crops did not take place until much later, between 1890 and 1910.

This is not to deny that Kuang-chou's rural economy was partially commercialized before that date. At least by 1890, standard market towns were declining in favor of the larger urban markets of Fatshan and Canton. City and countryside were being united. The rural peasant was coming into economic contact with the outer world. If supposition is permissible without precise data, it can be inferred that this was partly true even for the 1840's. Given the apparently high consumption of machine cotton in Nan-hai; the concentric size of Canton; the existence of relatively decent roads and efficient water communications, we can suppose that the geographic contiguity of the rural and urban landscapes was matched by an economic contiguity. This would have made the peasant partially vulnerable to new economic fluctuations, such as the 1847 depression, and not just to "traditional" changes in climate or irrigation. A corollary to this would be increased contact between village and city. Hostility is a result of intimacy. Increased contact might have meant increased hostility between town and country, which would have had a great deal of influence on the course taken by the anti-foreign movement in the 1840's and '50's.

Needless to say, these are hypothetical conclusions. Local gazetteers and contemporary accounts do not lend themselves to this sort of analysis. However, one type of indirect evidence (investment rates in Kwangtung's local academies) suggests that there was a tremendous growth of all forms of rental capital at the end of the eighteenth century, during the heyday of Canton's prosperity. Excess commercial income was invested in land, which accordingly became quite scarce after 1795. Between 1820 and 1850, however, a great deal of land suddenly became available. The fact that this was accompanied by a tremendous decline in the collection of rents indicated that countless freeholders had become tenants or laborers. The abundance of silver specie and the building of many small shops pointed to a glaring contrast between the city, or commercial, mode and the countryside, or agrarian, mode. Little wonder, then, that Canton attracted so many dispossessed and poverty-stricken peasants during this period — men and women who formed a floating, urban population of beggars and thieves.

APPENDIX TABLE 3

FORMS OF ENDOWMENT OF ACADEMIES AND LOCAL SCHOOLS[a]

	Fields (mou)	Endowment (taels)	Rents (piculs)	Rents (taels)	Shops (rooms)
1722	0.2	n.f.	0.2	1.3	n.f.
1735	2.8	0.5	0.2	2.4	1.0
1795	15.0	3.4	3.6	18.3	1.2
1820	10.8	5.0	13.8	12.8	2.8
1850	16.6	7.2	0.1	10.7	10.0
1861	0.2	0.5	0.2	0.2	n.f.
1874	1.5	9.5	0.2	14.7	3.0
1907	14.2	10.0	0.1	8.8	11.0

[a] Fields are represented in thousands of mou; endowment in tens of thousands taels; rents in tens of thousands of piculs of grain; rents in thousands of taels of silver; and shops in tens of rooms.

Appendix V

KWANGTUNG'S MILITARY RECEIPTS AND EXPENSES, 1854–1857 *

Receipts	*Taels*
"Regular" sources of income:	
Land tax	670,060
Portion of Canton customs revenue allotted for the *Arrow* war	191,200
Salt gabelle	20,000
Military allotments from the revenue of Kwangsi province	73,000
Miscellaneous funds from the treasury of Kuang-chou prefecture	47,527
Unexpended surpluses from military salaries, barracks' rations, etc.	25,115
Value of military supplies (gunpowder, shot, timber) contributed by other provinces	25,115
Funds forwarded by the provincial judge of Kwangsi	1,507
Funds forwarded by the provincial treasurer of Kwangtung	70,000
Subtotal	1,100,628
"Irregular" and local sources of income:	
Merchant loans to make up the treasury deficit	294,502
Assessments on local officials and gentry for the *Arrow* war	121,297

*All of these figures are based upon provincial military ledgers which were taken from Canton's yamens when the British captured the city. They are currently filed in London's Public Record Office, numbered FO 682/228/2, and bear the title: *Chün-hsü shou-chih ko k'uan yueh-pao che-ti* (Rough Drafts of Itemized Monthly Cash Receipts for Military Use). The period covered runs from Hsien-feng 4/5 (May 27–June 24, 1854) to Hsien-feng 7/2 (Feb. 24–March 25, 1857).

Receipts		Taels
Voluntary contributions from local officials, gentry, and others		603,645
Funds from the confiscation and seizure of local properties, and from judicial fines		167,131
Hsiang-shan's contributions for the *Arrow* war		15,380
Hui-chou's contributions for the *Arrow* war		14,873
Contributions raised in the "new city" (of Canton, i.e. the mercantile quarter) in May, 1855		256
Shun-te's contributions:		
"Public Office"	191,500	
Random voluntary contributions	381,182	
Contributions for the *Arrow* war	96,000	
		668,682
Subtotal		1,885,766
Total likin collected by the provincial authorities at the customs barriers west of Canton City		1,829,038
Total receipts		4,815,432

Expenses		
Authorized general expenditure [a]		1,244,706
Salaries and benefits:		
Miscellaneous salaries for provincial yamen personnel, the quartermaster corps and port clearance officers		15,486
Reward money to official troops		156,264
Reward money to Nan-hai militia		1,300
Military pensions and benefits for heirs of the deceased		59,139
Subtotal		232,189
Armaments:		
Muskets		124,403
Cannons		93,802
Gunpowder		122,082
Building and repairing gun emplacements and forts		22,726
Construction costs of work-sheds for boat building and repairing		6,814
Boats (crews, builders, rentals, construction costs)		2,530,219
Subtotal		2,900,046

[a] This category must have included regular military salaries and rations.

Expenses		*Taels*
Rations and provisions:		
Food for boatmen		155,929
Oil, coal, and dried provisions		63,375
Extraordinary army provisions elsewhere unaccounted for		2,118
	Subtotal	221,422
Transportation:		
Cost of transferring troops from Kiangnan		316
Cost of transporting a foreign gunboat to Hupei		2,041
Miscellaneous transportation costs		3,200
	Subtotal	5,557
Interest costs of servicing the merchant loan		9,407
	Total expenses	4,613,327

NOTE: Of the income, 23 percent was "regular"; 40, "irregular"; and 37, derived from likin collection. Of the "irregular" and local receipts, Shun-te county's share was approximately 35 percent. This meant, in effect, that this single *hsien* contributed, or was assessed, 14 percent of the costs of war and rebellion in Kwangtung province. Moreover, the total burden on the country was probably even higher, as some of the extraordinary property confiscation (which was obviously an important source of revenue) must have affected this area.

Of the total military expenses, approximately 590,000 taels represented the costs of the *Arrow* war; and 4,020,000 taels, those of civil war.

Appendix VI

THE RED TURBAN REVOLT*

Lung-men

September 20, 1854: Liu Kuan-hsiu attacked the county seat, and the district magistrate, Ch'iao Ying-keng, died defending the city gates.

November 21, 1854: The city was recovered by the acting magistrate and a member of the gentry named Li Shih-ch'üan.

January 6, 1855: The acting magistrate suffered a severe defeat.

Hua-hsien

October 11, 1854: Official troops and braves besieged the *hsien* capital.

December 25, 1854: The county seat was recovered.

January 21, 1855: Red Turbans led by Chu Tzu-i and Kan Hsien once more attacked the city.

Ts'eng-ch'eng

September 21, 1854: Militia led by a member of the gentry, Ch'en Wei-yueh, recovered the city.

January 17, 1855: Bandits led by Huang Huai-hua attacked the city. T'ang Lun-ying's local militia killed 90 of the bandits.

Hsin-hui

October 5, 1854: The siege was broken, and the bandits driven off.

October 11, 1854: The rebels returned but were again dispersed by imperial troops.

November 4, 1854: Another attack repelled.

November 30, 1854: Local militia pacified the northeastern part of the district.

*Sources: Ch'en Po-t'ao, ed., *Tung-kuan hsien-chih* (Gazetteer of Tung-kuan District) (1919), chüan 35, 71, 72. Cheng Meng-yü, ed., *Hsü-hsiu nan-hai hsien-chih* (Revised Gazetteer of Nan-hai District) (1872), chüan 14, 15, 16, 17, 19. Liang Ting-fen, ed., *P'an-yü hsien-hsü-chih* (Revised Gazetteer of P'an-yü District), chüan 20, 21, 22, 24, 26. Shih Ch'eng, ed., *Kuang-chou fu-chih* (Gazetteer of Kuang-chou Prefecture) (1879), chüan 82. T'ien Ming-yueh, ed., *Hsiang-shan hsien-chih* (Gazetteer of Hsiang-shan District) (1879), chüan 15.

January 21, 1855: The capital was so tranquil that the troops there
were rewarded for their bravery and loyalty.

Hsin-ning

September 14, 1854: Hsü Chao-piao's bandits suffered a severe defeat
when the local magistrate, Yang Te-i, led the peasantry against them.

September 26, 1854: Yang Te-i again defeated Hsü.

December 20, 1854: The K'ai-p'ing bandit leader, T'an Ya-shou, was
captured and executed.

Hsiang-shan

September 9, 1854: Bandits led by Kuang Ts'an-feng occupied Hsiao-
hao-yung.

September 15, 1854: Further rebel victories.

October 11, 1854: Kuan Shih-piao's Shun-te gang attacked and besieged
the city of Hsiao-huang-p'u in Hsiang-shan, but they were driven
off by village braves.

October 21, 1854: Hsiao-hao-yung was relieved by militia under the
gentry leader, Ho Hsin-t'ao.

November 24, 1854: Armed peasants pacified the area around
Ch'üan-lu.

Hsiang-shan seemed to have had no central militia organization.
However, there were many instances of gentry forming local militia in
single walled villages.

Tung-kuan

June 17, 1854: Ho Liu captured the country seat.

June 25, 1854: Ho defeated a contingent of official troops.

July 2, 1854: The officials regained nominal control of the county seat.

July 4, 1854: A larger group of Red Turbans began to assemble south
of the *hsien* capital. However, the gentry of that area (*sha-t'ien*) collected braves and scattered the rebels.

August 11, 1854: Ho captured Ts'eng-ch'eng. At the same time, a new
group of rebels under a man named Liu Wan-yu moved into Tung-
kuan.

September 1, 1854: Militia organized by Hua T'ing-chieh, the county
magistrate, captured and executed Liu.

February 7, 1855: Ho Liu returned defeated from Ts'eng-ch'eng to
plunder the Shih-lung area. Peasants assembled by the gentry defeated and scattered Ho's band.

The local gazetteer suggests that Ho Liu, a member of the Triad Society, was driven into open revolt by the zealousness of a local gentry leader named Ch'en Ming-kuei, who denounced Ho as a potential rebel, burned his home, and posted a reward for his head.

Although Tung-kuan suffered much devastation, the efforts of the local magistrate, Hua T'ing-chieh, eventually restored order to the county. Helped by some of the local gentry, he created a militia bureau in the "local school" at the "northwest corner" of the county (*Hsi-pei-yü she-hsüeh*). Other gentry leaders followed suit. Ch'en Ming-kuei, for example, organized a control system of "white banners" around Shih-lung, and eventually mustered over ten thousand militiamen.

Nan-hai

October 27, 1854: The gentry leader Lin Fu-sheng took and destroyed the bandit headquarters at Niu-lan-kang.

January 17, 1855: Fatshan was recovered by imperial troops.

January 28, 1855: Lin Fu-sheng successfully wiped out the rebels at Hsin-ts'un.

January 30, 1855: The bandits in the "western villages" area were completely defeated.

There were several other large militia organizations in addition to the Ta-li league: the "Bureau for Nurturing Humaneness" (*Huai-jen-chü*), founded by I Wei-chi at Sha-wan; the defense "span" at T'u-lu, created by Chao Ch'eng-hsi; and so forth.

P'an-yü

November 3, 1854: Troops and braves assaulted Fo-ling-shih where the Red Turbans had entrenched themselves in the "local schools."

December 7, 1854: Lu Ch'ang's band was destroyed by troops and braves led by the famous Wei Tso-pang.

January 8, 1855: Inconclusive battle at Hsin-tsao.

January 20, 1855: Huang Yung led troops against the bandits in Honam. He killed their chief, Lin Kuang-lung, and the rest scattered.

January 31, 1855: Honam was pacified.

P'an-yü was a major battleground for the Red Turban armies, which were staged there to attack Canton. Some of the county's gentry moved into the provincial capital, working for a central bureau headed by a *chü-jen* named Ch'en P'u. But outside of the city, three major militia offices were established during the summer and fall of 1854.

The area just north of the Manchu parade grounds was known as the "North Road" (*pei-lu*) and centered on the market town of Fo-ling-shih. As soon as the revolt began, the gentry there quickly and spontaneously formed a multitude of small militia groups, which were eventually united under the "Pacification Bureau" (*An-ho-chü*), which was run by Ts'eng Lin-shu. The militia that this bureau trained was often used in joint attacks with banner troops.

The area around Po-lo was organized by Chung Ch'i-yao into a *yueh* (covenant) of "the clear and peaceful villages" (*Ch'ing-p'ing-she*). From there, Chung formed an alliance with the "seven covenants" (*ch'i-yueh*) of Tung-kuan.

The southern villages of the *hsien* were organized into militia by the wealthy patriarch, the famous Wu K'uei-yang. He had been an important local notable since the 1830's, often summoning the villages and clans together to deliberate on serious questions. In 1841, he used this technique to raise public funds for local self-defense. When the Red Turbans revolted, he again summoned the village associations and had them all recruit and train local *t'uan-lien*. Wu K'uei-yang himself arranged for relief kitchens and provisions, even selling his own enormous grain supplies at low prices in order to provide relief. Nevertheless, that part of the county was swept under by Ch'en Hsien-liang's rebels. Only the region around "East Mountain" (*tung-shan*) remained a gentry base. By then, Wu K'uei-yang's *t'uan-lien* were completely under the control of himself and his clan. An ancillary bureau, the *Sha-chiao tsung-chü*, which was in charge of *sha-t'ien* rents, was managed by K'uei-yang's younger brother, Wu Chün-yang.

The contribution and likin bureau, which was called the "Association for Great Profit" (*Kuang-i-hui*), was headed by two other clansmen, Wu Pin and Wu Chi-shu. Eventually, of course, this complex defense organization mustered the 35,000 braves that defeated Ch'en Hsien-liang.

Notes

Abbreviations Used in Notes

CR	Chinese Repository
FO	Foreign Office Archives; filed in Public Record Office, London
IWSM	*Ch'ou-pan i-wu shih-mo*
TK	Tao-kuang reign period (1821–1850)
HF	Hsien-feng reign period (1851–1861)
HSHC	T'ien Ming-yueh, ed., *Hsiang-shan hsien-chih*
KCFC	Shih Ch'eng, ed., *Kuang-chou fu-chih*
NHHC	Cheng Men-yü, ed., *Hsü-hsiu nan-hai hsien-chih*
PYHC	Liang Ting-fen, ed., *P'an-yü hsien-hsü-chich*
STHC	Chou Ch'-ao-huai, ed., *Shun-te hsien-chih*
TKHC	Ch'en Po-t'ao, ed., *Tung-kuan hsien-chih*
WO	War Office Archives; filed in Public Record Office, London
YPCC	Ch'i Ssu-ho, ed., *Ya-p'ien chan-cheng*

1. There are so many reliable accounts of these events that documentation is almost unnecessary. Some of the sources that I have relied on are: H. B. Morse, *The International Relations of the Chinese Empire: The Period of Conflict, 1834–1860* (Shanghai, 1910), chap. 10. Edgar Holt, *The Opium Wars in China* (London, 1964), chaps. 9–10. Chiang T'ing-fu, "Ch'i-shan yü ya-p'ien chan-cheng" (Ch'i-shan and the Opium War), *Ch'ing-hua hsüeh-pao*, 6.3:1–26 (Oct., 1931). Hsiao, I-shan, *Ch'ing-tai t'ung-shih* (General History of the Ch'ing Period) (Taipei, 1963), vol. 2. W. H. Hall and W. D. Bernard, *The Nemesis in China, Comprising a History of the Late War in That Country with an Account of the Colony of Hong Kong* (London, 1855), 79–161. FO 17/46 ("1841, China, from Captain Charles Elliot, A. R. Johnson, and Robert Morrison"). FO 17/48 ("1841, China. March 25–August, from Plenipotentiaries"). WO 1/461 ("China, Hong Kong and India, 1841: Military").

2. Yen-yü Huang, "Viceroy Yeh Ming-ch'en and the Canton Episode (1858–1861)," *Harvard Journal of Asiatic Studies*, 6.1:46, n. 3 (March, 1941). Hsia Hsieh, *Chung-hsi chi-shih* (A Record of Sino-Western Affairs) (Taipei, 1962), 6:10-a. Liang T'ing-nan, *I-fen chi-wen* (An Account of the Barbarian Invasion) (1874), 3. The edition of this famous work in the Fu Ssu-nien library has no pagination. My references are, therefore, only to the particular *chüan*. E. H. Parker, *Chinese Account of the Opium War* (Shanghai, 1888), 32–37. KCFC, 81:35-b. Hall and Bernard, *Nemesis*, 190.

3. FO 17/48, Elliot–Gough, Incl. 1, Desp. 21, May 13, 1841.

4. Parker, *Chinese Account*, 31–32.

5. For Chinese discussions of I-shan's blunder and the strategy of the British attack, see: Parker, *Chinese Account*, 32–33; and Hsia Hsieh, *Chung-hsi chi-shih*, 6:10-a. On the *Nemesis*, see Hall and Bernard, *Nemesis*, 89–190.

6. Henri Cordier, "Les marchands hanistes de Canton," *T'oung Pao*, 2.3:284 (1902). Hsia Hsieh, *Chung-hsi chi-shih*, 6:10-b. FO 17/46, Elliot's voucher to Aberdeen, unnumbered dispatch, Nov. 25, 1841. This was an officially approved act. See: FO 682/912, "True Copy of Authorization given to the Prefect of Canton by I-shan, to Ransom the City, dated TK 21/4/7" (Chinese text).

7. Robert S. Rait, *The Life and Campaigns of Hugh, First Viscount Gough, Field-Marshal* (Westminster, 1903), 1:193.

8. Edward Bing-Shuey Lee, *Modern Canton* (Shanghai, 1936), chaps. 1–2 G. Allgood, *China War, 1860: Letters and Journal* (London, 1901), 23. A. J. du Bosch, *La Chine contemporaine, d'après les travaux les plus récents* (Paris,

1860), 204–214. *Kuang-chou chih-nan* (Guidebook to Canton) (Canton, 1934), 5. Huang Fo-i, *Kuang-chou-ch'eng fang-chih* (Local Gazetteer of the City of Canton) (1948), Vol. 1. B. C. Henry, *Ling-Nam, or Interior Views of Southern China, including Explorations in the Hitherto Untraversed Island of Hainan* (London, 1886), 59–60. *Shina shōbetsu zenshi* (Gazetteer of China by Provinces) (Tokyo, 1917), 1:156. FO 17/30, Gutzlaff's report, Incl. 1, Desp. 4, Jan. 10, 1839. Hall and Bernard, *Nemesis*, 174–175. The best description in English of the Pearl River delta can be found in: Gunther Barth, *Bitter Strength: A History of the Chinese in the United States: 1850–1870* (Cambridge, Mass., 1964), chap. 1.

9. FO 17/272, Wade's report, Incl. 1, Desp. 407, Oct. 19, 1857.

10. Hall and Bernard, *Nemesis*, 196.

11. YPCC, 4:21.

12. Arthur Waley, *The Opium War through Chinese Eyes* (London, 1958), 109–110, 186–196.

13. IWSM, TK 29:23-a to 23-b.

14. A Ying, comp., *Ya-p'ien chan-cheng wen-hsueh chi* (A Collection of Opium War Literature) (Peking, 1957), 734–736.

15. YPCC, 4:22, 27. Lin Tse-hsü, *Lin wen-kung ch'üan-chi* (The Collected works of Lin Tse-hsü; Taipei, 1963), 1.6:1-b.

16. J. Elliot Bingham, *Narrative of the Expedition to China* (London, 1842), 1:231–232. Rait, *Gough*, 1:126. D. McPherson, *Two Years in China: Narrative of the Chinese Expedition from Its Formation in April, 1840, till April, 1842* (London, 1842), 148.

17. KCFC, 81:39-a.

18. FO 17/40, Davis–Palmerston, Feb. 8, 1848. For a typical Chinese reference to this, see: Hall and Bernard, *Nemesis*, 196.

19. Rait, *Gough*, 1:155.

20. Hall and Bernard, *Nemesis*, 194.

21. Liang T'ing-nan, 1.

22. This account is based on a comparative use of the following sources: Kuang-tung-sheng wen-shih yen-chiu-kuan (The Research Institute of the Literature and History of Kwangtung Province), "Kuang-tung jen-min tsai san-yuan-li k'ang-ying tou-cheng chien-shih" (A Concise History of the Anti-English Struggle of the Cantonese People at San-yuan-li), in Lieh Tao, ed., *Ya-p'ien chan-cheng shih lun-wen chuan-chi* (A Collection of Essays on the History of the Opium War) (Peking, 1958), 113–141. Ch'en Hsi-ch'i, *Kuang-tung san-yuan-li jen-min te k'ang-ying tou-cheng* (The Anti-British Struggle of the People of San-yuan-li in Kwangtung) (Canton, 1956). Hsiao I-shan, *Ch'ing-tai*, 2:948–949. Hsia Hsieh, *Chung-hsi chi-shih*, 6:11-b, and 13:8-a. Liang T'ing-nan, 3. Suzuki Chusei, "Shimmatsu jōgai-undō no kigen" (Origins of the Antiforeign Movement During the Later Ch'ing Period), *Shigaku Zasshi*, 62.10:1–29 (Oct., 1953). A Ying, 736–738. Holt, *Opium Wars*, 129–130. Rait, *Gough*, 1:180. Bingham, *Narrative*, 2:242, 323. Hall and Bernard, *Nemesis*, 190. CR, 5:192–193 (May, 1836–Dec., 1836).

23. Kuang-tung-sheng, "Kuang-tung jen-min," 286.

24. NHHC, 26:6-b. A Ying, 735. IWSM, TK 29:23-b.

25. A Ying, 1. In one popular legend (*Chung-lun wen-chai pi-lu*, 8:7-b) Kuan-yin helps the Cantonese defeat the British attackers.

26. Translated in Parker, *Chinese Account*, 35–36.

Notes to Chapter 2 (pp. 22–28)

1. For a much more thorough examination in English of the history of China's militia, see the excellent study by Philip Kuhn, to which I am greatly indebted: "The Militia in Nineteenth Century China," (Ph.D. thesis, Harvard University, 1963). Also see: Suzuki Tadashi, "Min-dai katei kō" (A Study of the Militia During the Ming Period), *Shikan*, 37:23–40 (1952).

2. KCFC, 81:14-a to 16-b.

3. KCFC, 81:16-b to 17-b. HSHC, 14:44-a. TKHC, 38:25-a.

4. HSHC, 20:5-b.

5. NHHC, 15:8-a.

6. NHHC, 15:10-a.

7. H. B. Morse, *The International Relations of the Chinese Empire: The Period of Conflict, 1834–1860* (Shanghai, 1910), 195. Hsin-pao Chang, *Commissioner Lin and the Opium War* (Cambridge, Mass., 1964), chap. 4.

8. YPCC, 2:168.

9. FO 17/46, Elliot-Palmerston, Desp. 46. E. H. Parker, *Chinese Account of the Opium War* (Shanghai, 1888), 12.

10. Barbara E. Ward, "A Hong Kong Fishing Village," *Journal of Oriental Studies*, 1:195–214 (1954). Edward H. Schafer, *The Vermilion Bird*, chap. 11.

11. Lin Tse-hsü, 1:3-b (see chap. 1, n. 15, above).

12. KCFC, 81:34-b. Parker, *Chinese Account*, 13–16. IWSM, TK 31:6-a to 6-b. Lin Tse-hsü, 1:3-b (see chap. 1, n. 15).

13. Charles Gutzlaff, *The Life of Taou-Kwang, Late Emperor of China, with Memoirs of the Court of Peking* (London, 1852), 67. Chiang T'ing-fu, "Ch'i-shan," 181 (see chap. 1, n. 1). Kung-chuan Hsiao, *Rural China: Imperial Control in the Nineteenth Century* (Seattle, 1960), 300. Franz Michael, "Military Organization and Power Structure of China during the Taiping Rebellion," *Pacific Historical Review*, 18:469–483 (Nov., 1949).

14. Lin Tse-hsü, 8:1-a to 20-b (see chap. 1, n. 15). Laai Yi-faai, "The Part Played by the Pirates of Kwangtung and Kwangsi Provinces in the T'ai-p'ing Insurrection" (Ph.D. thesis, University of California, Berkeley, 1950), 39. Liang T'ing-nan, 3 (see chap. 1, n. 2).

15. YPCC, 2:121.

16. Arthur Waley, *The Opium War through Chinese Eyes* (London, 1958), 51–52.

17. Sung Lung-yuan, *Tao-te-ching chiang-i* (An Explanation of the Tao-te-ching) (Taipei, n.d.), 6-a.

18. For a delightful account of some of these devices, see: Waley, *Opium War*. Also see: Lin Tse-hsü, 1:22-b (see chap. 1, n. 15).

19. Liang T'ing-nan, 3 (see chap. 1, n. 2). Parker, *Chinese Account*, 22–23.

20. Chiang T'ing-fu, "Ch'i-shan," 181–183 (see chap. 1, n. 1).

21. IWSM, TK 23:14-a.

22. Hsia Hsieh, *Chung-hsi chi-shih*, 6:5-a to 5-b (see chap. 1, n. 2).

23. Hsiao I-shan, *Ch'ing-tai*, 2:948 (see chap. 1, n. 1).

24. IWSM, TK 30:9-a.

Notes to Chapter 3 (pp. 29–41)

1. Kung-chuan Hsiao, *Rural China: Imperial Control in the Nineteenth Century* (Seattle, 1960). T'ung-tsu Ch'ü, *Local Government in China under the Ch'ing* (Cambridge, Mass., 1962). Franz Michael, introduction to: Stanley Spector, *Li Hung-chang and the Huai Army: A Study in Nineteenth-Century Chinese Regionalism* (Seattle, 1964), xxi–xliii. Chung-li Chang, *The Chinese Gentry: Studies on Their Role in Nineteenth-Century Chinese Society* (Seattle, 1955), table 33.

2. For a general discussion of this cycle, see: James T. K. Wu, "The Impact of the Taiping Rebellion on the Manchu Fiscal System," *Pacific Historical Review*, 19:265–275 (1950).

3. Hsiao, *Rural China*, 68.

4. David Edward Owen, *British Opium Policy in China and India* (New Haven, 1934), 53–61, 113–114. Hsin-pao Chang, *Commissioner Lin and the Opium War* (Cambridge, Mass., 1964), chaps. 3 and 4. Hsü Sung-chou, "Ya-p'ien shu-ju chung-kuo k'ao" (An Examination of Opium Imports into China), in *Chung-kuo chin-tai shih lun-ts'ung* (A Collection of Articles on Modern Chinese History) (Taipei, 1958), 156–158. H. H. Kane, *Opium-smoking in America and China: A Study of its Prevalence, and Effects, Immediate and Remote, on the Individual and the Nation* (New York, 1882), 111–115.

5. Chiang T'ing-fu, comp., *Chin-tai chung-kuo wai-chiao shih-liao chi-yao* (Selected Materials on Modern Chinese Diplomatic History) (Taipei, 1958), 1:24. My discussion in general leans heavily on Hsin-pao Chang's account, chaps. 4 and 5.

6. Chiang T'ing-fu, comp., *Chin-tai chung-kuo*, 24–25.

7. *Ibid.*, 25–26.

8. *Ibid.*, 27–28.

9. *Ibid.*

10. *Ibid.*, 29–32. P. C. Kuo, *A Critical Study of the First Anglo-Chinese War, with Documents* (Shanghai, 1935), chap. 5. Hsiao I-shan, *Ch'ing-tai*, 2:913 (see chap. 1, n. 1).

11. Chiang T'ing-fu, comp., *Chin-tai chung-kuo*, 32–36. P. C. Kuo, *Critical Study*, chap. 5. Holt, *The Opium Wars in China* (London, 1964), 71. Hsiao I-shan, *Ch'ing-tai*, 2:914 (see chap. 1, n. 1).

12. Chang, *Commissioner Lin*, 89.

13. P. C. Kuo, *Critical Study*, chap. 6.

14. *Ibid.*, 58. This is Kuo's translation.

15. Hsiao I-shan, *Ch'ing-tai*, 2:915–919 (see chap. 1, n. 1).

16. *Ibid.* B. C. Henry, *Ling-Nam, or Interior Views of Southern China, including Explorations in the Hitherto Untraversed Island of Hainan* (London, 1886), chap. 7.

17. Liang T'ing-nan, 1 (see chap. 1, n. 2).

18. CR, 7:112, 232, 336, 437–441 (May, 1838–April, 1839).

19. Chang, *Commissioner Lin*, 117.

20. *Ibid.*, 97.

21. CR, 9:55–56, 560–572 (May, 1840–Dec., 1840). P. C. Kuo, *Critical Study*, chap. 9.

22. Arthur Waley, *The Opium War through Chinese Eyes* (London, 1958), 26–27.

23. Lin Tse-hsü, 4:2-a (see chap. 1, n. 15).

24. Lord Jocelyn, *Six Months with the Chinese Expedition, or Leaves from a Soldier's Note-book* (London, 1841), 4–5.

25. FO 17/155, Incl. 1, Desp. 71, May 21, 1849.

26. TKHC, 34:11-b.

27. *Ibid.*, 52:19-b. HSHC, 15:8-b.

28. TKHC, 71:1-b. HSHC, 15:31-a.

29. CR, 9:167 (May, 1840–Dec., 1840). Philip Kuhn, "The Militia in Nineteenth Century China," (Harvard University, 1963), 114.

30. HSHC, 16:4-a.

31. PYHC, 24:11-b.

32. NHHC, 13:57-b.

33. *Ibid.*, 17:9-a.

34. TKHC, 71:16-a.

35. *Ibid.*, 52:21-a. HSHC, 16:2-a.

36. PYHC, 20:31-a, 22:9-a.

37. Liang T'ing-nan, 3 (see chap. 1, n. 2). YPCC, 3:391, 539.

38. Sir John Francis Davis, *China, During the War and Since the Peace* (London, 1852), 1:34.

39. *Ibid.*, 24:13-a. STHC, 17:9-b. A Ying, 739–740 (see chap. 1, n. 14).

40. Hsia Hsieh, *Chung-hsi chi-shih*, 13:1-a to 2-a (see chap. 1, n. 2).

41. *Ibid.* Kuang-tung-sheng, "Kuang-tung jen-min," 277–280 (see chap. 1, n. 22).

42. There were several cases of rape and kidnapping around San-yuan-li and Fatshan, followed by militia attacks on British troops, two or three days before the actual San-yuan-li incident. See: IWSM, TK 31:7-a to 8-a. KCFC, 81:40-b. Hsia Hsieh, *Chung-hsi chi-shih*, 6:9-a (see chap. 1, n. 2). Kuang-tung-sheng, "Kuang-tung jen-min," 280 (see chap. 1, n. 22).

43. Kuang-tung-sheng, "Kuang-tung jen-min.," 281. YPCC, 4:24.

44. Kuang-tung-sheng, "Kuang-tung jen-min," 292. YPCC, 4:18–19.

45. NHHC, 19:10-b. Kuang-tung-sheng, "Kuang-tung jen-min," 299. YPCC, 4:24.

46. IWSM, TK 29:23-b; TK 31:7-b. Kuang-tung-sheng, "Kuang-tung jen-min," 299.

47. Kuang-tung-sheng, "Kuang-tung jen-min," 282.

48. *Ibid.*, 279.

49. *Ibid.*, 281–282.

Notes to Chapter 4 (pp. 42–51)

1. This historical account is drawn primarily from: Harold J. Wiens, *China's March Toward the Tropics* (Hamden, Conn., 1954), chap. 4. Hisayuki Miyakawa, "The Confucianization of South China," in A. F. Wright, ed., *The Confucian*

Persuasion (Stanford, 1960), 21–46. Chi Li, *The Formation of the Chinese People: An Anthropological Inquiry* (Cambridge, Mass., 1928). Above all, I have used Edward H. Schafer's new book, *Vermilion Bird: T'ang Images of the South* (Berkeley and Los Angeles, 1967). Professor Schafer was kind enough to let me read his prepublication manuscript.

2. Edward H. Schafer, *The Golden Peaches of Samarkand: A Study of T'ang Exotics* (Berkeley and Los Angeles, 1963), 28–32.

3. J. K. Fairbank and S. Y. Teng, "On the Ch'ing Tributary System," in *Ch'ing Administration: Three Studies* (Cambridge, Mass., 1961), 135–144.

4. Shigeshi Kato, "On the Hang or the Associations of Merchants in China," *Memoirs of the Research Department of the Toyo Bunko*, 8:45–83 (1936). Etienne Balazs, *Chinese Civilization and Bureaucracy: Variations on a Theme* (New Haven and London, 1964), chaps. 1, 2, 4. Hosea Ballou Morse, *The Gilds of China, with an Account of the Gild Merchant or Co-hong of Canton* (London, 1909), 24–27. John Steward Burgess, *The Guilds of Peking* (New York, 1928), 211–213.

5. This discussion of the Canton trade is generally based on the following works: T'ien-tse Chang, *Sino-Portuguese Trade, 1514–1544: A Synthesis of Portuguese and Chinese Sources* (Leiden, 1934). Chang Te-ch'ang, "Ch'ing-tai ya-p'ien chan-cheng ch'ien chih chung-hsi yen-hai t'ung-shang" (Maritime Trade Between China and the West During the Ch'ing Period Before the Opium War), *Ch'ing-hua hsüeh-pao* (Tsing Hua Journal), 10.1:97–145 (1935). *Description of the City of Canton with an Appendix Containing an Account of the . . . Chinese Empire . . .* (Canton, 1839). Liang Jen-ts'ai, *Kuang-tung ching-chi ti-li* (Economic Geography of Kwangtung) (Peking, 1956). J. K. Fairbank, *Trade and Diplomacy on the China Coast: The Opening of the Treaty Ports, 1842–1854* (Cambridge, Mass., 1953), 2 vols. Ch'eng Wei-hsin, "Sung-tai kuang-chou-shih tui wai mao-i te ch'ing-hsing" (The Nature of the Canton Market and Foreign Trade During the Sung Dynasty), *Shih-huo* (Economics), 1.12:26 (May 16, 1935). Hosea Ballou Morse, *The International Relations of the Chinese Empire: The Period of Conflict, 1834–1860* (Shanghai, 1910), and *The Trade and Administration of China*, 3rd ed. (London, 1921). Michael Greenberg, *British Trade and the Opening of China, 1800–1842* (Cambridge, England, 1951). Louis Dermigny, *La Chine et l'occident: le commerce à Canton au XVIIIe siècle, 1719–1833* (Paris, 1964), 4 vols.

6. H. F. MacNair, *Modern Chinese History: Selected Readings* (Shanghai, 1923), 48. G. Allgood, *China War, 1860: Letters and Journal* (London, 1901), 24.

7. FO 17/30, Incl. 1, Desp. 4, Jan. 10, 1839. FO 228/143, Incl. 1, Desp. 169, Oct. 28, 1852.

8. Henri Pirenne, "Stages in the Social History of Capitalism," in Bendix and Lipset, eds., *Class, Status, and Power: A Reader in Social Stratification* (London, 1954), 504–506.

9. Etienne Balazs, "The Birth of Capitalism in China," *Journal of the Economic and Social History of the Orient*, 3:196–216 (1960). Ping-ti Ho, "The Salt Merchants of Yang-chou: a Study of Commercial Capitalism in Eighteenth Century China," *Harvard Journal of Asiatic Studies*, 17:130–168 (1954).

10. Everett E. Hagen, *On the Theory of Social Change: How Economic Growth Begins* (Homewood, Ill., 1962), 60–66.

11. WO 1/461, Elliot's letter to the Governor-General of India, dated June 21,

1841, and enclosed in dispatch from the India Board to Lord Stanley, November 6, 1841. FO 17/48, Elliot–Palmerston, Desp. 17, April 16, 1841.

12. FO 17/48, Elliot–Palmerston, Desp. 17, April 16, 1841.

13. FO 17/46, Confidential letter from Elliot while in London to the Earl of Aberdeen, unnumbered, dated Nov. 18, 1841.

14. FO 17/48, Elliot-Gough, Incl. 3, Desp. 21, May 24, 1841.

15. R. S. Rait, *The Life and Campaigns of Hugh, First Viscount Gough, Field-Marshal* (Westminster, 1903), 1:168, 171.

16. FO 17/47, Elliot–Palmerston, Desp. 12, March 2, 1841.

17. FO 17/48, Elliot–Palmerston, Desp. 17, April 16, 1841.

18. W. H. Hall and W. D. Bernard, *The Nemesis in China, Comprising a History of the Late War in That Country with an Account of the Colony of Hong Kong* (London, 1847), 173.

19. IWSM, TK 23:14-a.

20. YPCC, 4:24–25.

21. *Ibid.*, 4:91. Hsia Hsieh, *Chung-hsi chi-shih*, 13:1-a. Kung-chuan Hsiao, *Rural China: Imperial Control in the Nineteenth Century* (Seattle, 1960), 489–490. Lin Tse-hsü, 2:5-a (see chap. 1, n. 15). This problem is also analyzed in John J. Nolde, "The 'Canton City Question,' 1842–1849: A Preliminary Investigation into China's Antiforeignism and Its Effect upon China's Diplomatic Relations with the West" (Ph.D. thesis, Cornell, 1956), 34–49.

22. FO 17/48, Elliot-Palmerston, Desp. 17, April 16, 1841.

23. IWSM, TK 9:21-a to 21-b.

24. Liang Chia-pin, *Kuang-tung shih-san hang k'ao* (The Hong Merchants of Canton) (Taipei, 1960), 300–305.

25. Ping-ti Ho, *The Ladder of Success in Imperial China: Aspects of Social Mobility, 1368–1911* (New York, 1962), 83. CR, 2:238–239 (May, 1833–April, 1834). T. F. Tsiang (Chiang T'ing-fu), "Government and Co-hong of Canton," *Chinese Social and Political Science Review*, 15.4:606 (Jan., 1932). The early development of the Wu clan is described in detail in Wolfram Eberhard, *Social Mobility in Traditional China* (Leiden, 1962), part 2.

26. Liang T'ing-nan, 3 (see chap. 1, n. 2). Hall and Bernard, *Nemesis*, 95–96.

27. FO 17/46, Memorial by Ch'i-shan, Translated by the British, Incl. 2, Desp. 6, May 1, 1841. Liang T'ing-nan, 3 (see chap. 1, n. 2).

28. Hall and Bernard, *Nemesis*, 134, 207. Arthur Waley, *The Opium War through Chinese Eyes* (London, 1958), 36. Lin Tse-hsü, 6:2-a to 2-b; 8:34-b; 9:1-a (see chap. 1, n. 15). YPCC, 4:27.

29. Lin Tse-hsü, 8:31-a to 35-b. Waley, *Opium War*, 94–95, 101–102.

30. Chang Te-ch'ang, 10. 1:106 (1935) (see n. 5 above).

31. Lin Tse-hsü, 1:5-a (see chap. 1, n. 15). Chiang T'ing-fu, comp., *Chin-tai Chung-kuo*, 1:24 (see chap. 3, n. 5).

32. W. H. Medhurst, *China: Its State and Prospects, with Special Reference to the Spread of the Gospel* (London, 1838), 278–282.

33. *Ibid.*, 289.

34. Lin Tse-hsü, 8:34-b (see chap. 1, n. 15).

35. E. Holt, *The Opium Wars in China* (London, 1964), 79.

36. TKHC, 34:18-b.

37. Hall and Bernard, *Nemesis*, 133, 139.

38. IWSM, TK 29:9-b, 23-a; 31:8-a. YPCC, 4:22.

39. Chu Hsi, ed., *Ssu-shu chi-chu* (Collected Glosses of the Four Books) (Taipei, 1959), 17.

40. Stanley Coben, "A Study in Nativism: The American Red Scare of 1919–1920," *Political Science Quarterly*, 79.1:52–75 (March, 1964).

Notes to Chapter 5 (pp. 52–58)

1. Hsia Hsieh, *Chung-hsi chi-shih*, 6:10-b (see chap. 1, n. 2).

2. Liang T'ing-nan, 3 (see chap. 1, n. 2).

3. Sir John F. Davis, *China, During the War and Since the Peace* (London, 1852), 1:125–127. For the Chinese version of this famous letter from one Chinese official to a close friend, describing the fall of the city, see: Hsia Hsieh, *Chung-hsi chi-shih*, 6:15–20 (see chap. 1, n. 2).

4. Liang T'ing-nan, 3 (see chap. 1, n. 2).

5. FO 682/912, "True Copy of Authorization given to the Prefect of Canton, by I-shan, etc., to ransom the City, date TK 21/4/7 (May 27, 1841): Chinese text."

6. IWSM, TK 29:1-a to 2-b.

7. Hsia Hsieh, *Chung-hsi chi-shih*, 6:11-b to 12-a (see chap. 1, n. 2).

8. A Ying, 247–248 (see chap. 1, n. 14).

9. See, for example, NHHC, 19:10-b.

10. H. B. Morse, *The International Relations of the Chinese Empire: The Period of Conflict, 1834–1860* (Shanghai, 1910), 160.

11. W. C. Hunter, *The " Fan Kwae" at Canton before Treaty Days, 1825–1844* (London, 1882), 119–120.

12. Gordon W. Allport, "Prejudice: A Problem in Psychological and Social Causation," in Talcott Parsons and Edward A. Shils, eds., *Toward a General Theory of Action* (Glencoe, Ill., 1952), 365–387. Centre International de Synthèse, *La Foule, Exposés par George Bohn, Georges Hardy, Paul Alphandéry, Georges Lefebvre, and E. Dupréel* (Paris, 1934), 88. Herbert Blumer, "The Nature of Race Prejudice," in E. T. Thompson and E. C. Hughes, eds., *Race, Individual and Collective Behaviour* (Glencoe, Ill., 1958), 484–493. Wilmoth A. Carter, "Epithets," in Thompson and Hughes, *Race*, 375–380.

13. Gordon W. Allport, *The Nature of Prejudice* (Boston, 1954), 20–23. This general process has also been called "external structuration." See: Hadley Cantril, *The Psychology of Social Movements* (New York, 1963), 51–62.

14. Traces of this fear can be found in many gentry placards. See, for example: YPCC, 4:16–17.

15. YPCC, 4:16, 22, 167. Kuang-tung-sheng, "Kuang-tung jen-min," 279 (see chap. 1, n. 22). Ch'en Hsi-ch'i, *Kuang-tung san-yuan-li*, 21 (see chap. 1, n. 22).

16. FO 17/154, Bonham–Palmerston, Desp. 51, April 23, 1849.

17. Paul A. Cohen, *China and Christianity: The Missionary Movement and the Growth of Chinese Antiforeignism, 1860–1870* (Cambridge, Mass., 1963), 90–91.

18. Karl W. Deutsch, *Nationalism and Social Communication: An Inquiry into the Foundations of Nationality* (New York, 1953), 23–25.

19. Liang T'ing-nan, 3 (see chap. 1, n. 2). Hsiao I-shan, *Ch'ing-tai*, 2:948; 3:45 (see chap. 1, n. 1). IWSM, TK 30:9-a.

20. Deutsch, *Nationalism*, 51.

21. Kuang-tung-sheng, "Kuang-tung jen-min," 290 (see chap. 1, n. 22).

22. IWSM, TK 79:43-a.

23. E. H. Schafer, *The Vermilion Bird: T'ang Images of the South* (Berkeley and Los Angeles, 1967), chap. 12.

24. Ch'en Hsü-ching, "Kuang-tung yü Chung-kuo" (Kwangtung and China), *Tung-fang tsa-chih*, 36.2:41–45 (Jan., 1939).

25. For a discussion of the relationship between contacts and anti-foreignism, see: Kung-chuan Hsiao, *Rural China: Imperial Control in the Nineteenth Century* (Seattle, 1960), 491.

26. E. J. Hobsbawm, *Primitive Rebels, Studies in Archaic Forms of Social Movement in the Nineteenth and Twentieth Centuries* (New York, 1963), 118–121.

27. Allport, *Nature of Prejudice*, 57–58.

28. *La Foule*, 84–91 (see n. 12 above). Hobsbawm, *Primitive Rebels*, chap. 5.

29. Kuang-tung-sheng, "Kuang-tung jen-min," 288 (see chap. 1, n. 22).

Notes to Chapter 6 (pp. 61–70)

1. A Ying, 739 (see chap. 1, n. 14).

2. IWSM, TK 29:24-b to 25-a.

3. YPCC, 4:17.

4. *Ibid.*, 4:24.

5. IWSM, TK 28:23-b; TK 29:23-b. W. H. Hall and W. D Bernard, *The Nemesis in China, Comprising a History of the Late War in That Country with an Account of the Colony of Hong Kong* (London, 1847), 162–3.

6. IWSM, TK 28:23-a to 24-b; TK 29:10-a and 24-a. FO 17/48, Elliot–Palmerston, Desp. 16, April 6, 1841. Hsia Hsieh, *Yueh-fen chi-shih* (A Record of the Miasma in Kwangtung and Kwangsi). 13 chüan (1869), 2:2-b. TKHC, 70:7-a. NHHC, 17:6-a.

7. YPCC, 4:23.

8. NHHC, 15:18-b to 19-a. Kuang-tung-sheng, "Kuang-tung jen-min," 294 (see chap. 1, n. 22).

9. Kuang-tung-sheng, "Kuang-tung jen-min," 293.

10. PYHC, 19:8-b.

11. NHHC, 19:10-b to 11-a.

12. Kuang-tung-sheng, "Kuang-tung jen-min," 293 and 295 (see chap. 1, n. 22).

13. D. A. Low, "The Advent of Populism in Buganda," *Comparative Studies in Society and History*, 4.4:433 (July, 1964).

14. CR, 4:414 (May, 1835–April, 1836).

15. NHHC, 15:18-b to 19-a. HSHC, 15:36-a to 37-a.

16. NHHC, 14:47-a.

17. *Ibid.*, 1:16-a to 18-a.

18. IWSM, TK 29:23-b to 24-a.

19. *Ibid.*, TK 67:38-a.

20. KCFC, 64:11-b.

21. IWSM, TK 40:27-a to 27-b.

22. *Ibid.*, TK 30:15-a to 16-a.

23. *Ibid.*, TK 29:22-a to 25-a. Citation from 22-a.

24. *Ibid.*, TK 31:4-b to 9-a.

25. *Ibid.*, TK 32:15-a to 17-a; TK 33:11-b to 14-a.

26. CR, 11:64 (Jan.–Dec., 1842); 12:328 (Jan.–Dec., 1843). IWSM, TK 40:27-b to 30-a.

27. Translated in CR, 11:576 (Jan.–Dec., 1842).

28. Mencius, *Chin hsin*, 2.14.

29. YPCC, 4:18.

30. Kuang-tung-sheng, "Kuang-tung jen-min," 292–3 (see chap. 1, n. 22). YPCC, 4:18–19.

31. YPCC, 4:18–19.

32. *Ibid.*

33. Ping-ti Ho, *The Ladder of Success in Imperial China: Aspects of Social Mobility, 1368–1953* (Cambridge, Mass., 1959), 35–37.

34. YPCC, 4:18–19.

35. *Ch'ing-shih* (History of the Ch'ing Dynasty) (Taipei, 1961), 4829. Hsieh Hsing-yao, *T'ai-p'ing t'ien-kuo shih-shih lun-ts'ung* (Collected Historical Essays on the Taiping Heavenly Kingdom) (Shanghai, 1935), 137–144. Chang Hsiang-wen, *Nan-yuan ts'ung-kao* (Collected Drafts from a Southern Garden) (Peiping, 1929–1935), 8:9-a to 11-b.

36. YPCC, 4:28–31.

37. IWSM, TK 67:10-b.

38. IWSM, TK 67:8-a to 10-a. Philip Kuhn, "The Militia in Nineteenth Century China" (Harvard University, 1963), 117–121.

39. IWSM, TK 67:36-b to 39-a.

40. Kuhn, "Militia," 115–117.

41. YPCC, 4:29–30. Kuhn, "Militia," 121–122.

42. J. F. Davis, *China, During the War and Since the Peace* (London, 1852), 2:29–33. TKHC, 34:23-b. Kuhn, "Militia," 122.

Notes to Chapter 7 (pp. 71–80)

1. There are several excellent accounts of the city question. Especially valuable are Nolde's thesis: John J. Nolde, "The 'Canton City Question,' 1842–1849: A Preliminary Investigation into Chinese Antiforeignism and Its Effect upon China's Diplomatic Relations with the West" (Cornell University, 1956); and his "The 'False Edict' of 1849," *Journal of Asian Studies*, 20:299–315 (1960–1961).

2. Nathan A. Pelcovits, *Old China Hands and the Foreign Office* (New York, 1948), 2–3. See also Arthur Redford, *Manchester Merchants and Foreign Trade, 1794–1853* (Manchester, 1934), chap. 9. Hsin-pao Chang, *Commissioner Lin and the Opium War* (Cambridge, Mass., 1964), chap. 2.

3. Pelcovits, *Old China Hands*, 14.

4. Liverpool East India and China Association, *China: Correspondence between*

the Liverpool East India and China Association and Lord Viscount Palmerston in Reference to the Hostile Proceedings at Canton in 1847 (Liverpool, n.d.), 12.

5. Pelcovits, *Old China Hands*, 4 and 16.

6. Elie Halevy, *The Age of Peel and Cobden: A History of the English People, 1841–1852* (London, 1947), chaps. 1–3.

7. Harley Farnsworth MacNair, *Modern Chinese History: Selected Readings* (Shanghai, 1923), sec. 27. Hosea Ballou Morse, *The International Relations of the Chinese Empire: The Period of Conflict, 1834–1860* (Shanghai, 1910), 356.

8. John K. Fairbank, *Trade and Diplomacy on the China Coast: The Opening of the Treaty Ports, 1842–1854* (Cambridge, Mass., 1953), 1:chap. 15.

9. Masataka Banno, *China and the West, 1858–1861: The Origins of the Tsungli Yamen* (Cambridge, Mass., 1964), 7.

10. Hsia Hsieh, *Chung-hsi chi-shih*, 6:12-a to 12-b (see chap. 1, n. 2). Kuang-tung-sheng, "Kuang-tung jen-min," 286–287 (see chap. 1, n. 22). CR, 10:527–528 (Jan.–Dec., 1841). IWSM, TK 20:15-b to 19-a.

11. Kung-chuan Hsiao, *Rural China: Imperial Control in the Nineteenth Century* (Seattle, 1960), 433–436. Morse, *International Relations*, 372.

12. Yen-yü Huang, "Viceroy Yeh Ming-ch'en and the Canton Episode (1858–1861)" *Harvard Journal of Asiatic Studies*, 6.1:47–48. Nolde, "Canton City Question," 183–193.

13. FO 17/59, Pottinger-Aberdeen, Desp. 71, December 20, 1842. W. H. Hall and W. D. Bernard, *The Nemesis in China, Comprising a History of the Late War in That Country with an Account of the Colony of Hong Kong* (London, 1847), 377. Morse, *International Relations*, 360–371. Fairbank, *Trade and Diplomacy*, 83.

14. For a good account of these events, see: Nolde, "False Edict."

15. FO 17/71, Pottinger-Aberdeen, Desp. 163, Dec. 14, 1843; Ch'i-ying to Pottinger, Incl. 1 in above dispatch. Morse, *International Relations*, 328.

16. W. C. Costin, *Great Britain and China, 1833–1860* (Oxford, 1937), 115–134.

17. Translated by the British in FO 228/51, MacGregor–Davis, Desp. 53, June 6, 1845.

18. *Ibid.*, Desp. 73, Sept. 27, 1845.

19. *Ibid.*, Desp. 93, Nov. 19, 1845.

20. *Ibid.*, Desp. 107, Dec. 18, 1845; Desp. 112, Dec. 31, 1845.

21. FO 228/61, MacGregor–Davis, Desp. 11, Jan. 22, 1846.

22. Hsia Hsieh, *Chung-hsi chi-shih*, 13:13-b (see chap. 1, n. 2).

23. FO 228/61, "Public Proclamation" translated by the British, Incl. 1, Desp. 8, Jan. 21, 1846.

24. Hsia Hsieh, *Chung-hsi chi-shih*, 13:2-b to 3-a (see chap. 1, n. 2). KCFC, 81:43-a. Hsiao I-shan, *Ch'ing-tai*, 3:458 (see chap. 1, n. 1). Lu Ch'in-ch'ih, "Ying-fa lien-chün chan-chü kuang-chou shih-mo" (A Complete Account of the Anglo-French Occupation of Canton), *Shih-hsüeh nien-pao*, 2.5:267 (Dec., 1938).

25. FO 228/61, MacGregor–Davis, Desp. 6, Jan. 16, 1846. Morse, *International Relations*, 377–378.

26. FO 228/61, Ch'i-ying's proclamation translated by the British, Incl. 1, Desp. 13, Jan. 23, 1846.

27. *Ibid.*, Ch'i-ying's proclamation, Desp. 25, March 25, 1846; Ch'i-ying's proclamation, Incl. 1, Desp. 23, Feb. 5, 1846.

28. Costin, *Great Britain*, 124.
29. IWSM, TK 75:13-a to 14-b.
30. *Ibid.*, TK 75:34-a to 39-a.
31. *Ibid.*, TK 75:35-b.
32. *Ibid.*
33. *Ibid.*, TK 75:36-b to 37-a.
34. *Ibid.*, TK 75:37-a.
35. *Ibid.*, TK 75:37-a to 37-b.
36. *Ibid.*, TK 75:37-b.
37. *Ibid.*, TK 75:38-b to 39-a.

Notes to Chapter 8 (pp. 81–89)

1. FO 17/120, Incls. 1, 4, and 5, in Desp. 1, July 9, 1846. John J. Nolde has examined this incident very carefully in his thesis, "The 'Canton City Question,' 1842–1849: A Preliminary Investigation into Chinese Antiforeignism and Its Effect upon China's Diplomatic Relations with the West" (Cornell University, 1956).
2. FO 17/120, Palmerston-Davis, Desp. 3, Oct. 3, 1846.
3. *Ibid.*, Desp. 5, Oct. 17, 1846.
4. *Ibid.*, Ch'i-ying–MacGregor, Incl. 1, Desp. 7, July 19, 1846.
5. *Ibid.*, Davis–Ch'i-ying, Incl. 2, Desp. 8, Aug. 14, 1846.
6. *Ibid.*, Incl. 5 and 6, Desp. 7, July 19, 1846.
7. *Ibid.*, "Proclamation of the Local Schools, dated September 15," translated by the British, Incl. 2, Desp. 12.
8. *Ibid.*, Ch'i-ying–MacGregor, Incl. 14, Desp. 1, July 12, 1846.
9. IWSM, TK 76:15-a to 15-b.
10. FO 17/120, Ch'i-ying–Davis, Incl. 1, Desp. 13, Sept. 23, 1846.
11. *Ibid.*, Incl. 1, Desp. 12, Sept. 17, 1846.
12. *Ibid.*, Davis–Ch'i-ying, Incl. 2, Desp. 9, Aug. 26.
13. *Ibid.*, Ch'i-ying–Davis, Incl. 1, Desp. 10, Sept. 6.
14. *Ibid.*, Ch'i-ying–Davis, Incl. 1, Desp. 13, Sept. 23.
15. *Ibid.*, Davis–Palmerston, Desp. 13, Sept. 26.
16. *Ibid.*, Incl. 3, Desp. 40, Feb. 8, 1847.
17. *Ibid.*, Incl. 3, Desp. 7, July 29, 1846; Incl. 40, Feb. 8, 1847.
18. John J. Nolde, "The 'False Edict' of 1849," *Journal of Asian Studies*, 20:299–315 (1960).
19. John Francis Davis, *China, During the War and Since the Peace* (London, 1852), 2: chap. 5. Nolde, "False Edict." W. C. Costin, *Great Britain and China, 1833–1860* (Oxford, 1937), 120–128.
20. FO 228/72, MacGregor–Davis, Desp. 64, May 20, 1847.
21. P'eng Tse-i, *et al.*, comp., *Chung-kuo chin-tai shou-kung-yeh shih tzu-liao, 1840–1949* (Historical Materials on Modern Chinese Handicraft Industries) (Peking, 1957), 1:509–511.
22. FO 228/73, MacGregor–Davis, Desp. 162, Aug. 10, 1847.
23. *Ibid.*, Desp. 252, and 253, Dec. 6, 1847.
24. *Ibid.*, Desp. 254, Dec. 7, 1847.

25. *Ibid.*, Incl. 1, Desp. 258, Dec. 9, 1847.
26. *Ibid.*
27. Costin, *Great Britain*, 125–134.
28. FO 228/73, Ch'i-ying's declarations of his arrests, Incl. 1, Desp. 261, Dec. 10, 1847.
29. *Ibid.*, MacGregor–Davis, Desp. 269, Dec. 27, 1847.
30. Translated in FO 228/85, MacGregor-Davis, Desp. 17, Jan 13, 1848.
31. IWSM, TK 78:26-b to 28-a.
32. *Ibid.*, 28-a to 28-b.
33. *Ibid.*, 28-b to 39-b.
34. *Ibid.*, 30-a.
35. *Ibid.*, 30-a to 32-a.
36. *Ibid.*, 32-a to 32-b.
37. *Ibid.*, 36-a. Also see: *Tung-hua ch'üan-lu* (Complete Records of the Tung-hua [Gate]), photolithographic reprint (Taipei, 1963), Tao-kuang 12:39-b. Hsiao I-shan, *Ch'ing-tai*, 3:359 (see chap. 1, n. 1).

Notes to Chapter 9 *(pp. 90–105)*

1. W. C. Costin, *Great Britain and China, 1833–1860* (Oxford, 1937) 134–152. John J. Nolde, "The 'False Edict' of 1849," *Journal of Asian Studies*, 20:299–315 (1960).
2. FO 17/144, Bonham–Palmerston, Desp. 69, July 20, 1848.
3. FO 17/145, Bonham–Palmerston, Desp. 113, Oct. 23, 1848.
4. FO 17/153, Hsü–Bonham, Incl. 1, Desp. 12, Dec. 29, 1848; Bonham–Hsü, Incl. 2 in above; Hsü-Bonham, Incl. 4 in above.
5. *Ibid.*, Bonham–Hsü, Incl. 3, Desp. 12, Jan. 20, 1849.
6. *Shih-liao hsün-k'an* (Historical Materials Published Thrice Monthly) (Peiping, 1931). Photolithographic reprint (Taipei, 1963), *ti*:339-b.
7. *Ibid.*, 340-b.
8. IWSM, TK 79:31-a.
9. *Ibid.*, 31-a to 32-b.
10. *Shih-liao*, *ti*:340-a to 340-b.
11. *Ibid.*
12. FO 17/153, Bonham–Palmerston, Desp. 22, Feb. 21, 1849. I have added the italics.
13. Nolde, "False Edict."
14. KCFC, 81:44-b. Yen-yü Huang, "Viceroy Yeh Ming-ch'en and the Canton Episode (1858–1861)," *Harvard Journal of Asiatic Studies*, 6.1:49, note 24. Hsiao I-shan, *Ch'ing-tai*, 3:460 (see chap. 1, n. 1). IWSM, TK 80:13-a.
15. Hsia Hsieh, *Chung-hsi chi-shih*, 13:4-b to 5-b (see chap. 1, n. 2).
16. CR, 18:162 (January–December, 1849). This was probably either the *Hai-kuang ssu* (Temple of the Light of the Sea), or the Temple of the God of the South Seas. See: Edward H. Schafer, *The Vermilion Bird: T'ang Images of the South* (Berkeley and Los Angeles, 1967).
17. CR, 18:163.
18. *Ibid.*, 217–218.

19. Hsia Hsieh, *Chung-hsi chi-shih*, 13:4-b to 5-b (see chap. 1, n. 2). "Ying-chi-li Kuang-tung ju-ch'eng shih-mo" (Complete Account of the British Entry into Canton), in Chao Chih-ch'ien, comp., *Yang-shih ch'ien-ch'i-pai erh-shih-chiu ho chai ts'ung-shu* (Collectanea from the Studio Where One Gazes in Respect at One Thousand, Seven Hundred and Twenty-nine Cranes) (photolithographic reprint, 1929), 4:2-b.

20. FO 17/153, Bonham–Palmerston, Desp. 28, March 19, 1849.

21. *Ibid.*

22. CR, 17:360–364 (Jan.–Dec., 1848).

23. *Shih-liao, ti*:341-b.

24. FO 228/99, Elmslie–Bonham, Desp. 36, March 5, 1849. CR, 18:167. Hsia Hsieh, *Chung-hsi chi-shih*, 13:14-a (see chap. 1, n. 2). IWSM, TK 80:14-a to 14-b. Liang Chia-pin, *Shih-san-hang*, 169 (see chap. 4, n. 24). FO 17/153, Bonham–Palmerston, Desp. 28, March 19, 1849.

25. FO 228/99, Elmslie–Bonham, Desp. 43, March 12, 1849.

26. IWSM, TK 80:14-a to 14-b.

27. WO 1/461, Elliot–Auckland, June 21, 1841.

28. FO 228/30, Lay–Pottinger, Desp. 22, Aug. 18, 1843.

29. FO 228/30, Lay–Pottinger, Desp. 65, Sept. 29, 1843.

30. *Ibid.*, Desp. 12, Nov. 14, 1843. FO 228/40, Lay–Pottinger, Desp. 1, Jan. 8, 1844.

31. FO 228/40, Lay–Pottinger, Desp. 2, Jan. 31, 1844. FO 228/51, MacGregor–Davis, Desp. 9, Feb. 4, 1845.

32. The consular reports for 1844 and 1845 are filled with references too numerous to cite here. For a contemporary's account of these monopolizing attempts, see John Francis Davis, *China, During the War and Since the Peace* (London, 1852), 2:48–109.

33. Elie Halevy, *The Age of Peel and Cobden: A History of the English People, 1841–1852* (London, 1947), 161–182.

34. Nathan A. Pelcovits, *Old China Hands and the Foreign Office* (New York, 1948), 12–13.

35. FO 228/73, MacGregor–Davis, Desp. 172, Aug. 18, 1847.

36. Hosea Ballou Morse, *The International Relations of the Chinese Empire: The Period of Conflict, 1834–1860* (Shanghai, 1910), 363–366. Lai Hsin–hsia, "Ti-i-tz'u ya-p'ien chan-cheng tui chung-kuo she-hui te ying-hsiang" (The Effects of the First Opium War on Chinese Society), in Lieh Tao, ed., *Ya-p'ien chan-cheng shih lun-wen chuan-chi* (A Collection of Essays on the History of the Opium War) (Peking, 1958), 114. CR, 12:331 (Jan.–Dec., 1843). Hsiao I-shan, *Ch'ing-tai*, 3:457 (see chap. 1, n. 1). Yi-faai Laai, "The Part Played by Pirates of Kwang-tung and Kwangsi Provinces in the T'ai-P'ing Insurrection," University of California, Berkeley, 1950), 43–48; 54–55.

37. FO 17/154, Incl. 1, Desp. 37, March 28, 1849. Morse, *International Relations*, 366.

38. Morse, *International Relations*, 313.

39. Liang Chia-pin, *Shih-san hang*, 168–169 (see chap. 4, n. 24).

40. Henri Cordier, "Les Marchands hanistes de Canton," *T'oung Pao*, 2.3:309–311.

41. G. William Skinner, *Chinese Society in Thailand: An Analytical History* (Ithaca, 1957), 42.

42. FO 228/143, Incl. 1, Desp. 169, Oct. 28, 1852.

43. FO 228/99, Elmslie–Bonham, Desp. 34, Feb. 28, 1849; Desp. 41, March 10, 1849.

44. Translated in FO 17/153, Bonham–Palmerston, Desp. 28, March 19, 1849

45. Hsia Hsieh, *Chung-hsi chi-shih*, 13:13-b to 14-a (see chap. 1, n. 2).

46. FO 17/153, Bonham–Palmerston, Desp. 32, March 22, 1849.

47. FO 17/154, Bonham–Palmerston, Desp. 40, March 30, 1849.

48. IWSM, TK 79:36-b to 38-b.

49. *Ibid.*, 39–b to 40-b. Nolde, "False Edict," 310.

50. IWSM, TK 79:43-a to 46-a.

51. *Ibid.*, 46-a to 47-a.

52. *Ibid.*

53. *Ibid.*, 47-a.

54. FO 17/154, Bonham–Palmerston, Desp. 45, April 18, 1849; Hsu–Bonham, Incl. 1 in above, April 1.

55. Nolde, "False Edict," 310–313.

56. FO 17/154, Bonham–Palmerston, Desp. 41, March 31, 1849.

57. *Ibid.*, Bonham–Hsü, Incl. 2, April 2, Desp. 45.

58. *Ibid.*, Hsü–Bonham, Incl. 3, April 6, Desp. 45.

59. *Ibid.*, Bonham–Hsü, Incl. 4, April 9, Desp. 45.

60. CR, 18:280. Hsia Hsieh, *Chung-hsi chi-shih*, 13:5-a (see chap. 1, n. 2). The dispatch referred to can be found in IWSM, TK 80:12-b to 13-b.

61. Harley Farnsworth MacNair, *Modern Chinese History: Selected Readings* (Shanghai, 1923), 229. Also see: IWSM, TK 80:14-b. Hsia Hsieh, *Chung-hsi chi-shih*, 13:6-a (see chap. 1, n. 2).

62. Translated in FO 17/155, Incl. 1, Desp. 66, May 18, 1849. This was a printed pamphlet, handed out on May 11 to regular subscribers of the *Peking Gazette*, explaining why the tablet was being erected to Hsü.

63. IWSM, TK 80:10-b.

64. Morse, *International Relations*, 398–399.

65. FO 17/155, Bonham–Palmerston, Incl. 1, Desp. 71, May 21, 1849; and Incl. 1, Desp. 78, May 24.

66. FO 228/112, Bowring–Bonham, Desp. 4, Jan. 8, 1850.

67. *Ibid.*, Desp. 10, Jan. 21, 1850.

68. FO 228/113, Meadows' report, Incl. 1, Desp. 179, Dec. 28, 1850.

69. "Ch'ing-ch'ao shih-liao" (Historical Materials on the Ch'ing Dynasty), *Ch'ing-ch'ao yeh-shih ta-kuan* (A Review of the Apocryphal History of the Ch'ing Dynasty) (Taipei, 1959), 177.

70. *Ibid.*, 176. Hsia Hsieh, *Chung-hsi chi-shih*, 13:6-a to 6-b (see chap. 1, n. 2).

71. Costin, *Great Britain*, 152.

Notes to Chapter 10 (pp. 109–116)

1. R. H. Tawney, *Land and Labour in China* (London, 1964), 32.

2. This information is largely derived from Han-seng Ch'en, *Agrarian Problems*

in Southernmost China (Shanghai, 1936), chap. 2. Ch'en's ideological bias probably caused him to overestimate the extent of clan ownership. Professor Eberhard has pointed out to me that the Japanese scholar Makino gives only 33 percent of all land in Kwangtung as clan land. There is a large repository of official land documents for Kwangtung at the Central Provincial Library's archives in Hsin-tien, Taiwan. These, I believe, date from 1926, but are so voluminous (and as yet unclassified) that they could make a book unto themselves.

3. Maurice Freedman, *Lineage Organization in Southeastern China* (London, 1958), 17, 27–30. Kung-chuan Hsiao, *Rural China: Imperial Control in the Nineteenth Century* (Seattle, 1960), 329. Hsiao-t'ung Fei, "Peasantry and Gentry: An Interpretation of Chinese Social Structure and Its Changes," in R. Bendix and S. Lipset, eds., *Class, Status and Power: A Reader in Social Stratification* (London, 1954), 639–640.

4. Freedman, *Lineage Organization*, 54. Myron Cohen, "The Hakka or 'Guest People': Linguistic Diversity as a Sociocultural Variable in Southeastern China" (M.A. thesis, Columbia University, 1963), 57–59. Everett E. Hagen, *On the Theory of Social Change: How Economic Growth Begins* (Homewood, Ill., 1962), 68.

5. Hsien-chin Hu, *The Common Descent Group in China and Its Functions* (New York, 1948), 90.

6. Wolfram Eberhard, *Social Mobility in Traditional China* (Leiden, 1962), 224.

7. Cited and Translated in Hsiao, *Rural China*, 354–355. Also see: 362–363.

8. Hu, *Descent Group*, Appendix 60. Professor Eberhard has pointed out that interclan fights were also often settled by common meetings in local Kuan-ti temples.

9. Hu, *Descent Group*, Appendix 10.

10. Daniel Kulp, *Country Life in South China: The Sociology of Familism* (New York, 1925), 1:114–115. Liu Hsing-t'ang, "Fu-chien te hsüeh-tsu tsu-chih" (Clan Organization in Fukien), *Shih-huo*, 4.8:43 (Sept. 16, 1936).

11. Freedman, *Lineage Organization*, 8. J. Scarth, *Twelve Years in China: The People, the Rebels, and the Mandarins* (Edinburgh, 1860), 66.

12. CR, 4:412–415 (May, 1835–April, 1836); 6:496 (May, 1837–April, 1838). Thomas Taylor Meadows, *The Chinese and Their Rebellions* (London, 1856), 47, note.

13. Hsiao, *Rural China*, 364. Freedman, *Lineage Organization*, 5, 105–113. Hsiao, *Rural China*, 365. Hu, *Descent Group*, 94.

14. Citing Lin Yueh-hua, in Freedman, *Lineage Organization*, 65.

15. *Ibid.*, 78.

16. *Ibid.*, 47.

17. *Ibid.*, 48.

18. Hu, *Descent Group*, Appendix 59.

19. Freedman, *Lineage Organization*, 91.

20. See, for example: Ping-ti Ho, *The Ladder of Success in Imperial China: Aspects of Social Mobility, 1368–1911* (New York, 1962), chap. 5.

21. Hu, *Descent Group*, 17–18.

22. For a description of clan leaders, see: Kulp, *Country Life*, 110–117; Olga Lang, *Chinese Family and Society* (New Haven, 1946), 175.

23. For a description of this process occurring later in Fukien, see: Freedman, *Lineage Organization,* 68.

24. Ch'en, *Agrarian Problems,* 40.

25. Seiji Imabori, "Shindai nōsen kikō no kindaika ni tsuite" (On the Modernization of Rural Organizations in the Ch'ing Period), *Rekishigaku kenkyū,* 191 and 192. This article is discussed and refuted in Sasaki Masaya, "Shun-te-hsien kyōshin to tōkai juroku-sa" (The Gentry of Shun-te District and the Sixteen Delta Lands of the Eastern Sea), *Kindai chūgoku kenkyū,* 3:163–232. For a discussion of the relationship between secret societies and lineages, see: Myron Cohen, "Hakka," 6.

26. E. J. Hobsbawm, *Primitive Rebels: Studies in Archaic Forms of Social Movement in the 19th and 20th Centuries* (New York, 1963), 4.

Notes to Chapter 11 (pp. 117–125)

1. TKHC, 33:20-a to 22-b; 34:22-b. STHC, 23:3-b. KCFC, 81:30-a. IWSM, TK 5:13-b to 17-a. CR, 1:80 (May, 1832–April, 1833). Henri Cordier, *Les sociétés secrètes chinoises* (Paris, 1888), 4.

2. Hsiao I-shan, *Chin-tai pi-mi she-hui shih-liao* (Historical Materials on Modern Secret Societies) (Peiping, 1935), 2:6-a and 10-a.

3. Cordier, *Sociétés secrètes,* 13. B. Favre, *Les Sociétés secrètes en Chine* (Paris, 1933), chap. 5. CR, 14:59–69 (Jan.–Dec., 1845). J. S. M. Ward and W. G. Stirling, *The Hung Society, or the Society of Heaven and Earth* (London, 1925–1926), chap. 5. Hsiao I-shan, *Pi-mi she-hui,* 2:1-b to 2-a.

4. Hsiao I-shan, *Ch'ing-tai,* 3:2–4 (see chap. 1, n. 1). C. K. Yang, *Religion and Chinese Society: A Study of Contemporary Social Functions of Religion and Some of their Historical Factors* (Berkeley and Los Angeles, 1961), 220. Wei Yuan, *Sheng-wu chi* (A Record of Imperial Military Exploits) (1842). Photolithographic reprint (Taipei, 1963), 7:41-a to 45-a. CR, 1:29–31, and 207. Charles Gutzlaff, *China Opened, or a Display of the Topography, etc., of the Chinese Empire* (London, 1838), 1:157–158. J. J. M. de Groot, *Sectarianism and Religious Persecution in China: A Page in the History of Religions* (Amsterdam, 1903), 2:485–550. Kung-chuan Hsiao, *Rural China: Imperial Control in the Nineteenth Century* (Seattle, 1960), 291–293. Hsiao I-shan, *Pi-mi she-hui,* 2nd chüan. Paul Pelliot, review of Ward and Stirling's *The Hung Society,* in *T'oung Pao* 25:444–448 (1928).

5. Translated in Ward and Stirling, *The Hung Society,* 1:61–63.

6. *Ibid.,* 1:72. Also see: Gustave Schlegel, *Thian Ti Hwui, the Hung League* (Batavia, 1866), part 6.

7. Translated in Ward and Stirling, *The Hung Society,* 1:71.

8. C. K. Yang, "The Functional Relationship Between Chinese Thought and Chinese Religion," in J. K. Fairbank, ed., *Chinese Thought and Institutions* (Chicago, 1957), 286. Morton H. Fried, *Fabric of Chinese Society* (New York, 1953), 230.

9. Lucien Bianco, "Classes laborieuses et classes dangereuses dans la Chine Impériale au XIXe siècle," *Annales, Economies, Sociétés et Civilisations,* 17.6:1175–1182 (Dec., 1962).

10. Marion Levy, *The Family Revolution in Modern China* (Cambridge, Mass., 1949), 58–59.

11. Translated in Ward and Stirling, *The Hung Society*, 1:58. Also see: 1: chap. 4; and 3: chap. 10.

12. For the distinction between "revolutionary" and "revolutionist," see: Byran A. Wilson, "Millennialism in Comparative Perspective," *Comparative Studies in Society and History*, 6.1:95 (Oct., 1963).

13. Yuji Muramatsu, "Some Themes in Chinese Rebel Ideologies," in, A. F. Wright, ed., *Confucian Persuasion*, (Stanford, 1960), 241–267.

14. *Description of the City of Canton* (Canton, 1839), 10–13.

15. Cited in: Hsiao I-shan, *Pi-mi she-hui*, 1:3-a.

16. G. William Skinner, *Chinese Society in Thailand: An Analytical History* (Ithaca, 1957), chap. 4. G. W. Skinner, *Leadership and Power in the Chinese Community of Thailand* (Ithaca, 1958), 5. Maurice Freedman, "Immigrants and Associations: Chinese in Nineteenth-Century Singapore," *Comparative Studies in Society and History*, 3.1:33 (Oct., 1960).

17. For an analysis of "rational perpetuative nativism," see: Ralph Linton, "Nativistic Movements," in William A. Lessa and Evon Z. Vogt, eds., *Reader in Comparative Religion: An Anthropological Approach* (Evanston, 1958), 469.

18. Thomas T. Meadows, *The Chinese and Their Rebellions* (London, 1856), 117. E. J. Hobsbawm, *Primitive Rebels, Studies in Archaic Forms of Social Movement in the Nineteenth and Twentieth Centuries* (New York, 1963), chap. 2.

19. Hsia Hsieh, *Yueh-fen chi-shih*, 1:2-a (see chap. 6, n. 6).

20. Yi-faai Laai, "The Part Played by the Pirates of Kwang-tung and Kwangsi Provinces in the T'ai-P'ing Insurrection" (University of California, Berkeley, 1950), 18–19.

21. De Groot, *Sectarianism*, 1:8. C. K. Yang, *Religion and Chinese Society*, 176.

22. Ernst Troeltsch, *The Social Teaching of the Christian Churches* (New York, 1960), 1:331.

23. Muramatsu, "Rebel Ideologies."

24. *Ibid.* Also see: Norman Cohn, "Medieval Millenarianism: Its Bearing on the Comparative Study of Millenarian Movements," *Comparative Studies in Society and History*, Suppl. II, 37.

25. C. K. Yang, *Religion in Chinese Society*, 176, 223, 235.

Notes to Chapter 12 (pp. 126–131)

1. Hatano Yoshihiro, "Taihei Tengoku ni kansuru nisan no mondai ni tsuite" (On Certain Problems Relating to the Taiping Heavenly Kingdom), *Rekishigaku kenkyū* (Historical Research), 150:32–42 (Mar., 1951).

2. IWSM, TK 25:32-a to 33-a. Yi-faai Laai, "The Part Played by the Pirates of Kwang-tung and Kwangsi Provinces in the T'ai-P'ing Insurrection" (University of California, Berkeley, 1950), 178. Hsiao I-shan, *Ch'ing-tai*, 3:5 (see chap. 1, n. 1).

3. Laai, "Pirates of Kwangtung," 62.

4. Hsieh Hsing-yao, *T'ai-p'ing t'ien-kuo ch'ien-hou kuang-hsi te fan-ch'ing yun-tung* (The Anti-Ch'ing Movement in Kwangsi Before and After the Taiping Rebellion) (Peking, 1950), pages 1–13. Arthur Hummel, *Eminent Chinese of the Ch'ing Period* (Washington, D.C., 1943 and 1944), 136–137. Laai, "Pirates of Kwangtung," 107–128.

5. Laai, "Pirates of Kwangtung," 106. Jean Chesneaux, "La Revolution Taiping d'après quelques travaux récents," *Revue Historique*, 209:33–57 (Jan./Mar 1953).

6. Laai, "Pirates of Kwangtung," chap. 3. Hsieh Hsing-yao, *Fan-ch'ing*, 14–15.

7. Hatano Yoshihiro, "Taihei Tengoku," 34–35.

8. George Shepperson, "The Comparative Study of Millenarian Movements," *Comparative Studies in Society and History*, Suppl. II (1962).

9. This, of course, is Mannheim's theory.

10. Theodore Hamberg, *The Chinese Rebel Chief Hung-Siu-Tsuen and the Origin of the Insurrection in China* (London, 1855), 14–23.

11. *Ibid.*, 34. Hamberg's translation.

12. *Ibid.*, 37. Hamberg's translation.

13. Thomas T. Meadows, *The Chinese and Their Rebellions* (London, 1856), chaps. 6 and 7.

14. Letter to Bonham, cited: Lindesay Brine, *The Taiping Rebellion in China* (London, 1862), 171.

15. Hsiao I-shan, *T'ai-p'ing t'ien-kuo ts'ung-shu* (Collected Writings of the Taiping Heavenly Kingdom) (Taipei, 1956), 1:92.

16. Hamberg, *Insurrection*, 46.

17. Hatano Yoshihiro, "Taihei Tengoku," 38. For another example of the connection between racism and messianism, see: Justus M. Van der Kroef, "Racial Messiahs," in E. T. Thompson and E. C. Hughes, eds., *Race, Individual and Collective Behavior* (Glencoe, Ill., 1958), 357–364.

18. Wang Chung-min, *et al.*, eds., *T'ai-p'ing t'ien-kuo* (The Taiping Heavenly Kingdom) (Shanghai, 1952), 2:624.

19. Hatano Yoshihiro, "Taihei Tengoku," 38–40.

Notes to Chapter 13 (pp. 132–138)

1. FO 228/113, Meadows' report, Incl. 1, Desp. 97, Aug. 16, 1850; Desp. 112, Sept. 3, 1850. FO 228/126, Meadows' reports, Inclosures in Desp. 9, Jan. 7, 1851. FO 228/127, Meadows' report, Incl. 1, Desp. 114, July 12, 1851; Desp. 97, June 14, 1851; Desp. 117, July 14, 1851; Desp. 143, Aug. 26, 1851; Desp. 152, Sept. 26, 1851; Desp. 174, Oct. 25, 1851; Desp. 192, Nov. 27, 1851.

2. FO 17/188, Parkes' report, Incl. 1, Desp. 42, March 29, 1852. FO 228/143, Parkes' report, Incl. 1, Desp. 111, July 21, 1852; Desp. 116, Aug. 10, 1852.

3. FO 228/143, Desp. 124, Aug. 21, 1852; Desp. 130, Aug. 27, 1852; Desp. 134, Sept. 1, 1852; Desp. 140, Sept. 11, 1852; Desp. 146, Sept. 23, 1852. FO 228/156, Parkes' report, Incl. 1, Desp. 29, Feb. 21, 1853.

4. Hsüeh Fu-ch'eng's account, cited in: Yen-yü Huang, "Viceroy Yeh Ming-ch'en and the Canton Episode (1858–1861)," *Harvard Journal of Asiatic Studies* (Mar., 1941), 51.

5. FO 17/190, Parkes' report, Incl. 2, Desp. 57, June 19, 1852. FO 17/191, Medhurst's report, Incl. 1, Desp. 84, July 22, 1852. FO 17/199, Bowring–Malmesbury, Desp. 16, Jan. 27, 1853. FO 228/156, Parkes–Bonham, Desp. 44, April 14, 1853. FO 682/288/2, "Account Book of the Government of Kwangtung Province, Income and Expenditures for Campaign versus Taiping, 1854–1857" (Chinese text). Edwin George Beal, Jr., *The Origin of Likin (1853–1864)* (Cambridge, Mass., 1958), 14.

6. FO 228/126, Meadows' report, Incl. 1, Desp. 57, March 17, 1851; Desp. 64, April 19, 1851. FO 17/193, Bowring–Malmesbury, Desp. 157, Nov. 11, 1852.

7. FO 17/187, Medhurst's report, Incl. 1, Desp. 31, Feb. 27, 1852. FO 17/188, Parkes' report, Incl. 3, Desp. 10, April 22, 1852. FO 17/191, Meadows' report, Incl. 1, Desp. 84, July 22, 1852. FO 228/158, Parkes–Bonham, Desp. 141, Oct. 8, 1853.

8. George W. Cooke, *China: Being the Times' Special Correspondence from China in the Years 1857–1858* (London, 1858), 435–436. KCFC, 81:41-a to 41-b. TKHC, 34:22-a. CR, 12:332. Also see: FO 17/234, Wade's translation of Tseng Wang-yen's memorial, Incl. 1, Desp. 331, Oct. 13, 1855.

9. HSHC, 15:33-a.

10. FO 17/234, Wade's translation of Tseng Wang-yen's memorial, Incl. 1, Desp. 331, Oct. 13, 1855. HSHC, 15:33-a. TKHC, 34:22-b. KCFC, 81:42-b.

11. FO 17/203, Bonham–Clarendon, Desp. 63, July 6, 1853. FO 228/156, Elmslie–Bowring, Desp. 118, Jan. 27, 1853.

12. FO 228/156, Parkes–Bonham, Desp. 44, April 4, 1853; Desp. 54, April 26, 1853. FO 17/202, Medhurst's report, Incl. 1, Desp. 47, June 5, 1853. FO 17/204, Bonham–Clarendon, Desp. 111, Sept. 27, 1853. FO 228/158, Parkes' report, Incl. 1, Desp. 124, Sept. 5, 1853. FO 17/203, Bonham–Clarendon, Desp. 72, July 28, 1853. FO 17/205, Bonham–Clarendon, Desp. 116, Oct. 10, 1853.

13. FO 17/204, Desp. 111, Sept. 27, 1853. FO 228/158, Parkes' report, Incl. 1, Desp. 124, Sept. 5, 1853.

14. FO 17/205, Bonham–Clarendon, Desp. 124, Oct. 26, 1853. FO 228/158, Parkes–Bonham, Desp. 141 (Oct. 8), 153 (Oct. 25), 162 (Nov. 9), 170 (Nov. 25); Elmslie–Bonham, Desp. 180, Dec. 24, 1853. FO 228/172, Parkes' report, Incl. 1, Desp. 5, Jan. 9, 1854; Desp. 16, Jan. 25, 1854.

15. KCFC, 82:3-b. J. Scarth, *Twelve Years in China: The People, the Rebels, and the Mandarins* (Edinburgh, 1850), 235–240. Huang, "Yeh Ming-ch'en," 53, n. 36.

Notes to Chapter 14 (pp. 139–148)

1. This account in general is based on: KCFC, 82:3-b to 24-a; and a comparative analysis of other gazetteers, outlined in the appendix. Unless otherwise cited, however, the prefectural gazetteer is my basic source for this section. Unfortunately I have been unable to obtain a copy of Ch'en K'un's *Yueh-tung chiao fei chi-lüeh* (Record of the Suppression of Rebels in Kwangtung) (Canton, 1871).

2. STHC, 23:5-b.

3. FO 228/172, Elmslie–Bonham, Desp. 73, June 14, 1854.

4. FO 17/215, Morrison's report, Incl. 1, Desp. 112, July 20, 1854.

5. FO 228/172, Robertson–Bowring, Desp. 86, July 24, 1854.

6. NHHC, 14:48-a. Arthur Hummel, *Eminent Chinese of the Ch'ing Period* (Washington, D.C., 1943 and 1944), 501–502.

7. FO 17/215, Morrison's report, Incl. 1, Desp. 112, July 31, 1854. Kuo T'ing-i, *T'ai-p'ing t'ien-kuo shih-shih jih-chih* (A Calendar of Historical Events of the Taiping Rebellion) (Taipei, 1963), 326–328.

8. J. Scarth, *Twelve Years in China: The People, the Rebels, and the Mandarins* (Edinburgh, 1860), 227.

9. NHHC, 17:14-b.

10. FO 17/215, Caldwell's translation, Incl. 1, Desp. 123, Aug. 26, 1854.

11. *Ibid.*, Morrison's report, Incl. 1, Desp. 112, Aug. 5, 1854. FO 17/216, Morrison's report, Incl. 1, Desp. 135, Aug. 31, 1854; Consular Memo, Incl. 1, Desp. 142, Sept. 8, 1854.

12. FO 17/216, Robertson–Hammond, Desp. 17, Oct. 10, 1854; Morrison's report, Incl. 1, Desp. 4, Sept. 25, 1854.

13. FO 17/217, Morrison's report, Incl. 1, Desp. 59, Nov. 10, 1854.

14. *Ibid.*, Morrison's report, Incl. 2, Desp. 59, Nov. 10, 1854; Robertson–Hammond, Desp. 75, Nov. 25, 1854. Also, Morrison's report, unnumbered Inclosure in same.

15. FO 228/172, Robertson–Bowring, Desp. 86, July 24; Desp. 91, Aug. 17, 1854. FO 17/226, Morrison's report, Incl. 12, Desp. 8, Jan. 4, 1855. FO 228/189, Bird's report, Incl. 1, Desp. 3, Jan. 4, 1855.

16. FO 17/218, Memo from Ch'en Hsien-liang to Bowring, Incl. 2, Desp. 235, Dec. 23, 1854.

17. FO 17/226, Morrison's report, Incl. 12, Desp. 8, Jan. 4, 1855.

18. FO 228/172, Robertson–Bowring, Desp. 84, July 18, 1854.

19. FO 17/218, Ch'en–Bowring, Incls. 1 and 2, Desp. 235, Dec. 23, 1854.

20. FO 17/227, Ch'en–Bowring, Incl. 1, Desp. 86, Feb. 14, 1855.

21. *Ibid.*, Bowring–Clarendon, Desp. 86, Feb. 14, 1855.

22. FO 17/228, Bowring–Clarendon, Desp. 108, Feb. 28, 1855.

23. FO 17/202, Parkes–Bonham, Incl. 2, Desp. 45, May 27, 1853.

24. Hsüeh Fu-ch'eng's account, cited: Yen-yü Huang, "Viceroy Yeh Ming-ch'en and the Canton Episode (1858–1861)," *Harvard Journal of Asiatic Studies* (Mar., 1941), 53, n. 37.

25. FO 17/218, Inclosures 1 to 4, Desp. 226, Dec. 6, 1854.

26. *Ibid.*, Bowring–Clarendon, Desp. 230, Dec. 11, 1854. For copies of Yeh and Bowring's correspondence, see Inclosures 1 and 2 in same.

27. FO 17/226, Robertson–Bowring, Incl. 1, Desp. 8, Jan. 4, 1855; Bowring–Clarendon, Desp. 31, Jan. 15; Morrison's report, Incl. 1, Desp. 33, Jan. 15.

28. FO 17/218, Morrison's report, Incl. 1, Desp. 231, Dec. 11, 1854. FO 228/189, Robertson–Bowring, Desp. 35, Jan. 23, 1855. FO 17/228, Robertson–Bowring, Incl. 1, Desp. 130, March 9, 1855. FO 228/190, Pedder's memo, Incl. 1, unnumbered Despatch, March 13, 1855.

29. FO 17/226, Morrison's report, Incl. 1, Desp. 33, Jan. 15, 1855; Bowring–Clarendon, Desp. 36, Jan. 19; Desp. 39, Jan. 20. FO 17/227, Pedder's report, Incl. 1, Desp. 87, Feb. 14, 1855.

Notes to Chapter 15 (pp. 149–156)

1. G. W. Cooke, *China: Being the Times' Special Correspondence from China in the Years 1857–1858* (London, 1858), 406–407. FO 17/231, Morrison's report, Incl. 1, Desp. 208, June 9, 1855. FO 17/233, Bowring–Clarendon, Desp. 297, Sept. 13, 1855. J. Scarth, *Twelve Years in China: The People, the Rebels, the Mandarins* (Edinburgh, 1860), 235–240.

2. IWSM, HF 19:16-a.

3. Cooke, *China*, 407.

4. FO 17/234, Wade's report, Incl. 1, Desp. 331, Oct. 13, 1855. FO 17/229, Morrison's report, Incl. 1, Desp. 15, April 15, 1855. FO 17/231, Morrison's report, Incl. 1, Desp. 208, June 9, 1855. FO 17/235, Morrison's report, Incl. 1, Desp. 368, Nov. 14, 1855.

5. Philip Kuhn, "The Militia in Nineteenth Century China" (Harvard University, 1963), 15–20, 126–140. Hsiao I-shan, *Ch'ing-tai*, 3:115–119 (see chap. 1, n. 1). Lo Erh-kang, "Ch'ing-chi ping wei-chiang-yu te ch'i-yuan" (Origin of Personal Armies During the Ch'ing Period), *Chung-kuo she-hui ching-chi shih chi-k'an* (Collectanea on the Economic and Social History of China), 5.2:235–250 (June, 1937).

6. Max Weber, in H. H. Gerth and C. W. Mills, eds., *From Max Weber: Essays on Sociology* (London, 1948), 183–184.

7. FO 228/157, Parkes' report, Incl. 1, Desp. 101, July 21, 1853.

8. STHC, 20:14-a; 23:6-a to 6-b.

9. *Ibid.*, 18:6-b.

10. *Ibid.*, 18:2-a to 2-b.

11. *Ibid.*, 3:1-a; 23:7-a to 7-b.

12. This description is based on: Sasaki Masaya, "Shun-te-hsien" (see chap. 10, n. 25). Also see: Makino Tatsumi, *Shina kazoku kenkyū* (A Study of the Chinese Clan) (Tokyo, 1944), 575.

13. STHC, 18:6-a; 23:9-b. The following discussion, unless otherwise indicated, is based on information given in Sasaki Masaya, "Shun-te-hsien."

14. STHC, 3:5-a to 6-a; 23:14-b.

15. Cited in: Sasaki Masaya, "Shun-te-hsien," 175.

16. Kuo-T'ing-i, *T'ai-p'ing t'ien-kuo*, 816 (see chap. 14, n. 7). TKHC, 35:13-b.

17. M. Freedman, *Lineage Organization in Southeastern China* (London, 1958), 76. R. H. Tawney, *Land and Labour in China* (London, 1964), 37. Kung-chuan Hsiao, *Rural China: Imperial Control in the Nineteenth Century* (Seattle, 1960), 408. Han-seng Chen, *Agrarian Problems in Southernmost China* (Shanghai, 1936), 47, 63.

18. T'ai-ch'u Liao, "School Land: A Problem of Educational Finance," *Yenching Journal of Social Studies*, 2.2:212–233 (Feb., 1940).

Notes to Chapter 16 (pp. 159–163)

1. FO 17/263, Placard dated Dec. 24, 1856, Incl. 2, Desp. 6, Jan. 3, 1857.

2. *Ibid.*, Wade's report, Incl. 1, Desp. 6, Jan. 3, 1857.

3. FO 17/272, Ward's report, Incl. 1, Desp. 407, Oct. 21, 1857.

4. *Ibid.*

5. IWSM, HF 17:44-b. This is also translated in: Yen-yü Huang, "Viceroy Yeh Ming-ch'en and the Canton Episode (1858–1861)," *Harvard Journal of Asiatic Studies* (Mar., 1941), 85, n. 151. FO 17/271, Parkes' report, Incl. 1, Desp. 362, Aug. 24, 1857; Wade's report, Incl. 1, Desp. 319, July 10, 1857. FO 228/240, Parkes–Elgin, July 25, 1857. FO 17/272, Chinese Secretary's Memo, Incl. 1, Desp. 370, Sept. 2, 1857; Desp. 385, Sept. 21; Desp. 390, Oct. 5; Desp. 399, Oct. 13; Wade's report, Desp. 407, Oct. 21.

6. G. W. Cooke, *China: Being the Times' Special Correspondence from China in the Years 1857–1858* (London, 1858), 16–42.

7. FO 17/271, Wade's report, Incl. 1, Desp. 319, July 10, 1857. FO 228/240, Parkes–Elgin, July 25, 1857.

8. FO 17/276, Elgin–Clarendon, Desp. 46, Sept. 24, 1857.

9. NHHC, 14:48-b. PYHC, 20:25-b. FO 17/271, Morrisons' report, Incl. 1, Desp. 336, July 25, 1857; Parkes' report, Incl. 2, Desp. 336, July 25. FO 17/277, Wade–Bowring, Incl. 1, Desp. 75, Dec. 9, 1857.

10. Stanley Lane-Poole, *The Life of Sir Harry Parkes* (London, 1894), 1: chaps. 12–13.

11. Hsia Ting-yü, "Ying-chi-li chan-chü kuang-chou chih i-shih-liao" (Historical Materials on the English Occupation of Canton), in *Kuo-li chung-shan ta-hsüeh yü-yen li-shih hsueh yen-chiu-so chou-k'an* (Weekly Journal of the Research Institute of Philology and History of National Chung-shan University), 10.110:45–48 (Dec. 18, 1929).

12. *Ibid.*

13. Arthur Hummel, *Eminent Chinese of the Ch'ing Period* (Washington, D.C., 1943 and 1944), 904–905.

14. Hsüeh Fu-ch'eng, cited in Huang, "Yeh Ming-ch'en," 71 and 74. IWSM, HF 17:38-a.

15. Liang Chia-pin, *Shih-san hang*, 198 (see chap. 4, n. 24).

16. *Ibid.*, 170. Huang, "Yeh Ming-ch'en," 75–82.

17. Lu Ch'in-ch'ih, "Ying-fa," 287 (see chap. 7, n. 24).

18. Laurence Oliphant, *Narrative of the Earl of Elgin's Mission to China and Japan in the Years 1857, 1858, 1859* (London, 1859), 1:151.

19. Lu Ch'in-ch'ih, "Ying-fa," 287 (see chap. 7, n. 24).

20. Oliphant, *Elgin's Mission*, 1:148–157.

21. FO 228/252, Regulations to be observed by the Chinese Commissioners in Canton, Incl. 3, Desp. 11, Jan. 12, 1858.

22. *Ibid.*

23. Oliphant, *Elgin's Mission*, 1:169.

24. Huang, "Yeh Ming-ch'en," 82, n. 142.

25. *Ibid.*, 77–78.

Notes to Chapter 17 (pp. 164–167)

1. *Ch'ing-shih* (History of the Ch'ing Dynasty) (Taipei, 1961), 4818–4819. STHC, 23:16-b to 23-a.

2. *Ch'ing-shih*, 4589–4590.

3. IWSM, HF 17:44-b.
4. STHC, 23:8-b. Hsia Hsieh, *Chung-hsi chi-shih*, 13:8-b (see chap. 1, n. 2).
5. TKHC, 72:18-b; 90:10-b. STHC, 23:9-a.
6. IWSM, HF 26:34-a.
7. FO 17/263, Placard dated Dec. 24, 1856, Incl. 2, Desp. 6, Jan. 3, 1857; *ibid.*, Wade's report, Incl. 1, Desp. 6, Jan. 3.
8. FO 17/267, Inclosures, Desp. 181, April 14, 1857. This dispatch encloses fifty letters to and from the Ch'en brothers and Su T'ing-k'uei. They were seized by Commodore Elliot when he captured a "militia" junk.
9. STHC, 18:14-b; 23:9-a; 2:34-b.
10. *Ibid.*, 18:4-b.
11. *Ibid.*, 3:4-b; 23:9-b. FO 228/284, Parkes' Report, Incl. 1, Desp. 112, May 21, 1860.
12. NHHC, 14:35-a to 35-b.
13. STHC, 23:9-b. Hsia Hsieh, *Chung-hsi chi-shih*, 13:21-b (see chap. 1, n. 2).

Notes to Chapter 18 (pp. 168–173)

1. Hsia Hsieh, *Chung-hsi chi-shih*, 13:7-b to 11-a, and 20-a (see chap. 1, n. 2). FO 228/259, Alcock–Elgin, Desp. 9, July 21, 1858; Parkes–Elgin, Desp. 37, June 4; Parkes–Elgin, Desp. 40, June 6; Desp. 43, June 18; Desp. 45, June 19, 1858.
2. FO 228/259, Parkes–Elgin, Incls. 1 and 2, Desp. 54, July 20, 1858.
3. *Ibid.*, Parkes–Elgin, Desp. 38, June 6, 1858. Also see enclosures in same.
4. *Ibid.*, copy of proclamation, Incl. 2, Desp. 54, July 20, 1858; Parkes' report, Incl. 4, Desp. 54.
5. IWSM, HF 19:19-a to 20-a.
6. FO 228/259, Parkes–Elgin, Desp. 43, June 18, 1858.
7. IWSM, HF 21:45-a to 47-b.
8. *Ibid.*, 47-b to 48-a.
9. IWSM, HF 19:13-a to 19-a.
10. *Ibid.*, HF 22:5-b.
11. *Ibid.*, 37-a to 41-a.
12. *Ibid.*, HF 20:25-a to 26-a.
13. *Ibid.*, 26-a to 27-b.
14. *Ibid.*, HF 22:17-b to 19-b.
15. *Ibid.*
16. *Ibid.*, 27-b to 28-a.
17. *Ibid.*, 41-a to 42-b.
18. FO 228/259, Parkes–Elgin, Desp. 40, June 6, 1858; Huang to the allied commission, Incl. 9, Desp. 47.
19. *Ibid.*, Parkes–Elgin, Desp. 45, June 19, 1858; Desp. 46, June 21. Kuo T'ing-i, *Chin-tai chung-kuo shih-shih jih-chih* (A Calendar of Historical Events of Modern China) (Taipei, 1963), 280.
20. FO 228/259, Parkes–Elgin, Desp. 47, July 3, 1858.
21. *Ibid.*, Incl. 3, Desp. 43, June 18, 1858.
22. Stanley Lane-Poole, *The Life of Sir Harry Parkes* (London, 1894), 1:283–284.

23. FO 228/259, Parkes–Elgin, Desp. 37, June 4, 1858; intelligence report, Incl. 1, Desp. 38, June 6. Hsia Hsieh, *Chung-hsi chi-shih*, 13:18-b to 19-a (see chap. 1, n. 2). IWSM, HF 26:33-b to 34-b.

24. Masataka Banno, *China and the West, 1858–1861: The Origins of the Tsungli Yamen* (Cambridge, Mass., 1964), chap. 2.

25. Immanuel Hsu, *China's Entrance into the Family of Nations: The Diplomatic Phase, 1858–1880* (Cambridge, Mass., 1960), 23–79.

26. IWSM, HF 26:33-b to 34-b, 37-a to 37-b.

27. *Ibid.*, HF 27:31-b.

28. *Ibid.*, 32-a to 32-b.

29. *Ibid.*, HF 28:33-a to 41-b. Kuo T'ing-i, *Chin-tai chung-kuo*, 282–283.

30. IWSM, HF 28:41-b to 42-b.

31. Kuo T'ing-i, *Chin-tai chung-kuo*, 282–283. IWSM, HF 30:3-b to 6-a.

32. IWSM, HF 30:18-b.

33. *Ibid.*, 37-b to 38-a.

34. *Ibid.*, 34-b to 37-b.

35. Hsia Hsieh, *Chung-hsi chi-shih*, 13:11-b to 12-a (see chap. 1, n. 2).

36. IWSM, HF 31:7-a to 7-b.

37. Kuo T'ing-i, *Chin-tai chung-kuo*, 285–287. Laurence Oliphant, *Narrative of the Earl of Elgin's Mission to China and Japan in the Years 1857, 1858, 1859* (London, 1859), 2:469–472.

38. FO 228/266, Alcock–Bowring, Desp. 7, Jan. 13, 1859; Desp. 13, Jan. 23. Lane-Poole, *Harry Parkes*, 1: chap. 14.

39. Oliphant, *Elgin's Mission*, 2:469.

40. Quoted in *ibid.*, 2:473–474. Banno, *China and the West*, chap. 14.

41. See, for example: FO 228/266, Alcock–Bowring, Desp. 7, Jan. 13, 1859.

Notes to Chapter 19 (pp. 174–176)

1. FO 228/268, Communication from Po Kuei to the commissioners, Incl. 1, Desp. 1, March 29, 1859; Proclamation by Hui-chou prefect, Incl. 5, Desp. 1, March 29.

2. FO 228/266, Alcock–Bowring, April 19, 1859. FO 228/268, Parkes–Bruce, Desp. 16, May 14, 1859.

3. FO 228/266, Petition from security merchants to Alcock, Incl. 1, Desp. 31, April, 1859. FO 228/370, Depositions of the executions of eighteen kidnappers, sent by Governor Lao to the allied commission, Incl. 2, Desp. 42, Nov. 10, 1859. FO 228/266, Alcock–Bowring, Desp. 31, April, 1859. FO 228/268, Parkes' report, Incl. 3, Desp. 1, March 29, 1859. FO 228/269, Parkes' report, Incl. 2, Desp. 37, Oct. 6, 1859. FO 228/267, Winchester–Bruce, Desp. 36, Oct. 8, 1859. FO 228/270, Parkes–Bowring, Desp. 45, Nov. 12, 1859. Stanley Lane-Poole, *The Life of Sir Harry Parkes* (London, 1894), 1:319. Maurice Freedman, "Immigrants and Associations: Chinese in Nineteenth-century Singapore," *Comparative Studies in Society and History*, 3.1:47 (Oct., 1960).

4. FO 228/263, Proclamation of the gentry of Canton, translated by the British, Incl. 1, Desp. 11, May 3, 1859.

5. FO 228/268, Parkes' memo, Incl. 3, Desp. 1, March 29, 1859; Incl. 1, Desp.

6, April 21. FO 17/216, Robertson–Hammond, Desp. 17, Oct. 10, 1854. Lane-Poole, *Harry Parkes*, 1:82–83. Laurence Oliphant, *Narrative of the Earl of Elgin's Mission to China and Japan in the Years 1857, 1858, 1859* (London, 1859), 1:95–96. William Lockhart, *The Medical Missionary in China: A Narrative of Twenty Years' Experience* (London, 1861), 185–186.

6. FO 228/263, Gentry proclamation, translated by the British, Incl. 1, Desp. 11, May 3, 1859.

7. FO 228/284, Parkes' report, Incl. 1, Desp. 116, July 6, 1860. Also see Inclosure 2 in same. FO 228/287, Winchester–Bruce, Desp. 73, Aug. 4, 1860; Desp. 83, Sept. 20; Pedder's report, Incl. 1, Desp. 99, Nov. 12, 1860; Winchester–Bruce, Desp. 101, Nov. 26. FO 228/268, Parkes–Bruce, Desp. 23, July 9, 1859. FO 228/266, Winchester–Bruce, Desp. 19, July 20, 1859. FO 228/269, Parkes' report, Incl. 1, Desp. 28, Aug. 6, 1859. FO 228/266, Winchester–Bruce, Desp. 22, Aug. 2, 1859; Lao's proclamation, Incl. 1, Desp. 23, Aug. 6, 1859. FO 228/269, Parkes' report, Incl. 1, Desp. 28, Aug. 6, 1859; Incl. 4, Desp. 29, Aug. 22; Parkes–Bruce, Desp. 32, Sept. 18.

8. FO 228/269, Parkes' report, Incl. 1, Desp. 29, Aug. 22, 1859; Lao's instructions to P'an-yü magistrate, Incl. 5, Desp. 32, Sept. 18, 1859; Parkes' report, Incl. 1, Desp. 37, Sept. 25.

9. FO 228/269, Parkes' report, Incl. 1, Desp. 28, Aug. 6, 1859.

10. FO 228/266, Robertson–Bruce, Desp. 27, Aug. 31, 1859.

11. FO 228/270, Parkes' report, Incl. 1, Desp. 62, Dec. 13, 1859.

12. FO 228/283, Parkes–Bruce, Desp. 82, Jan. 27, 1860.

13. FO 228/306, Mayers' report, Incl. 1, Desp. 46, July 5, 1861; Robertson–Bruce, June 7. FO 228/284, Parkes–Bruce, Desp. 103, March 12, 1860; Desp. 106, March 25; Desp. 115, June 20; Desp. 116, July 6; Parkes' memo, Incl. 1, Desp. 112, May 21.

14. FO 228/284, Petition from P'an-yü gentry to allied commission, Incl. 8, Desp. 106, March 25, 1861.

15. Lane-Poole, *Harry Parkes*, 1:444.

16. *Ibid.*, 451.

17. Peter G. Laurie, *A Reminiscence of Canton, June, 1859* (London, 1866), 43.

18. FO 228/306, Robertson–Bruce, Desp. 71, Oct. 21, 1861.

Selected Bibliography

Listed below are the principal Chinese, Japanese, and Western sources that I have consulted or cited.

Western Sources

Abeel, David. *Journal of a Residence in China and the Neighboring Countries from 1830–1833*. Revised from the American edition. London, 1835. 366 pp.

Aberle, David F. "A Note on Relative Deprivation Theory as Applied to Millenarian and other Cult Movements," *Comparative Studies in Society and History*, Suppl. II, 209–214 (1962).

Akira, Fujieda and Wilma Fairbank. "Current Trends in Japanese Studies of China and Adjacent Areas," *Far Eastern Quarterly*, 13.1:33–47 (Nov., 1953).

Allen, Nathan. *An Essay on the Opium Trade*. Boston: John P. Jewett, 1850. 68 pp.

Allgood, G. *China War, 1860: Letters and Journal*. London: Longmans, Green, 1901. 107 pp.

Allport, Gordon. *The Nature of Prejudice*. Boston: Beacon Press, 1954. 537 pp.

——. "Prejudice: A Problem in Psychological and Social Causation," in Talcott Parsons and Edward A. Shils, eds., *Toward a General Theory of Action*. Glencoe, Ill.: Free Press, 1952. Pp. 365–387.

An Alphabetical Guide to Certain War Office and Other Military Records in the Public Record Office. Public Record Office Lists and Indexes, LIII. New York: Kraus Reprint Corp., 1963.

Anderson, Flavia. *The Rebel Emperor*. Garden City, N.Y.: Doubleday, 1959. 352 pp.

Appleton, William W. *A Cycle of Cathay. The Chinese Vogue in England during the Seventeenth and Eighteenth Centuries*. New York: Columbia University Press, 1951. 182 pp.

Backhouse, Edmund, and J. O. P. Bland. *Annals and Memoirs of the Court of Peking*. Boston: Houghton Mifflin, 1914.

Balazs, Etienne. *Chinese Civilization and Bureaucracy: Variations on a*

Theme, tr. H. M. Wright, ed. Arthur F. Wright. New Haven: Yale University Press, 1964. 309 pp.

Banno, Masataka. *China and the West, 1858–1861: the Origins of the Tsungli Yamen.* Cambridge, Mass.: Harvard University Press, 1964. 367 and 45 pp.

Barth, Gunther. *Bitter Strength. A History of the Chinese in the United States, 1850–1870.* Cambridge, Mass.: Harvard University Press, 1964. 305 pp.

Beal, Edwin George, Jr. *The Origin of Likin (1853–1864).* Cambridge, Mass.: Harvard University Press, 1958. 201 pp.

Bendix, Reinhard. "The Lower Classes and the 'Democratic Revolution,' " *Industrial Relations*, 1.1:91–116 (Oct., 1961).

Bianco, Lucien. "Classes laborieuses et classes dangereuses dans la Chine Impériale au XIXe siècle," *Annales, Economies, Sociétés et Civilisations*, 17.6:1175–1182 (Dec., 1962).

Bingham, J. Elliot. *Narrative of the Expedition to China.* 2 vols. London, 1842.

Blake, Clagette. *Charles Elliot, R. N., 1801–1875.* London: Cleaver-Hume Press, 1960. 130 pp.

Boardman, Eugene. *Christian Influence upon the Ideology of the Taiping Rebellion, 1851–1864.* Madison, Wis.: University of Wisconsin Press, 1952.

Boeke, J. H. "The Village Community in Collision with Capitalism," in R. Bendix, and Seymour Lipset, eds. *Class, Status and Power, A Reader in Social Stratification.* London: Routledge, and Kegan Paul, 1954. 541–546.

Bosch, A. J. du. *La Chine contemporaine, d'après les travaux plus récents.* Traduction de l'allemand. Paris and Brussels, 1860. 272 pp.

Bowring, Sir John. *Autobiographical Recollections.* London, 1877. 401 pp.

Boxer, C. R. *Fidalgoes in the Far East, 1550–1770: Fact and Fancy in the History of Macao.* The Hague: Martinus Nijhoff, 1948. 297 pp.

——, ed. *South China in the Sixteenth Century.* London: Hakluyt Society, 1953. 388 pp.

Brine, Lindesay. *The Taiping Rebellion in China.* London, 1862. 394 pp.

Brock, Peter. *The Political and Social Doctrines of the Unity of Czech Brethren in the Fifteenth and Early Sixteenth Centuries.* The Hague: Mouton, 1957. 302 pp.

Brunnert, H. S., and V. V. Hagelstrom. *Present Day Political Organization of China*, tr. A. Beltchenko and E. E. Moran. Shanghai: Kelly and Walsh, 1912. 572 and 81 pp.

Bulwer, Henry Lytton. *The Life of Henry John Temple, Viscount Palmerston, with Selections from His Diaries and Correspondence.* 3 vols.: London, 1870.

Burgess, John Steward. *The Guilds of Peking*. New York: Columbia University Press, 1928. 270 pp.

Callery, M. M., and Yvan. *The History of the Insurrection in China*. tr. John Oxenford. London, 1854. 301 pp.

Cantril, Hadley. *The Psychology of Social Movements*. New York: John Wiley, 1963. 274 pp.

Carter, Thomas. *Historical Record of the Twenty-Sixth, or Cameronian Regiment*. London, 1867. 265 pp.

Centre International de Synthèse. *La Foule, Exposés par Georges Bohn, Georges Hardy, Paul Alphandéry, Georges Lefebvre, et E. Dupréel*. Paris: Felix Alcan, 1934. 143 pp.

Chang, Chung-li. *The Chinese Gentry. Studies on their Role in Nineteenth-Century Chinese Society*. Seattle: University of Washington Press, 1955.

——, and Stanley Spector, eds. *Guide to the Memorials of Seven Leading Officials of Nineteenth-Century China*. Seattle: University of Washington Press, 1955. 457 pp.

Chang, Hsin-pao. *Commissioner Lin and the Opium War*. Cambridge, Mass.: Harvard University Press, 1964. 311 pp.

Chang, Te-ch'ang. "Maritime Trade at Canton During the Ming Dynasty," *Chinese Social and Political Science Review*, 17.2:264–282 (July, 1933).

Chang, T'ien-tse. *Sino-Portuguese Trade from 1514–1644: A Synthesis of Portuguese and Chinese Sources*. Leiden: Brill, 1934. 157 pp.

Chen, Han-seng. *Agrarian Problems in Southernmost China*. Shanghai: Kelly and Walsh, 1936. 144 pp.

Chen, Ta. *Emigrant Communities in South China, A Study of Overseas Migration and Its Influence on Standards of Living and Social Change*. London: Oxford University Press, 1939. 287 pp.

Cheng, J. C. *Chinese Sources for the Taiping Rebellion, 1850–1864*. Hong Kong: Hong Kong University Press, 1963. 182 pp.

Chesneaux, Jean. "La Revolution Taiping d'après quelques travaux récents," *Revue Historique*, 209:33–57 (Jan./Mar., 1953).

Chi, Ch'ao-ting. *Key Economic Areas in Chinese History*. London: Allen & Unwin, 1936.

China, Correspondence between the Liverpool East India and China Association and Lord Viscount Palmerston in Reference to the Hostile Proceedings at Canton in 1847. Liverpool: Liverpool East India and China Association. 23 pp.

Chinese Repository. E. C. Bridgman and S. Wells Williams, eds. Macao or Canton: Vols. 1–20, 1832–1851.

Chu, Shih-chia. *A Catalog of Local Histories in the Library of Congress*. Washington: U. S. Government Printing Office, 1942. 552 pp.

Ch'ü, T'ung-tsu. "Chinese Class Structure and its Ideology," in John K.

Fairbank, ed., *Chinese Thought and Institutions*. Chicago: University of Chicago Press, 1957. Pp. 235–250.

———. *Local Government in China under the Ch'ing*. Cambridge, Mass.: Harvard University Press, 1962. 410 pp.

Coben, Stanley. "A Study in Nativism: the American Red Scare of 1919–20," *Political Science Quarterly*, 79:1:52–75 (Mar., 1964).

Cohen, Myron. "The Hakka or 'Guest People': Linguistic Diversity as a Sociocultural Variable in Southeastern China." M. A. thesis, Columbia University, 1963. 73 pp.

Cohen, Paul A. *China and Christianity: the Missionary Movement and the Growth of Chinese Antiforeignism, 1860–1870*. Cambridge, Mass.: Harvard University Press, 1963. 392 pp.

Cohn, Norman. "Medieval Millenarianism: Its Bearing on the Comparative Study of Millenarian Movements," *Comparative Studies in Society and History*, Suppl. II, 31–43 (1962).

———. *The Pursuit of the Millennium*. 2nd ed. New York: Harper, 1961. 481 pp.

Collis, Maurice. *Foreign Mud: Being an Account of the Opium Imbroglio at Canton in the 1830's and the Anglo-Chinese War that Followed*. London: Faber and Faber, 1946. 318 pp.

Cooke, George Wingrove. *China: Being the Times' Special Correspondence from China in the Years 1857–1858*. London, 1858. 457 pp.

Cordier, Henri. *Bibliotheca Sinica*. Rev. ed. 4 vols. Paris, 1904–1908. Supplementary Vol. Paris, 1924. Author Index, New York: Columbia University East Asiatic Library, 1953.

———. *Le Consulat de France à Canton au XVIIIᵉ siècle*. Leiden, 1908. 52 pp.

———. *L'Expedition de Chine de 1857–1858: Histoire Diplomatique. Notes et Documents*. Paris, 1905. 475 pp.

———. "Les marchands hanistes de Canton," *T'oung Pao*, 2.3:281–315 (1902).

———. *Les Sociétés secrètes chinoises*. Paris, 1888. 21 pp.

Costin, W. C. *Great Britain and China, 1833–1860*. Oxford: Oxford University Press, 1937. 362 pp.

Courcy, Rene de. *L'Insurrection Chinoise*. Paris, 1861. 78 pp.

Davis, Sir John Francis. *China, During the War and Since the Peace*. 2 vols. London, 1852. 327 and 342 pp.

——— *The Chinese: A General Description of China and Its Inhabitants*. 3rd ed. London, 1844. 263 pp.

Dermigny, Louis. *La Chine et l'occident; le commerce à Canton au XVIIIᵉ siècle, 1719–1833*. 4 vols. Paris: S.E.V.P.E.N., 1964.

Description of the City of Canton with an Appendix Containing an Account of the Population of the Chinese Empire, Chinese Weights and Measures, and the Imports and Exports of Canton. 2nd ed. Canton, 1839. 168 pp.

Deutsch, Karl W. *Nationalism and Social Communication; an Inquiry into the Foundations of Nationality.* New York: John Wiley, 1953. 292 pp.

Downing, C. Toogood. *The Fan-Qui in China in 1836–1837.* 3 vols. London, 1837. 316, 306, and 327 pp.

Dulles, Foster Rhea. *China and America, the Story of their Relations since 1784.* Princeton: Princeton University Press, 1946. 277 pp.

Eastman, Lloyd. "The Kwangtung Anti-foreign Disturbances during the Sino-French War," *Papers on China,* 13:1–31 (1959).

Eberhard, Wolfram. *Chinese Fairy Tales and Folk Tales.* London: Kegan Paul Trench and Trubner, 1937.

——. *Conquerors and Rulers. Social Forces in Medieval China.* 2nd ed. Leiden: E. J. Brill, 1965. 191 pp.

——. *Social Mobility in Traditional China.* Leiden: Brill, 1962. 302 pp.

Eisenstadt, S. N. "Internal Contradictions in Bureaucratic Politics," *Comparative Studies in Society and History,* 1.1:58–75 (Oct., 1958).

——. "Sociological Analysis of Historical Societies (Review Article)," *Comparative Studies in Society and History,* 6.4:481–489 (July, 1964).

Eitel, E. J. *Europe in China: The History of Hong Kong from the Beginning to the Year 1882.* London and Hong Kong, 1895. 575 pp.

Eliade, Mircea. "'Cargo-cults' and Cosmic Regeneration," *Comparative Studies in Society and History,* suppl. II, 139–143 (1962).

Elliott, Alan J. A. *Chinese Spirit-Medium Cults in Singapore.* London: London School of Economics, 1955. 179 pp.

Emerson, Rupert. "Paradoxes of Asian Nationalism," *Far Eastern Quarterly,* 13.2:131–142 (Feb., 1954).

Endacott, G. B., and A. Hinton. *Fragrant Harbor, A Short History of Hong Kong.* Hong Kong: Oxford University Press, 1962. 216 pp.

Epigrafi Cinesi di Quang-Ceu, Ossia della città chiamata volgarmente dagle Europei "Canton," tr. Hager. 2nd ed. Milan, 1818.

Essen, L. van der, and G. J. Hoogewerff. *Le Sentiment National dans les Pays-bas.* 2nd ed. Brussels: Editions universitaires, 1944. 106 pp.

Fairbank, John K. *Ch'ing Documents: An Introductory Syllabus.* 2nd ed. rev. Cambridge, Mass.: Harvard University Press, 1959.

——. "Meadows on China: A Centennial Review," *Far Eastern Quarterly,* 14:3:365–371 (May, 1955).

——. "Patterns behind the Tientsin Massacre," *Harvard Journal of Asiatic Studies,* 20:480–511 (1957).

——. "Synarchy under the Treaties," in J. K. Fairbank, ed., *Chinese Thought and Institutions.* Chicago: University of Chicago Press, 1957. Pp. 204–231.

——. *Trade and Diplomacy on the China Coast, the Opening of the Treaty*

Ports, 1842–1854. 2 vols. Cambridge, Mass.: Harvard University Press, 1953. 489 and 88 pp.

——. "Tributary Trade and China's Relations with the West," *Far Eastern Quarterly*, 1:2:129–149 (Feb., 1942).

——. *The United States and China.* Rev. ed. Cambridge, Mass.: Harvard University Press, 1958.

——, and Masataka Banno. *Japanese Studies of Modern China, A Bibliographical Guide to Historical and Social Science Research on the 19th and 20th Centuries.* Rutland, Vt., and Tokyo: Charles E. Tuttle, 1955. 331 pp.

——, Edwin O. Reischauer, and Albert M. Craig. *East Asia: The Modern Transformation.* Boston: Houghton Mifflin, 1965. 955 pp.

——, and S. Y. Teng. *Ch'ing Administration: Three Studies.* Cambridge, Mass.: Harvard University Press, 1961. 246 pp.

——, and Mary C. Wright. "Documentary Collections in Modern Chinese History, Introduction," *Journal of Asian Studies*, 17:1:55–111 (Nov., 1957).

Fallers, Lloyd A. "Populism and Nationalism: A Comment on D. A. Low's 'The Advent of Populism in Buganda,' " *Comparative Studies in Society and History*, 6.4:445–448 (July, 1964).

Faure, B. *Les Sociétés secrètes en Chine.* Paris: Courtrai, 1933. 222 pp.

Fay, C. R. *Life and Labour in the Nineteenth Century.* Cambridge: Cambridge University Press, 1947. 320 pp.

Fei, Hsiao-t'ung. *China's Gentry: Essays in Rural-Urban Relations.* Rev. and ed. by Margaret Park Redfield. Chicago: University of Chicago Press, 1953. 289 pp.

——. "Peasantry and Gentry: An Interpretation of Chinese Social Structure and Its Changes," in R. Bendix and S. Lipset, eds., *Class, Status and Power: A Reader in Social Stratification.* London: Routledge and Kegan Paul, 1954. Pp. 631–650.

Feuerwerker, Albert. "From 'Feudalism' to 'Capitalism' in Recent Historical Writings from Mainland China," *Journal of Asian Studies*, 18:107–115 (1958).

Fishbourne, E. G. F. *Impressions of China and the Present Revolution: Its Progress and Prospects.* London, 1855. 441 pp.

FO 17: Foreign Office, General Correspondence, China. Filed in the Public Record Office, London.

FO 228: Foreign Office, Embassy and Consular Archives, China. Filed in the Public Record Office, London.

FO 677: Foreign Office, Superintendent of Trade, Records, China. Filed in the Public Record Office, London.

FO 682: Foreign Office, Papers in the Chinese Language. Filed in the Public Record Office, London.

FO 802: Foreign Office, References and Indices of General Correspondence, China. Filed in the Public Record Office, London.

Fortune, Robert. *A Residence Among the Chinese: Inland, on the Coast, and at Sea, Being a Narrative of Scenes and Adventures During a Third Visit to China, from 1853–1856.* London, 1857. 440 pp.

Fox, Grace. *British Admirals and Chinese Pirates, 1832–1869.* London: Kegan Paul, Trench, Trubner and Co., 1940. 227 pp.

Freedman, Maurice. "Immigrants and Associations: Chinese in Nineteenth-century Singapore," *Comparative Studies in Society and History*, 3.1:25–48 (Oct., 1960).

——. *Lineage Organization in Southeastern China.* London: The Athlone Press, 1958. 151 pp.

Fried, Morton H. *Fabric of Chinese Society.* New York: Praeger, 1953.

Gamble, Sidney D. "Daily Wages of Unskilled Chinese Laborers, 1807–1902," *Far Eastern Quarterly*, 3.1:41–73 (Nov., 1943).

Gao, Hwei-shung. "Police Administration in Canton," *Chinese Social and Political Science Review*, 10.2:332–354 (Apr., 1926).

Gerth, H. H., and C. Wright Mills, eds. *From Max Weber: Essays in Sociology.* London: Kegan Paul, 1948. 490 pp.

Greenberg, Michael. *British Trade and the Opening of China, 1800–1842.* Cambridge: Cambridge University Press, 1951. 221 pp.

Groot, J. J. M. de. *Sectarianism and Religious Persecution in China. A Page in the History of Religions.* 2 vols. Amsterdam, 1903.

Gutzlaff, Charles. *China Opened, or, a Display of the Topography, etc., of the Chinese Empire.* 2 vols. London, 1838. 510 and 570 pp.

——. *Journal of Three Voyages along the Coast of China in 1831, 1832, and 1833, with Notices of Siam, Corea and the Loo-choo Islands.* 3rd ed. London, 1840. 312 pp.

——. *The Life of Taou-Kwang, Late Emperor of China, with Memoirs of the Court of Peking.* London, 1852. 279 pp.

——. *A Sketch of Chinese History, Ancient and Modern.* 2 vols. London, 1834. 436 and 461 pp.

Hagen, Everett E. *On the Theory of Social Change: How Economic Growth Begins.* Homewood, Ill.: Dorsey Press, 1962. 557 pp.

Hail, William James. *Tseng Kuo-fan and the Taiping Rebellion.* New Haven: Yale University Press, 1927.

Halevy, Elie. *The Age of Peel and Cobden: A History of the English People, 1841–1852.* Tr. E. I. Watkin. London: Ernest Benn, 1947. 374 pp.

Hall, W. H., and W. D. Bernard. *The Nemesis in China, Comprising a History of the Late War in That Country with an Account of the Colony of Hong Kong.* London, 1855. 399 pp.

Hamberg, Theodore. *The Chinese Rebel Chief Hung-Siu-Tsuen and the Origin of the Insurrection in China.* London, 1855. 98 pp.

Hayes, Carlton J. H. *Nationalism: A Religion.* New York: Macmillan, 1960. 187 pp.

Henry, B. C. *Ling-Nam, or Interior Views of Southern China, Including Explorations in the Hitherto Untraversed Island of Hainan.* London, 1886, 511 pp.

Hirth, F. "The Hoppo-Book of 1753," *Journal of the North China Branch of the Royal Asiatic Society, New Series,* 17:221–236 (1882).

Ho, Alfred K. L. "The Grand Council in the Ch'ing Dynasty," *Far Eastern Quarterly,* 11:167–182 (1951).

Ho, Ping-ti. *The Ladder of Success in Imperial China: Aspects of Social Mobility, 1368–1911.* New York: Columbia University Press, 1962. 385 pp.

——. "The Salt Merchants of Yang-chou: A Study of Commercial Capitalism in Eighteenth-Century China," *Harvard Journal of Asiatic Studies,* 17:130–168 (1954).

——. *Studies on the Population of China, 1368–1953.* Cambridge, Mass.: Harvard University Press, 1959.

Hobsbawm, E. J. *Primitive Rebels, Studies in Archaic Forms of Social Movement in the 19th and 20th Centuries.* 2nd ed. New York: Praeger, 1963. 208 pp.

Holt, Edgar. *The Opium Wars in China.* London: Putnam, 1964. 303 pp.

Holt, John B. "Holiness Religion: Cultural Shock and Social Reorganization," in J. Milton Yinger, ed., *Religion, Society and the Individual: An Introduction to the Sociology of Religion.* New York: Macmillan, 1957. 653 pp.

Hsiao, Kung-chuan. *Rural China: Imperial Control in the Nineteenth Century.* Seattle: University of Washington Press, 1960. 783 pp.

Hsieh, Kuo-ching. "Removal of Coastal Population in Early Tsing Period," *Chinese Social and Political Science Review,* 15.4:559–596 (Jan., 1932).

Hsieh, Pao-chao. *The Government of China (1644–1911).* Baltimore: Johns Hopkins Press, 1925.

Hsieh, Ting-yu. "Origin and Migrations of the Hakkas," *Chinese Social and Political Science Review,* 13:202–227 (1929).

Hsu, Francis L. K. "Influence of South-Seas Emigration on Certain Chinese Provinces," *Far Eastern Quarterly,* 5.1:47–59 (Nov., 1945).

Hsu, Immanuel C. Y. *China's Entrance into the Family of Nations: the Diplomatic Phase, 1858–1880.* Cambridge, Mass.: Harvard University Press, 1960. 255 pp.

Hu, Hsien-chin. *The Common Descent Group in China and Its Functions.* New York: Viking Fund Publications in Anthropology, 1948. 201 pp.

Huang, Yen-yü. "Viceroy Yeh Ming-ch'en and the Canton Episode (1858–1861)," *Harvard Journal of Asiatic Studies,* 6.1:37–127 (Mar., 1941).

Huc, R. P. *A Journey through the Chinese Empire.* 2 vols. New York:

Harper and Bros., 1856. 421 and 422 pp.

Hucker, Charles O. *China: A Critical Bibliography.* Tucson: University of Arizona Press, 1962. 125 pp.

Hughes, E. R. *The Invasion of China by the Western World.* New York: Macmillan, 1938. 324 pp.

Hummel, Arthur. *Eminent Chinese of the Ch'ing Period.* 2 vols. Washington, D.C.: United States Government Printing Office, 1943 and 1944. 1103 pp.

Hunter, W. C. *The "Fan-Kwae" at Canton before Treaty Days 1825–1844.* London, 1882. 160 pp.

Hutin, Serge. *Histoire mondiale des sociétés secrètes.* Paris: Productions de Paris, 1960. 415 pp.

Index to Foreign Office, Embassy and Consular Archives, China. 3 vols., n.d. Filed in the Public Record Office, London.

Irick, Robert L., Ying-shih Yü, and Kwang-ching Liu. *American-Chinese Relations, 1784–1941: A Survey of Chinese-Language Materials at Harvard.* Cambridge, Mass.: Harvard University Press, 1960. 296 pp.

Iwao, Seiichi, ed. *List of the Foreign Office Records Preserved in the Public Record Office in London Relating to China and Japan.* Tokyo: Toho Gakkai, 1958.

Jacobs, Norman. *The Origin of Modern Capitalism and Eastern Asia.* Hong Kong: Hong Kong University Press, 1958.

Jocelyn, Robert, Viscount. *Six Months with the Chinese Expedition, or Leaves from a Soldier's Note-Book.* London, 1841. 155 pp.

Kane, H. H. *Opium-Smoking in America and China: A Study of its Prevalence, and Effects, Immediate and Remote, on the Individual and the Nation.* New York, 1882. 156 pp.

Kato, Shigeshi. "On the Hang or the Associations of Merchants in China," *Memoirs of the Research Department of the Toyo Bunko*, 8:45–83 (1936).

Keer, J. G. "Description of the Great Examination Hall at Canton," *Journal of the North China Branch of the Royal Asiatic Society, New Series*, 3:63–69 (Dec., 1866).

Kirby, E. Stuart. *Introduction to the Economic History of China.* London: Allen and Unwin, 1954. 202 pp.

Kuhn, Philip. "The Militia in Nineteenth Century China." Ph.D. thesis, Harvard University, 1963.

Kulp, Daniel. *Country Life in South China: The Sociology of Familism.* Vol. 1, *Phoenix Village, Kwangtung, China.* New York: Columbia University Press, 1925. 367 pp.

Kuo, P. C. *A Critical Study of the First Anglo-Chinese War, with Documents.* Shanghai: Commercial Press, 1935. 315 pp.

Laai, Yi-faai. "The Part Played by the Pirates of Kwangtung and Kwangsi

Provinces in the T'ai-p'ing Insurrection." Ph.D. thesis, University of California, Berkeley, 1950. 362 pp.

———. "River Strategy: a Phase of the Taiping's Military Development," *Oriens*, 10:302–329 (1952).

———, Franz Michael, and John C. Sherman. "The Use of Maps in Social Research: a Case Study in South China," *Annals of the Association of American Geographers* (Jan., 1962).

Lane-Poole, Stanley. *Sir Harry Parkes in China*. London, 1901. 386 pp.

———. *The Life of Sir Harry Parkes*. Vol. 1, *Consul in China*. London, 1894. 512 pp.

Lang, Olga. *Chinese Family and Society*. New Haven: Yale University Press, 1946. 395 pp.

Laufer, Berthold. "The Development of Ancestral Images in China," in William A. Lessa and Evon Z. Vogt, eds., *Reader in Comparative Religion, An Anthropological Approach*. Evanston: Row, Peterson, 1958. Pp. 404–409.

Laurie, Peter G. *A Reminiscence of Canton, June 1859*. London, 1866. 58 pp.

Leavenworth, Charles S. *The Arrow War With China*. London: S. Low, Marston, and Co., 1901.

Lee, Edward Bing-Shuey. *Modern Canton*. Shanghai: The Mercury Press, 1936. 176 pp.

Leong, Y. K., and L. K. Tao. *Village and Town Life in China*. London: G. Allen and Unwin, 1915. 155 pp.

Levenson, Joseph R. *Confucian China and its Modern Fate*. 3 vols. Berkeley and Los Angeles: University of California Press, 1958, 1964, and 1965.

Levy, Marion J., Jr. "Contrasting Factors in the Modernization of China and Japan," *Economic Development and Cultural Change*, 2:161–197 (1953).

———. *The Family Revolution in Modern China*. Cambridge, Mass.: Harvard University Press, 1949.

Li, Chi. *The Formation of the Chinese People: An Anthropological Inquiry*. Cambridge, Mass.: Harvard University Press, 1928. 283 pp.

Li, Chien-nung. *The Political History of China, 1840–1928*. tr. S. Y. Teng and Jeremy Ingalls. Princeton: Van Nostrand, 1956.

Li, Hsiu-ch'eng. *Autobiography of one of Hung Hsiu-ch'üan's Lieutenants, Ordered by Tseng Kuo-fan: Li Hsiu-cheng, the Chung Wang*, tr. W. T. Lay. Shanghai, 1865. 104 pp.

Liao, T'ai-ch'u. "School Land: A Problem of Educational Finance," *Yenching Journal of Social Studies*, 2.2:212–233 (Feb., 1940).

Lin Yueh-hwa. *The Golden Wing: A Sociological Study of Chinese Familism*. London: Kegan Paul, 1948. 234 pp.

Linton, Ralph. "Nativistic Movements," in William A. Lessa and Evon Z.

Vogt, eds., *Reader in Comparative Religion, an Anthropological Approach.* Evanston: Row, Peterson, 1958. Pp. 466–474.

Lipset, S. M. *Agrarian Socialism: The Cooperative Commonwealth Federation in Saskatchewan.* Berkeley and Los Angeles: University of California Press, 1950. 315 pp.

List of Foreign Office Records to 1878 Preserved in the Public Record Office. Public Record Office Lists and Indexes, No. LII. H. M. Stationery Office, 1929.

Liu, Hui-chen Wang. "An Analysis of Chinese Clan Rules: Confucian Theories in Action," in David S. Nivison and Arthur F. Wright, eds. *Confucianism in Action.* Stanford: Stanford University Press, 1959. Pp 165–181.

Loch, Henry Brougham. *Personal Narrative of Occurrences during Lord Elgin's Second Embassy to China, 1860.* London, 1869. 298 pp.

Lockhart, William. *The Medical Missionary in China: A Narrative of Twenty Years' Experience.* London, 1861. 104 pp.

Lord Palmerston's Foreign Policy in and out of Europe by a Late Resident in China. London, 1857. 62 pp.

Low, D. A. "The Advent of Populism in Buganda," *Comparative Studies in Society and History*, 6.4:424–444 (July, 1964).

Lyman, Stanford M. "Chinese Secret Societies in the Occident: Notes and Suggestions for Research in the Sociology of Secrecy," *Canadian Review of Sociology and Anthropology*, 1.2:79–102 (1964).

——, W. E. Willmott, and Berching Ho. "Rules of a Chinese Secret Society in British Columbia," *Bulletin of the School of Oriental and African Studies*, University of London, 27.3:530–539 (1964).

Ma, Feng-ch'en. "Manchu-Chinese Social and Economic Conflicts in Early Ch'ing," in E-tu Zen Sun and John de Francis, eds., *Chinese Social History*. Washington, D.C.: American Council of Learned Societies, 1956. Pp. 33–51.

Mackie, J. Milton. *Life of Tai-Ping-Wang.* New York, 1857. 370 pp.

MacNair, Harley Farnsworth. *Modern Chinese History: Selected Readings.* Shanghai: Commercial Press, 1923. 922 pp.

Mancall, Mark. "Major-General Ignatiev's Mission to Peking, 1859–1860," *Papers on China*, 10:55–96 (1956).

Map of Gough's attack on May 25, 1841. London: Quartermaster-General's Office, 1841.

Maxwell, Sir Herbert. *The Life and Letters of George William Frederick, Fourth Earl of Clarendon.* 2 vols. London: E. Arnold, 1913.

Mayer, Harold M., and Clyde F. Kohn, eds., *Readings in Urban Geography.* Chicago: University of Chicago Press, 1959. 625 pp.

McPherson, D. *Two Years in China: Narrative of the Chinese Expedition From Its Formation in April, 1840, till April, 1842.* London, 1842. 391 pp.

Meadows, Thomas Taylor. *The Chinese and Their Rebellions*. London, 1856. 656 pp.

———. *Desultory Notes on the Government and People of China*. London, 1847. 250 pp.

Medhurst, W. H. *China: Its State and Prospects, with Especial Reference to the Spread of the Gospel*. London, 1838. 582 pp.

Meisner, Maurice. "The Development of Formosan Nationalism," *The China Quarterly*, 15:91–106 (July–Sept., 1963).

Michael, Franz. "Military Organization and Power Structure of China during the Taiping Rebellion," *Pacific Historical Review*, 18:469–483 (Nov., 1949).

Michie, Alexander. *The Englishman in China during the Victorian Era*. 2 vols. London: W. Blackwood and Sons, 1900. 442 and 510 pp.

Millot, Stanislas. "Extraits des chroniques de Kouang Tcheou Wan," *Bulletin de l'Association Amicale Franco-Chinoise*, 1.6:438–455 (Oct., 1909).

Miyakawa, Hisayuki. "The Confucianization of South China," in A. F. Wright, ed., *The Confucian Persuasion*. Stanford: Stanford University Press, 1960. Pp. 21–46.

Morison, J. L. *The Eighth Earl of Elgin: A Chapter in Nineteenth-Century Imperial History*. London: Hodder and Stoughton, 1928. 317 pp.

Morse, Hosea Ballou. "Currency in China," *Journal of the North China Branch of the Royal Asiatic Society*, Vol. XXXVIII.

———. *The International Relations of the Chinese Empire: The Period of Conflict, 1834–1860*. London: Longmans, Green, 1910. 727 pp.

———. *In the Days of the Taipings: Being the Recollections of Ting Kien-chang, otherwise Meisun*. Salem, Mass.: Essex Institute, 1927. 434 pp.

———. *The Gilds of China, with an Account of the Gild Merchant or Co-hong of Canton*. London: Longmans, Green, 1909.

———. *The Trade and Administration of China*. 3rd ed. London: Longmans, Green, 1921. 505 pp.

Muramatsu, Yuji. "Some Themes in Chinese Rebel Ideologies," in A. F. Wright, ed., *Confucian Persuasion*. Stanford: Stanford University Press, 1960.

Murphy, Rhoads. "The City as a Center of Change: Western Europe and China," *Annals of the Association of American Geographers*, 44:349–362 (Dec., 1954).

Nevins, John L. *China and the Chinese: A General Description of the Country and Its Inhabitants; Its Civilization and Form of Government; Its Religions and Social Institutions; Its Intercourse with Other Nations; and Its Present Condition and Prospects*. New York, 1869. 456 pp.

Nolde, John J. "The 'Canton City Question,' 1842–1849: A Preliminary Investigation into Chinese Antiforeignism and Its Effect upon China's

Diplomatic Relations with the West." Ph.D. thesis, Cornell University, 1956.

——. "The 'False Edict' of 1849," *Journal of Asian Studies*, 20:299–315 (1960).

Oliphant, Laurence. *Narrative of the Earl of Elgin's Mission to China and Japan in the Years 1857, 1858, 1859.* 2 vols. London, 1958.

Owen, David Edward. *British Opium Policy in China and India.* New Haven: Yale University Press, 1934. 399 pp.

Parker, Edward Harper, tr. *Chinese Account of the Opium War.* Shanghai, 1888. 82 pp.

Pelcovits, Nathan A. *Old China Hands and the Foreign Office.* New York: American Institute of Pacific Relations, 1948. 349 pp.

Pickering, W. A. "Chinese Secret Societies," *Journal of the Straits Branch of the Royal Asiatic Society*, Part I; 1:63–84 (July, 1878); Part II; 3:1–18 (July, 1879).

Pirenne, Henri. "Stages in the Social History of Capitalism," in R. Bendix and S. Lipset, eds., *Class, Status and Power: A Reader in Social Stratification.* London: Routledge and Kegan Paul, 1954. Pp. 501–517.

Playfair, G. M. H. *The Cities and Towns of China: A Geographical Dictionary.* Hong Kong, 1879. 417 pp.

Pritchard, Earl H. "The Crucial Years of Early Anglo-Chinese Relations, 1750–1800." Pullman, Wash.: Research Studies of the State College of Washington, 4.3–4:95–442 (Sept. and Dec., 1936).

Rait, Robert S. *The Life and Campaigns of Hugh, First Viscount Gough, Field-Marshal.* 2 vols. Westminster: A. Constable, 1903.

Redfield, Robert. "The Social Organization of Tradition," *Far Eastern Quarterly*, 15.1:13–21 (Nov., 1955).

Redford, Arthur. *Manchester Merchants and Foreign Trade, 1794–1858.* Manchester: Manchester University Press, 1934. 251 pp.

Reischauer, Edwin, and John K. Fairbank. *East Asia: The Great Tradition.* Boston: Houghton Mifflin, 1960.

Ribeiro, René. "Brazilian Messianic Movements," *Comparative Studies in Society and History*, suppl. II, 55–59 (1962).

Rowe, David Nelson, ed. *Index to Ch'ing Tai Ch'ou Pan I Wu Shih-mo.* Hamden, Conn.: Shoe String Press, 1960. 855 pp.

——. "Recent Acquisitions of Chinese Diplomatic Archives, Institute of Modern History, Academia Sinica, Taiwan, Republic of China," *Journal of Asian Studies*, 16.3:489–494 (May, 1962).

Scarth, J. *Twelve Years in China: The People, the Rebels, and the Mandarins.* Edinburgh, 1860. 328 pp.

Schafer, Edward H. *The Vermilion Bird: T'ang Images of the South.* Berkeley and Los Angeles: University of California Press, 1967.

Schlegel, Gustave. *Thian Ti Hwui, The Hung League*. Batavia, 1866.

Shepperson, George. "The Comparative Study of Millenarian Movements," *Comparative Studies in Society and History*, Suppl. II, 44–52 (1962).

——. "Nyasaland and the Millennium," *Comparative Studies in Society and History*, Suppl. II, 144–159 (1962).

Shih, Vincent Yu-chung. "The Ideology of the T'ai-p'ing T'ien-kuo," *Sinologica*, 3.1:1–16 (1951).

——. "Interpretations of the Taiping Tien-kuo by Non-Communist Chinese Writers," *Far Eastern Quarterly*, 10.3:248–257 (May, 1951).

——. "Some Chinese Rebel Ideologies," *T'oung Pao*, 44.1–3:150–226 (1956).

Simmel, Georg. *The Sociology of Georg Simmel*. Translated, edited with an introduction by Kurt H. Wolff. Glencoe, Ill.: The Free Press, 1950. 445 pp.

Skinner, G. William. *Chinese Society in Thailand: an Analytical History*. Ithaca, N.Y.: Cornell University Press, 1957. 459 pp.

——. *Leadership and Power in the Chinese Community of Thailand*. Ithaca, N.Y.: Cornell University Press, 1958. 363 pp.

——. "Marketing and Social Structure in Rural China," Part I, *Journal of Asian Studies*, 24.1:3–42 (Nov., 1964); Part II, *Journal of Asian Studies*, 24.2:195–228 (Feb., 1965).

Smelser, Neil J. *Social Change in the Industrial Revolution: An Application of Theory to the British Cotton Industry*. Chicago: University of Chicago Press, 1959. 440 pp.

Spector, Stanley. *Li Hung-chang and the Huai Army: A Study in Nineteenth-Century Chinese Regionalism*. Seattle: University of Washington Press, 1964. 359 pp.

Stanton, William. *The Triad Society or Heaven and Earth Association*. Hong Kong: Kelly and Walsh, 1900. 124 pp.

Staunton, Sir George Thomas. *Memoirs*. London, 1856. 232 pp.

Sun, E-tu Zen, and John de Francis. *Bibliography on Chinese Social History*. New Haven: Far Eastern Publications of Yale University, 1952.

Swisher, Earl. "Chinese Intellectuals under Western Impact, 1838–1900," *Comparative Studies in Society and History*, 1.1:26–37 (Oct., 1958).

Tawney, R. H. *Land and Labour in China*. 3rd impression. London: George Allen and Unwin, 1964. 207 pp.

Taylor, G. E. "The Taiping Rebellion, Its Economic Background and Social Theory," *Chinese Social and Political Science Review*, 16.4:545–614 (Jan., 1933).

Teng, S. Y. *New Light on the History of the Taiping Rebellion*. Cambridge, Mass.: Harvard University Press, 1950. 132 pp.

——, and Knight Biggerstaff. *An Annotated Bibliography of Selected Chinese*

Reference Works. Cambridge, Mass.: Harvard University Press, 1950. 326 pp.

———, and John K. Fairbank. *China's Response to the West.* 2 vols. Cambridge, Mass.: Harvard University Press, 1954. 296 and 84 pp.

Thompson, Edgar T., and Everett C. Hughes, eds. *Race, Individual and Collective Behavior.* Glencoe, Ill.: The Free Press, 1958. 619 pp.

Troeltsch, Ernst. *The Social Teaching of the Christian Churches.* Translated by Olive Wyon. 2 vols. New York: Harper, 1960. 1019 pp.

The Truth about Opium-Smoking. Proceedings at a Conference on Opium Smoking held at Exeter Hall in London by Rev. Moule, Rev. Sadler, *et al.* London, 1882. 124 pp.

Tsiang, T. F. (Chiang T'ing-fu). "The Government and Co-hong of Canton, 1839," *Chinese Social and Political Science Review,* 15.4:602–607 (Jan., 1932).

Tuveson, Ernest. "The Power of Believing (Review Article)," *Comparative Studies in Society and History,* 4.4:446–477 (July, 1963).

Twitchett, Denis. "The Fan Clan's Charitable Estate, 1050–1760," in David Nivison and Arthur F. Wright, eds., *Confucianism in Action.* Stanford: Stanford University Press, 1959. Pp. 97–133.

Vargas, Ph. de. "William C. Hunter's Books on the Old Canton Factories," *Yenching Journal of Social Studies,* 2.1:91–117 (July, 1939).

Waley, Arthur. *The Opium War through Chinese Eyes.* London: George Allen and Unwin, 1958. 257 pp.

Wallis, Wilson D. "Socio-Cultural Sources of Messiahs," in Milton Yinger, ed., *Religion, Society and the Individual.* New York: Macmillan, 1957. 653 pp.

Wang, Yü-ch'üan. "The Rise of Land Tax and the Fall of Dynasties in Chinese History," *Pacific Affairs,* 9.2:1–220 (1936).

Ward, Barbara E. "A Hong Kong Fishing Village," *Journal of Oriental Studies,* 1:195–214 (1954).

Ward, J. S. M., and W. G. Stirling. *The Hung Society, or the Society of Heaven and Earth.* 3 vols. London: Baskerville Press, 1925–1926. 178, 193, and 148 pp.

Weber, Max. *The Religion of China, Confucianism and Taoism,* tr. and ed. Hans H. Gerth. 2nd printing. Glencoe, Ill.: Free Press, 1959. 308 pp.

Wiens, Harold J. *China's March Toward the Tropics.* Hamden, Conn.: Shoe String Press, 1954. 441 pp.

Williams, Lea E. *Overseas Chinese Nationalism: the Genesis of the Pan-Chinese Movement in Indonesia, 1900–1916.* Glencoe, Ill.: Free Press, 1960. 229 pp.

Williams, S. Wells. *The Middle Kingdom: A Survey of the Geography, Government, Literature, Social Life, Arts, and History of the Chinese Empire and its Inhabitants.* 2 vols. London, 1848. 1204 pp.

Wilson, Andrew. *The "Ever-Victorious Army."* London, 1868. 395 pp.

Wilson, Bryan A. "Millennialism in Comparative Perspective," *Comparative Studies in Society and History*, 5.1:93–114 (Oct., 1963).

Wu, Hung-chu. "China's Attitude Toward Foreign Nations and Nationals Historically Considered," *Chinese Social and Political Science Review*, 10.1:13–45 (Jan., 1926).

Wu, James T. K. "The Impact of the Taiping Rebellion on the Manchu Fiscal System," *Pacific Historical Review*, 19:265–275 (Aug., 1950).

Wynne, Mervyn Llewelyn. *Triad and Tabut. A Survey of the Origin and Diffusion of Chinese and Mohammedan Secret Societies in the Malay Peninsula, A.D. 1800–1935.* Singapore: Government Printing Office, 1941. 540 pp.

Yang, C. K. "The Functional Relationship Between Chinese Thought and Chinese Religion," in John K. Fairbank, ed., *Chinese Thought and Institutions*. Chicago: University of Chicago Press, 1957. Pp. 269–290.

——. *Religion in Chinese Society: A Study of Contemporary Social Functions of Religion and Some of Their Historical Factors.* Berkeley and Los Angeles: University of California Press, 1961. 473 pp.

Yap, P. M. "The Mental Illness of Hung Hsiu-Ch'üan, Leader of the Taiping Rebellion." *Far Eastern Quarterly*, 13.3:287–304 (May, 1954).

Yinger, J. Milton. *Religion, Society and the Individual: An Introduction to the Sociology of Religion.* New York: Macmillan, 1957. 653 pp.

Yuan, Chung-teng. "Reverend Issachar Jacox Roberts and the Taiping Rebellion," *Journal of Asian Studies*, 23.1:55–68 (Nov., 1963).

Yuan, Tung-li. *China in Western Literature.* New Haven: Yale University Press, 1958.

——. *Economic and Social Development of Modern China. A Bibliographical Guide.* New Haven: Human Relations Area Files, 1956.

Chinese and Japanese Sources

A Ying 阿英, comp. *Ya-p'ien chan-cheng wen-hsüeh chi* 鸦片战争文学集 A Collection of Opium War Literature). 2 vols. Peking, 1957. 1,010 pp.

Chang Chung-fu 張忠紱 . "Ya-p'ien chan-cheng ch'ien ch'ing-t'ing pan-li wai-chiao chih chi-kuan yü shou-hsü 鴉片戰爭前清廷 辦理外交之 機關與手續 (The office and Procedure for Dealing with Diplomatic Affairs of the Ch'ing Court Before the Opium War), *Wai-chiao yueh-pao* 外交月報 (Foreign Affairs), 2.2:1–7 (Feb., 1933).

Chang Hsiang-wen 張相文 . *Nan-yuan ts'ung-kao* 南園叢稿 (Collected Drafts from a Southern Garden). Peiping, 1929–1935

Chang Te-ch'ang 張德昌 . "Ch'ing-tai ya-p'ien chan-cheng ch'ien chih chung-hsi yen-hai t'ung-shang" 清代鴉片戰爭前之中西沿海通商 (Maritime Trade Between China and the West During the Ch'ing Dynasty

Before the Opium War), *Ch'ing-hua hsüeh-pao* 清華學報 (Tsing Hua Journal), 10.1:97–145 (1935).

Chao Li-sheng 趙儷生 , comp. *Chung-kuo nung-min chan-cheng shih lun-wen-chi.* 中國 農民 戰爭 史論文集 (A Collection of Essays on the History of Chinese Peasant Wars). Shanghai, 1954. 162 pp.

Ch'en Hsi-ch'i 陳錫棋 . *Kuang-tung san-yuan-li jen-min te k'ang-ying tou-cheng* 广东三元里人民的抗英斗爭 (The Anti-British Struggle of the People of San-yuan-li in Kwangtung). Canton, 1956. 87 pp.

Ch'en Hsü-ching 陳序經 . "Kuang-tung yü Chung-kuo" 廣東與中國 (Kwangtung and China), *Tung-fang tsa-chih* 東方雜誌 (Eastern Miscellany), 36.2:41–45 (Jan., 1939).

Ch'en Po-ta 陳伯達 . *Chin-tai Chung-kuo ti-tsu kai-shuo* 近代中國地租概說 (Outline of the Land Rents of Modern China). Peking, 1949. 89 pp.

Ch'en Po-t'ao 陳伯陶 , ed. *Tung-kuan hsien-chih* 東莞縣志 (Gazetteer of Tung-kuan District. 102 chüan. 1919.

Cheng Meng-yü 鄭夢玉 , ed. *Hsü-hsiu nan-hai hsien-chih* 續修南海縣志 (Revised Gazetteer of Nan-hai District). 27 chüan. 1872.

Ch'eng Wei-hsin 程維新 . "Sung-tai kuang-chou-shih tui wai mao-i te ch'ing-hsing" 宋代 廣州市 對 外貿易 的情形 (The Nature of of the Canton Market and Foreign Trade During the Sung Dynasty), *Shih-huo* 食貨 (Economics), 1.12:26–31 (May 16, 1935).

Ch'i Ssu-ho 齊思和 , et al., eds. *Ya-p'ien chan-cheng* 鴉片戰爭 (The Opium War). 6 vols. Shanghai, 1954. 3,757 pp.

Chia Chih-fang 賈植芳 . *Chin-tai Chung-kuo ching-chi she-hui* 近代中國經濟社會 (The Economy and Society of Modern China). Shanghai, 1949. 297 pp.

Chiang T'ing-fu (T. F. Tsiang) 蔣廷黻 . "Ch'i-shan yü ya-p'ien chan-cheng" 琦善與鴉片戰爭 (Ch'i-shan and the Opium War), *Ch'ing-hua hsüeh-pao* 6.3:1–26 (Oct., 1931).

——, comp. *Chin-tai chung-kuo wai-chiao shih-liao chi-yao* 近代中國外交史料輯要 (Selected Materials on Modern Chinese Diplomatic History). 3 vols. Taipei: Taiwan Commercial Press, 1958.

Ch'ing-ch'ao yeh-shih ta-kuan 清朝野史大觀 (A review of the Apocryphal History of the Ch'ing Dynasty). 6 vols. Taipei, 1959. An anonymous compilation of apocrypha.

Ch'ing-shih 清史 (History of the Ch'ing Dynasty), ed. Chang Ch'i-yun 張其昀 *et al.* 8 vols. Taipei: National War College in association with the Institute of Chinese Culture, 1961.

Chou Ch'ao-huai 周朝槐 , ed. *Shun-te hsien-chih* 順德縣志 (Gazetteer of Shun-te District). 25 chüan. 1929.

Ch'ou-pan i-wu shih-mo 籌辦夷務始末 (A Complete Account of Our Management of Barbarian Affairs) Photolithographic reproduction,

Taipei, 1963. Tao-kuang period (1836–1850), 80 chüan. Hsien-feng period (1851–1861), 80 chüan.

Chu Hsi 朱熹 , ed. *Ssu-shu chi-chu* 四書集注 (Collected Glosses of the Four Books). Taipei, 1959.

Ch'üan-kuo hsin-shu-mu 全國新書目 (National Guide to New Books), monthly review. Peking, 1957–1960.

Hatano Yoshihiro 波多野善夫. "Taihei Tengoku ni kansuru nisan no mondai ni tsuite" 太平天國に關する二三の問題について (On certain Problems Relating to the Taiping Heavenly Kingdom), *Rekishigaku kenkyū* 歷史學研究 (Historical Research), 150:32–42 (Mar., 1951).

Hsia Hsieh 夏燮. *Chung-hsi chi-shih* 中西紀事 (A Record of Sino-Western Affairs). 24 chüan in 8 ts'e; first preface Tao-kuang 30, 12th month (1851), second preface to rev. ed. 1859, last preface 1865. Photolithographic reproduction, Taipei, 1962. 242 pp.

——. *Yueh-fen chi-shih* 粵氛紀事 (A Record of the Miasma in Kwangtung and Kwangsi). 13 chüan, 1869.

Hsia Nai 夏鼐. "T'ai-p'ing t'ien-kuo ch'ien-hou ch'ang-chiang ke sheng chih t'ien-fu wen-t'i" 太平天國前後長江各省之田賦問題 (The Problem of Land Taxes in the Yangtze Provinces During and After the Taiping Rebellion) in *Chung-kuo chin-tai shih lun-ts'ung* 中國近代史論叢 (A Collection of Articles on Modern Chinese History). Taipei, 1958. 2nd ts'e: pp. 145–204.

Hsia Ting-yü 夏定域. "Ying-chi-li chan-chü kuang-chou chih i-shih-liao" 英吉利佔據廣州之役史料 (Historical materials on the English Occupation of Canton), in *Kuo-li chung-shan ta-hsüeh yü-yen li-shih hsüeh yen-chiu-so chou-k'an* 國立中山大學語言歷史學研究所週刊 (Weekly Journal of the Research Institute of Philology and History of National Chung-shan University), 10.110:45–48 (Dec. 18, 1929).

Hsiao I-shan 蕭一山. *Chin-tai pi-mi she-hui shih-liao* 近代秘密社會史料 (Historical Materials on Modern Secret Societies). 6 chüan. Peiping, 1935.

——. *Ch'ing-tai t'ung-shih* 清代通史 (General History of the Ch'ing Period). 5 vols. Taipei, 1963.

——. *T'ai-p'ing t'ien-kuo ts'ung-shu* 太平天國叢書 (Collected Writings of the Taiping Heavenly Kingdom). 2 vols. Taipei, 1956.

Hsieh Hsing-yao 謝興堯. *T'ai-p'ing t'ien-kuo ch'ien-hou kuang-hsi te fanch'ing yun-tung* 太平天國前後廣西的反清運動 (The Anti-Ch'ing Movement in Kwangsi Before and After the Taiping Rebellion). Peking, 1950. 236 pp.

——. *T'ai-p'ing t'ien-kuo shih-shih lun-ts'ung* 太平天國史事論叢 (Collected Historical Essays on the Taiping Heavenly Kingdom). Shanghai, 1935. 259 pp.

Hsieh Shou-ch'ang 謝壽昌 *et al.*, eds. *Chung-kuo ku-chin ti-ming ta tz'u-tien* 中國古今地名大辭典 (The Larger Dictionary of Ancient and Modern Chinese Place Names). Taipei, 1957. 1,410 pp.

Hsien Yü-ch'ing 冼玉清 . *Kuang-tung wen-hsien ts'ung-t'an* 廣東文獻 叢談 (A Collection of Cantonese Biographical and Literary Notes). Hong Kong, 1965. 104 pp.

Hsing-hua ch'iao-tsu 杏花樵子 (A Confused and Apricot Woodcutter). *Yueh-fei shih-mo chi-lüeh* 粵匪始末紀畧 (A Complete Record of the Bandits of Kwangsi and Kwangtung). 1 ts'e. 1864.

Hsü Sung-chou 徐頌周 . "Ya-p'ien shu-ju chung-kuo k'ao" 鴉片輸入 中國考 (An Examination of Opium Imports into China), in *Chung-kuo chin-tai shih lun-ts'ung* 中國近代史論叢 (A Collection of Articles on Modern Chinese History). Taipei, 1958. 3rd ts'e: pp. 156–158.

Huang Fo-i 黃佛頤 . *Kuang-chou ch'eng fang-chih* 廣州城坊志 (Local Gazetteer of the City of Canton). 6 vols. Photolithographic reprint, 1948.

Juan Yuan 阮元 . *Kuang-tung t'ung-chih* 廣東通志 (Gazetteer of Kwangtung Province). 334 chüan. 1822. Photolithographic reprint, Taipei, 1959.

Kuang-chou chih-nan 廣州指南 (Guidebook to Canton). Canton, 1934. 533 pp.

Kuang-tung-sheng wen-shih yen-chiu-kuan 廣東省文史研究館 (The Research Institute of the Literature and History of Kwangtung Province). "Kuang-tung jen-min tsai san-yuan-li k'ang-ying tou-cheng chien-shih" 廣東人民在三元里抗英鬪爭簡史 (A Concise History of the Anti-English Struggle of the Cantonese People at San-yuan-li), in Lieh Tao 列島 ed., *Ya-p'ien chan-cheng shih lun-wen chuan-chi* 鴉片戰爭 史論文專集 (A Collection of Essays on the History of the Opium War). Peking, 1958. Pp. 276–295.

Kuang-tung ti-fang tzu-chih 廣東地方自治 (Local Self-government in Kwangtung). Shanghai, n.d. 275 pp.

Kuo T'ing-i 郭廷以 . *Chin-tai chung-kuo shih-shih jih-chih* 近代中國 史事日誌 (A Calendar of Historical Events of Modern China). 2 vols. Taipei, 1963. 1,450 pp.

——. *T'ai-p'ing t'ien-kuo shih-shih jih-chih* 太平天國史事日誌 . (A Calendar of Historical Events of the Taiping Rebellion). Taipei, 1963. 266 pp.

Lai Hsin-hsia 來新夏 . "Ti-i-tz'u ya-p'ien chan-cheng tui chung-kuo she-hui te ying-hsiang" 第一次鴉片戰爭對中國社會的影響 (The Effects of the First Opium War on Chinese Society), in Lieh Tao 列島, ed., *Ya-p'ien chan-cheng shih lun-wen chuan-chi* 鴉片戰爭史論文專集 (A Collection of Essays on the History of the Opium War). Peking, 1958. Pp. 113–141.

Li Wen-chih, 李文治 *et al.*, comp. *Chung-kuo chin-tai nung-yeh shih tzu-liao* 中國近代農業史資料 (Materials on the History of Modern Chinese Agriculture). Vol. 1: 1840–1911. Peking, 1957. 1,023 pp.

Liang Chia-pin 梁嘉彬. *Kuang-tung shih-san hang k'ao* 廣東十三行考 (The Hong Merchants of Canton). 2nd ed., Taipei, 1960. 342 pp.

Liang Jen-ts'ai 梁仁彩. *Kuang-tung ching-chi ti-li* 廣東經濟地理 (An Economic Geography of Kwangtung). Peking, 1956. 102 pp.

Liang Ting-fen 梁鼎芬, ed. *P'an-yü hsien-hsü-chih* 番禺縣續志 (Revised Gazetteer of P'an-yü District). 45 chüan. 1931.

Liang T'ing-nan 梁廷枬. *I-fen chi-wen* 夷氛記聞 (An Account of the Barbarian Invasion). 5 chüan. 1874.

Lin-Tse-hsü 林則徐. *Lin wen-kung ch'üan-chi* 林文公全集 (The Collected Works of Lin Tse-hsü). 2 vols. Taipei, 1963.

Liu Hsing-t'ang 劉興唐. "Fu-chien te hsüeh-tsu tsu-chih" 福建的血族組織 (Clan Organization in Fukien), *Shih-huo*, 4.8:35–46 Sept. 10, 1936).

Liu Po-chi 劉伯驥. *Kuang-tung shu-yuan chih-tu* 廣東書院制度 (The System of Academies in Kwangtung). Taipei, 1958. 476 pp.

Lo Erh-kang 羅爾綱. "Ch'ing-chi ping wei-chiang-yu te ch'i-yuan" 清季兵為將有的起源 (Origin of Personal Armies During the Ch'ing Period), *Chung-kuo she-hui ching-chi shih chi-k'an* 中國社會經濟史集刊 (Collectanea of the Economic and Social History of China), 5.2:235–250 (June, 1937).

——. "T'ai-p'ing t'ien-kuo ke-ming ch'ien te jen-k'ou ya-p'o wen-t'i" 太平天國革命前的人口壓迫問題 (The Problem of Population Pressure Prior to the Taiping Rebellion), in *Chung-kuo chin-tai shih lun-ts'ung* 中國近代史論叢 Taipei, 1958. 2nd ts'e; pp. 16–87.

——. *T'ai-p'ing t'ien-kuo shih pien-wei chi* 太平天國史辨偽集 (A Collection of Discussions on Forged Facts, Objects, and Books about the Taiping Heavenly Kingdom). Shanghai, 1950. 264 pp.

Lo Han 羅漢. "T'ien-ti-hui wen-chien" 天地會文件 (Triad Documents), *Kuang-chou hsüeh-pao* 廣州學報 (Canton Journal), 1.1:1–16 (Jan. 1, 1937).

Lo Hsiang-lin 羅香林. "Ya-p'ien chan-cheng yueh-tung i-min k'ang-ying shih-liao" 鴉片戰爭粵東義民抗英史料 (Historical Materials on the Opposition of the Righteous People of Kwangtung to the English During the Opium War), *She-hui k'e-hsüeh ts'ung-k'an* 社會科學叢刊 (Journal of Sociology), 2.2:145–164 (1936).

Lu Ch'in-ch'ih 陸欽墀. "Ying-fa lien-chün chan-chü kuang-chou shih-mo" 英法聯軍佔據廣州始末 (A Complete Account of the Anglo-French Occupation of Canton), *Shih-hsüeh nien-pao* 史學年報 (Historical Annual), 2.5:265–304 (Dec., 1938).

Makino Tatsumi 牧野巽. *Shina kazoku kenkyū* 支那家族研究 (A Study of the Chinese Clan). Tokyo, 1944. 724 pp.

Masui Tsuneo 増井經夫. "Kanton no kyoshi" 廣東の墟市 (The Local Markets of Kwangtung), *Tōa Ronsō* 東亞論叢 (Essays on East Asia), 4:263–283 (May, 1941).

P'eng Tse-i 彭澤益 *et al.*, comp. *Chung-kuo chin-tai shou-kung-yeh shih tzu-liao, 1840–1949.* 中國近代手工業史資料 (Historical Materials on Modern Chinese Handicraft Industries). 4 vols. Peking, 1957.

Sasaki Masaya 佐々木正哉. *Ahen sensō no kenkyū* 鴉片戰爭の研究 (Research on the Opium War). Tokyo, 1964. 319 pp.

——. "Hsien-feng ninen Yin-hsien no kōryō bōdō" 咸豐二年鄞縣の 抗糧暴動 (The Anti-tax Uprisings in Yin-hsien in the Second year of the Hsien-feng reign), *Kindai chūgoku kenkyū* 近代中國研究 (Research on Modern China), 5:185–300 (1963).

——. "Shun-te-hsien kyōshin to tōkai juroku-sa" 順德縣鄉紳と東海 十六沙 (The Gentry of Shun-te District and the Sixteen Delta Lands of the Eastern Sea), *Kindai Chūgoku kenkyū*, 3:163–232.

Shih Ch'eng 史澄, ed. *Kuang-chou fu-chih* 廣州府志 (Gazetteer of Kuang-chou Prefecture). 163 chüan. 1879.

Shih-liao hsün-k'an 史料旬刊 (Historical Materials Published Thrice Monthly). Peiping: Palace Museum, 1931. Photolithographic reprint, Taipei, 1963. 793 pp.

Shina shōbetsu zenshi 支那省別全誌 (Gazetteer of China by Provinces). Vol. 1. Tokyo, 1917. 1,220 pp.

Sung Lung-yuan 宋龍淵. *Tao-te-ching chiang-i* 道德經講義 (An Explanation of the Tao-te-ching). Presented to the K'ang-hsi Emperor in 1703. Photolithographic reprint, Taipei, n.d.

Suzuki Chusei 鈴木中正. "Shimmatsu jōgai-undō no kigen" 清末 攘外運動の起源 (Origins of the Antiforeign Movement During the Later Ch'ing Period), *Shigaku Zasshi* 史學雜誌 (Journal of History), 62.10:1–29 (Oct., 1953).

Suzuki Tadashi 鈴木正. "Min-dai katei kō" 明代家丁考 (A Study of the Militia During the Ming Period), *Shikan* 史觀 (Historical Views), 37:23–40 (1952).

Ta-ch'ing li-ch'ao shih-lu 大清歷朝實錄 (Veritable Records of Successive Reigns of the Ch'ing Dynasty). Photo-offset, Taipei, 1964.

Taga Akigoro 多賀秋五郎. "Kindai Chūgoku ni okeru zokujuku no seikaku" 近代中國における族塾の性格 (The Clan School in Modern China), *Kindai Chūgoku kenkyū*, 5:207–254 (1963).

——. *Sōfu no kenkyū* 宗譜の研究 (An Analytical Study of Chinese Genealogical Books). Tokyo: Toyo Bunko, 1960. 890 pp.

T'ao Yuan-chen 陶元珍. "Tu Ch'i-shan yü ya-p'ien chan cheng" 讀 「琦善與鴉片戰爭」 (Upon Reading "Ch'i-shan and the Opium War"), in

Chung-kuo chin-tai shih lun-ts'ung   中國近代史論叢   (Collected Articles on Modern Chinese History). Taipei, 1958. 3rd ts'e: pp. 198–204.

T'ien Ming-yueh 田明曜, ed. *Hsiang-shan hsien-chih* 香山縣志 (Gazetteer of Hsiang-shan District). 22 chüan. 1879.

Tung-hua ch'üan-lu 東華全錄 (Complete Records of the Tung-hua [Gate]), comp. Wang Hsien-ch'ien 王先謙. 252 ts'e. Editor's preface, 1884. Photolithographic reprint, Taipei, 1963. Tao-kuang period, 2 vols., 13 chüan. Hsien-feng period, 2 vols., 69 chüan.

Uedo Toshio 植田捷雄. "Ahen sensō to shimmatsu kammin no shosō" 阿片戰爭と清末官民の諸相 (The Actual Attitude of Chinese Officials and Commoners Towards the Opium War), *Kokusaihō gaikō zasshi* 國際法外交雜誌 (International Law Journal), 50.3:235–271 (July, 1951).

Wang Chung-min 王重民 *et al.*, eds. *T'ai-p'ing t'ien-kuo* 太平天國 (The Taiping Heavenly Kingdom). 8 vols. Shanghai, 1952. 3,405 pp.

Wang Erh-min 王爾敏. *Ch'ing-chi ping-kung-yeh te hsing-ch'i* 清季兵工業的興起 (The Rise of the Armaments Industry During the Late Ch'ing Period). Taipei, 1964. 223 pp.

Wang Hsing-jui 王興瑞. "Kuang-tung i-ke nung-ts'un hsien chieh-tuan te ching-chi she-hui" 廣東一個農村現階段的經濟社會 (The Economy and Society of a Contemporary Kwangtung Farming Town), *Shih-huo*, 3.2:43–49 (Dec. 16, 1935).

Wang Tuan-lu 王端履. "Chung-lun wen-chai pi-lu" 重論文齋筆錄 (Random Records from the Literary Studio of Grave Essays), 12 chüan. in *Ch'ing-tai pi-chi ts'ung-k'an* 清代筆記叢刊 (Collected Printings of Random Essays of the Ch'ing Period). Shanghai, 1936. Vol. 76–78.

Wang Ying 王瑛. "T'ai-p'ing t'ien-kuo ke-ming ch'ien tuo t'u-ti wen-t'i te i p'ien" 太平天國革命前多土地問題的一瞥 (A Glance at Several Land Problems Before the Taiping Rebellion), *Shih-huo*, 2.3:39–44 (July, 1935).

Wei Chien-yu 魏建猷. "Ch'ing-tai wai-kuo yin-yuan chih liu-ju chi ch'i ying-hsiang" 清代外國銀圓之流入及其影響 (The Importation of Foreign Specie During the Ch'ing Period, and its Effects), in *Chung-kuo chin-tai shih lun-ts'ung*, 3rd ts'e: pp. 159–175.

Wei Yuan 魏源. *Sheng-wu chi* 聖武記 (A Record of Imperial Military Exploits). 14 chüan. Preface to 1st edition, 1842. Photolithographic reprint, Taipei. 1963.

Ya-p'ien chan-cheng shih-ch'i ssu-hsiang shih tzu-liao hsüan-chi 鴉片戰爭時期思想史資料選輯 (A Compilation of Materials on the Intellectual History of the Opium War Period), compiled by the Modern History Research Institute of the Chinese Academy of Sciences. Peking, 1963. 108 pp.

Yen Chung-p'ing 嚴中平. "Chung-kuo mien-yeh chih fa-chan" 中國棉業之發展 (The Development of the Chinese Cotton Industry), in *Chung-kuo chin-tai shih lun-ts'ung* (Collected Essays on Modern Chinese History). Taipei, 1958. 2nd ts'e: pp. 245–271.

Ying-chi-li Kuang-tung ju-ch'eng shih-mo 英吉利廣東入城始末 (Complete Account of the British Entry into Canton), in Chao Chih-ch'ien 趙之謙, comp., *Yang-shih ch'ien-ch'i-pai erh-shih-chiu ho chai ts'ung-shu* 仰視千七百二十九鶴齋叢書 (Collectanea from the Studio Where One Gazes in Respect at One Thousand, Seven Hundred and Twenty-nine Cranes). 4th ts'e. Photolithographic reprint, 1929.

Yü Ping-ch'üan 余秉權, ed. *Chung-kuo shih-hsüeh lun-wen yin-te: 1902–1962* 中國史學論文引得 : 1902–1962 (Chinese History: Index to Learned Articles: 1902–1962). Hong Kong, 1962. 573 pp.

Glossary

A-ch'ieh 阿切
An-ho-chü 安和局

Ch'a Wen-kang 蔡文綱
Chang Chao-kuang 張紹光
Chang Chih-tung 張之洞
Chang Heng 張衡
Chang Hsi-yü 張熙宇
Chang Pao 張保
Chang Wei-p'ing 張維屏
Ch'ang-an 長安
Ch'ang-shou ssu 長壽寺
ch'ang-t'ien 長田
Chao Ch'eng-hsi 招成照
Chao Fu-ts'ai 趙福才
chao-hui 照會
Chao Kuang-t'ao 招廣濤
Chao T'o 趙佗
Ch'ao-chou fu 潮州府
Ch'ao-yang 潮陽
Ch'en Chao-lin 沈兆霖
Ch'en Chi 陳吉
Ch'en Chin-kang 陳金缸
Ch'en Hsien-liang 陳顯良
Ch'en Hsüan 陳宣
Ch'en K'ai 陳開
Ch'en Kuan-kuang 陳觀光
Ch'en Kuei-chi 陳桂籍
Ch'en Li 陳澧

Ch'en Li-nan 陳禮南
Ch'en Ming-kuei 陳銘珪
Ch'en Pei-yuan 陳北垣
Ch'en P'u 陳璞
Ch'en Sung 陳松
Ch'en Sung-nien 陳松年
Ch'en T'ang 陳棠
Ch'en Wei-yueh 陳維嶽
Ch'en Yü-hsien 陳裕賢
Ch'en Yuan-k'ai 陳元楷
cheng 征
Cheng K'uei-hung 鄭逵鴻
cheng-p'ai 正派
Cheng Ying-yuan 鄭應元
Ch'eng Hsüan 程選
chi-fang-tsai 機房仔
chi-t'ien 祭田
ch'i 旗
Ch'i Kung 祁墳
ch'i-kung 氣功
Ch'i-shan 琦善
Ch'i-ying 耆英
ch'i-yueh 七約
chia (family) 家
chia (unit) 甲
chia-chang 家長
Chia-ch'ing 嘉慶
chia-t'ing 家庭
Chia-ying chou 嘉應州

Chiang Hung-yuan　江宏源
Chiang Pen-chen　江本真
Chiang-ts'un　江村
Ch'iao Ying-keng　喬應庚
chien-shang　奸商
chien-sheng　監生
Ch'ien Chiang　錢江
Ch'ien-lung　乾隆
Chin Ching-mao　金菁茅
chin-shih　進士
Ch'in Shih Huang-ti　秦始皇帝
chin-wen　今文
Ch'ing (dynasty)　清
ch'ing (green)　青
ch'ing (measure)　頃
Ch'ing-lien　青蓮
Ch'ing-p'ing-she　清平社
Ch'ing-yuan　清遠
Ch'iung-chou fu　瓊州府
chou　州
Chou Ping-chün　周秉鈞
Chou Tuan-p'ei　周端佩
Chu Feng-piao　朱鳳標
Chu Hsi　朱熹
Chu Kuo-hsiung　朱國雄
Chu I-kuei　朱一貴
Chu Mao-li　朱毛里
Chu Tsun　朱嶟
Chu Tzu-i　朱子儀
Ch'un-feng　淳豐
chung　忠
Chung Chan-ch'i　鍾占琪
Chung Ch'i-yao　鍾其耀
Chung-shan　中山
Ch'ung-ho　冲鶴
chü　局
chü-jen　舉人

Ch'ü Ch'iu　區球
Ch'ü-chou　衢州
Ch'üan-lu　全祿
chün　軍
chün-tzu　君子

En-chou　恩洲
En-p'ing　恩平
Fan-ch'ing fu-ming　反清復明
fan-kuei　番鬼
Fan Jui-chao　范瑞照
fang-chang　房長
fen　奮
feng-shui　風水
Fo-ling　佛嶺
Fo-ling-shih　佛嶺市
Fo-shan (Fatshan)　佛山
fu　府
Fu-ch'ao　福潮
fu-le-she　福樂社
fu-ping　府兵

Hai-feng　海豐
Hakka (K'e-chia)　客家
Han　漢
han-chien　漢奸
hang (hong)　行
hao-shih-che　好事者
Heng-yang　衡陽
Ho　何
Ho-feng　和豐
Ho Hsin-t'ao　何信縚
Ho Kuei-ch'ing　何桂清
Ho Lien-ch'i　何運漢
Ho Liu　何六
Ho Po-fen　何博份
Ho Ta-chang　何大璋
Ho T'ing-kuang　何廷珖

Ho Yü-ch'eng　何玉成

Honam (Ho-nan)　河南

Hsi-hu　西湖

Hsi-pei-yü she-hsüeh　西北隅社學

Hsia Hsieh　夏燮

hsiang　鄉

Hsiang-shan　香山

hsiao　孝

Hsiao-hao-yung　小濠涌

Hsiao huang-p'u　小黃圃

Hsiao-tao　小刀

Hsiao-wan-pao　小灣堡

hsieh　邪

Hsieh Cho-en　謝卓恩

Hsieh Hsi-en　謝錫恩

hsieh-p'ai　邪派

Hsieh Shih-en　謝世恩

Hsieh Tse-sen　謝澤森

hsien　縣

Hsien-feng　咸豐

Hsin-an　新安

Hsin ch'ing-yun wen-she　新青雲文社

Hsin-feng she-hsüeh　濘峯社學

Hsin-hui　新會

Hsin-i　信宜

Hsin-ning　新寧

Hsin-tsao　新造

Hsin-ts'un　新村

hsin-tuan　鮮端

hsiu-ts'ai　秀才

Hsü Chao-piao　徐兆表

Hsü Ch'iu　許球

Hsü Hsiang-kuang　許祥光

Hsü Kuang-chin　徐廣晉

Hsü Nai-chao　許乃釗

Hsü Nai-chi　許乃濟

hsü-sheng　虛聲

Hsü Ta-hsiang　徐大祥

Hsü T'ien-po　徐添伯

Hsü T'ing-kuei　許廷桂

Hsü Ying-jung　許應鏄

Hsüeh-hai-t'ang　學海堂

hsüeh-t'ien　學田

hu　戶

hu-ch'ou-ting　戶抽丁

Hu-kuang　湖廣

hu-pao kan-chüeh　互保甘結

Hua-hsien　花縣

Hua-sha-na　花沙納

Hua T'ing-chieh　華廷傑

Huai-jen-chü　懷仁局

Huang Ch'ao　黃巢

Huang-ch'ing ching-chieh　皇清經解

Huang-chu-ch'i　黃竹岐

Huang Chüeh-tzu　黃爵滋

Huang En-t'ung　黃恩彤

Huang Huai-hua　黃槐花

Huang P'ei-fang　黃培芳

Huang-shu　黃書

Huang Tsung　黃琮

Huang Tsung-han　黃宗漢

Huang Tsung-hsi　黃宗羲

Huang Yung　黃鏞

Hui-chou fu　惠州府

hui-fei　會匪

Hui-lai she-hsüeh　惠來社學

hui-t'ien　會田

hung (rebellion)　訌

hung (red)　紅

hung-chin　紅巾

Hung Hsiu-ch'üan　洪秀全

Hung-men　洪門

hung-ping　洪兵

Liang-kuang　兩廣

Liang Lun-shu　梁綸樞

Liang T'ing-nan　梁廷枏

Liang T'ing-tung　梁廷棟

Liang Ts'ai-ying　梁彩煐

lieh-chuan　列傳

Lien-chou tu　廉州府

Lien-hu　蓮湖

Lien-sheng　聯陞

Lien Ssu-hu　練四虎

Lin Ch'i-fa　林起發

Lin Fu-hsiang　林福詳

Lin Fu-sheng　林福盛

Lin Hsiang-huai　林向槐

Lin Kuang-lung　林洸瀧

Lin Po-t'ung　林伯桐

Lin Shih-ch'eng　林士成

Lin Shuang-wen　林爽文

Lin Tse-hsü　林則徐

Ling-nan (Lingnam)　嶺南

Ling Shih-pa　凌十八

Liu　劉

liu-chih　柳枝

Liu Hsin　劉潯

Liu Kuan-hsiu　劉觀秀

liu-mang　流氓

Liu Wan-yu　劉萬有

Liu Yen　劉嚴

Liu Ying-ts'ai　劉英才

liu yü sheng-ch'eng　流寓省城

Lo Chia-cheng　羅家正

Lo-ko-wei　羅格圍

Lo Pao-kuang　羅葆光

Lo Ping-chang　駱秉章

Lo-ting chou　羅定州

Lo Tun-yen　羅惇衍

Lu Ch'ang　盧昌

Lu K'un　盧坤

Lung-men　龍門

Lung Pao-hsien　龍葆誠

Lung-shan　龍山

Lung T'ing-huai　龍廷槐

Lung Yuan-hsi　龍元僖

Ma Fu-an　馬福安

Ma Ying-chieh　馬映階

Ma Yuan　馬援

mai-kuo　賣國

Man　蠻

Mei-ling　梅嶺

mi-yu　密友

min chih i-chih　民之意志

min-pen　民本

min-tsu chu-i　民族主義

Ming-lun-t'ang　明倫堂

Mu-chang-a　穆彰阿

mu-fu　幕府

Mu-k'o-te-na　穆克德訥

mu-yu　幕友

nan　男

Nan-hai (Nam-hoi)　南海

Nan-hai-chün　南海軍

Nan-yueh　南越

nao　腦

nei-ho　內河

ni　逆

Ni-ch'eng　泥城

Niu-lan-kang　牛欄岡

Ou-yang ch'üan　歐陽泉

pa-ku　八股

Pa-kua　八卦

pai-hsing chih i 百姓之義

Pai-lien 白蓮

Pai Ling 百齡

pai-pai 拜拜

Pai-yun-shan 白雲山

P'an 潘

P'an Cheng-wei 潘正煒

P'an K'ai 潘楷

P'an Ming-ch'iu 潘鳴球

P'an Nien-tsu 潘念祖

P'an Shih-ying 潘世榮

P'an-yü (Poonyu) 番禺

pang-pang hui 棒棒會

pao 保

pao-chang 保長

pao-chia 保甲

pao-shang 包商

pei-lu 北路

ping (army) 兵

ping (petition) 稟

Po Kuei 柏貴

Po-lo 波羅

Po-lu-tung shu-yuan 白鹿洞書院

Po-mai-hsia-pi 伯麥霞畢

Punti (Pen-ti) 本地

Sai-shang-a 賽尚阿

San-ho-hui 三合會

San-shui 三水

San-tien-hui 三點會

San-yuan-li 三元里

Sha-chiao tsung-chü 沙茭總局

sha-chü 沙局

sha-fu 沙夫

Sha-mien (Shameen) 沙面

sha-so 沙所

sha-t'ien 沙田

Sha-wan 沙丸

shan huoh 煽惑

shang-ch'eng 商城

Shao-ch'ing fu 肇慶府

Shao-chou fu 韶州府

Shao-lin 少林

she 社

she-hsüeh 社學

She Pao-shun 佘葆純

shen-shih 紳士

Shen Ti-hui 沈棣輝

sheng-ch'eng 省城

Sheng-p'ing kung-so 昇平公所

Sheng-p'ing she-hsüeh 昇平社學

sheng-yuan 生員

Shih-ching (Shektsing) 石井

Shih-kang shu-yuan 石閩書院

Shih-ku shu-yuan 石鼓書院

Shih-lung 石龍

shu-yuan 書院

Shuang-shan ssu 雙山寺

Shun-te 順德

Shun-te t'uan-lien tsung-chü
    順德團練總局

Ssu-hsü lien-fang chü 絲墟聯防局

Ssu-ma Kuang 司馬光

Su Lang-jao 蘇朗篘

Su T'ing-k'uei 蘇廷魁

Su Tung-p'o 蘇東坡

Sung Lung-yuan 宋龍淵

Sung Ta-ch'ao 宋達潮

Ta-fo ssu 大佛寺

Ta-lan 大攬

Ta-li 大瀝

Ta-liang 大良

ta-ning 大寧

'a-tsung 大總

'a-tsung-tz'u 大宗祠

ta-t'ung 大同

Ta-yü-ling 大庾嶺

t'ai-chi-ch'üan 太極拳

T'ai-hsüeh 太學

T'ai-p'ing 太平

T'ai-p'ing t'ien-kuo 太平天國

T'an Chiu 譚釚

T'an Lu 譚路

T'an Ya-shou 譚亞受

T'ang 唐

T'ang-hsia 唐夏

T'ang Lun-ying 湯榆英

T'ang T'ai-tsung 唐太宗

Tanka (Tan-hu) 蛋户

tao 盜

Tao-kuang 道光

T'ao Pa 陶八

Tao te ching 道德經

Teng An-pang 鄧安邦

Teng-hai 澄海

Teng T'ing-chen 鄧廷楨

ti-kuo 敵國

ti-pao 地保

tiao-t'ing 調停

t'ieh-pan 鐵板

t'ien 天

T'ien Fang 田芳

t'ien-hsia 天下

T'ien-ti-hui 天地會

ting 丁

Ting-hai 定海

Ts'ao Lü-t'ai 曹履泰

tsei 賊

Tseng-Kuo-fan 曾國藩

Tseng Wang-yen 曾望顏

Ts-eng-ch'eng 增城

Ts'eng Lin-shu 曾麟書

Tso Meng-heng 左夢衡

Tso Tsung-t'ang 左宗棠

Tsou Hsin-lan 鄒斯蘭

tsu 族

tsu-tang 族黨

tsung 總

Tsung-hua 從化

t'u-fei 土匪

T'u-lu 土爐

t'uan-lien 團練

t'uan-lien ta-ch'en 團練大臣

tui 隊

Tung-hai shih-liu sha 東海十六沙

Tung-hua 東華

Tung-kuan 東莞

Tung-kuan 東關

Tung-p'ing kung-she 東平公社

tung-shan 東山

Tung-yuan 東園

T'ung-chih 同治

t'ung-feng 同豐

t'ung-hsiang 同鄉

t'ung-hsüeh 同學

t'ung-nien 同年

T'ung-sheng 同昇

t'ung-sheng 童生

T'ung-wen 同文

tzu 子

tz'u 祠

tz'u-t'ang 祠堂

Tz'u Yang-chiu 賜羊酒

wai-ch'iang nei-kan 外強內乾

wan-sung-yuan 萬松園

Wang An-shih 王安石

Wang Chen-tung　王鎮東
Wang Ch'ing-feng　王清奉
Wang Fu-chih　王夫之
Wang Hsi-ying　王錫瀛
Wang Shao-kuang　王紹光
Wang Shao-kuei　王韶貴
Wang Shih-ch'ung　王世充
wei (spurious)　偽
wei (span)　圓
Wei Tso-pang　衛佐邦
Wei Yuan　魏源
Wen-ming shu-yuan　文明書院
Whampoa (Huang-pu)　黃埔
Wo-lung-hui　臥龍會
Wu-ch'ang　武昌
Wu Chi-shu　鄔繼樞
Wu-chou　梧州
Wu Ch'ung-yueh (Howqua)　伍崇曜
Wu Chün-yang　鄔鈞颺
wu-hsia hsiao-shuo　武俠小説
Wu K'uei-yang　鄔夔颺
Wu Pin　鄔彬
Wu Ssu-shu　吳恩樹
Wu-tou-mi-tao　五斗米道
wu-wei　無為
wu-yeh yu-min　無業游民

Yang-ch'eng　羊城
Yang Chin　楊金
Yang Fang　楊芳
Yang Hsiu-ch'ing　楊秀清
Yang K'ang　楊康
Yang Li-ta　楊利達
Yang Te-i　楊德懿
Yang Yung-yen　楊永衍
Yao　猺
Yeh-man　野蠻
Yeh Ming-ch'en　葉名琛
Yen Feng-an　嚴逢安
Yen Hao-ch'ang　顏浩長
Yen Po-tao　顏伯燾
Yen Yuan　顏元
yin　淫
Ying-te　英德
Yuan K'uo-yü　袁廓宇
Yuan Yü-lin　袁玉麟
yueh　約
Yueh-hsiu shu-yuan　粵秀書院
Yueh-hua shu-yuan　越華書院
yung　勇
Yung-cheng　雍正

Index